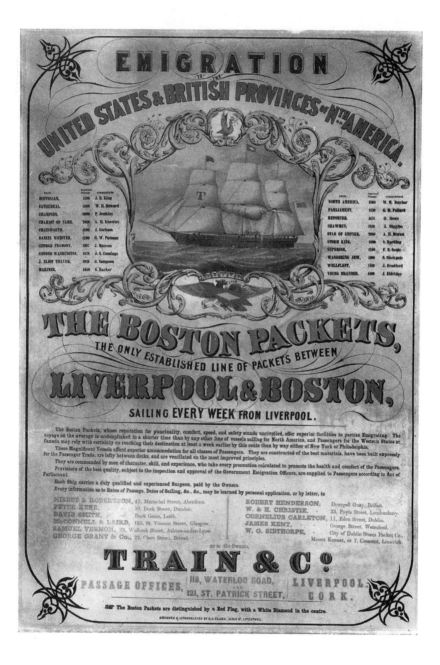

EMIGRATION

to the

UNITED STATES & BRITISH PROVINCES of Nth AMERICA.

SHIPS.	Register Tonnage	COMMANDERS
BOSTONIAN,	1100	J. B. King
CATHEDRAL,	1000	W. H. Howard
CHAMPION,	2000	P. Jenkins
CHARIOT OF FAME,	2050	A. H. Knowles
CHATSWORTH,	1500	J. Gorham
DANIEL WEBSTER,	1200	G. W. Putman
GEORGE PEABODY,	1397	J. Manson
GEORGE WASHINGTON,	1678	J. S. Cumings
J. ELIOT THAYER,	1915	G. Sampson
MARINER,	1450	G. Barker

SHIPS.	Register Tonnage	COMMANDERS
NORTH AMERICA,	1463	W. M. Dunbar
PARLIAMENT,	1250	G. M. Pollard
REPORTER,	1474	O. Howe
SHAWMUT,	1213	J. Higgins
STAR OF EMPIRE,	2050	A. H. Brown
STORM KING,	1480	S. Harding
SUPERIOR,	1240	F. B. Soule
WANDERING JEW,	1206	S. Stockpole
WELLFLEET,	1150	J. Bradford
YOUNG BRANDER,	1490	J. Eldridge

THE BOSTON PACKETS,

THE ONLY ESTABLISHED LINE OF PACKETS BETWEEN

LIVERPOOL & BOSTON,

SAILING EVERY WEEK FROM LIVERPOOL.

The Boston Packets, whose reputation for punctuality, comfort, speed, and safety stands unrivalled, offer superior facilities to parties Emigrating. The voyage on the average is accomplished in a shorter time than by any other line of vessels sailing for North America, and Passengers for the Western States or Canada may rely with certainty on reaching their destination at least a week earlier by this route than by way either of New York or Philadelphia.

These Magnificent Vessels afford superior accommodation for all classes of Passengers. They are constructed of the best materials, have been built expressly for the Passenger Trade, are lofty between decks, and are ventilated on the most improved principles.

They are commanded by men of character, skill, and experience, who take every precaution calculated to promote the health and comfort of the Passengers.

Provisions of the best quality, subject to the inspection and approval of the Government Emigration Officers, are supplied to Passengers according to Act of Parliament.

Each Ship carries a duly qualified and experienced Surgeon, paid by the Owners.

Every information as to Rates of Passage, Dates of Sailing, &c., &c., may be learned by personal application, or by letter, to

NISBET & ROBERTSON,	47, Marischal Street, Aberdeen.
PETER KERR,	10, Dock Street, Dundee.
DAVID SMITH,	Dock Gates, Leith.
McCONNELL & LAIRD,	155, St. Vincent Street, Glasgow.
SAMUEL VERNON,	39, Wollock Street, Ashton-under-Lyne.
GEORGE GRANT & Co.,	23, Clare Street, Bristol.

ROBERT HENDERSON,	Donegall Quay, Belfast.
W. & H. CHRISTIE,	23, Foyle Street, Londonderry.
CORNELIUS CARLETON,	11, Eden Street, Dublin.
JAMES KENT,	George Street, Waterford.
W. G. SIBTHORPE,	City of Dublin Steam Packet Co., Mount Kenoer, or 7, Crescent, Limerick.

or to the Owners,

TRAIN & Co.

PASSAGE OFFICES, 119, WATERLOO ROAD, LIVERPOOL, and 121, ST. PATRICK STREET, CORK.

The Boston Packets are distinguished by a Red Flag, with a White Diamond in the centre.

DESIGNED & LITHOGRAPHED BY H.H. FRASER, DALE ST. LIVERPOOL.

John A. Butler

Atlantic Kingdom

America's Contest with Cunard
in the Age of Sail and Steam

BRASSEY'S, INC.
Washington, D.C.

Library of Congress Cataloging-in-Publication Data
Butler, John A., 1927–
Atlantic kingdom : America's contest with Cunard in the age of sail
and steam / John A. Butler—1st ed.
p. cm.
Includes bibliographical references and index.
ISBN 1-57488-383-6
1. Merchant marine—United States—History.
2. Shipping—United States—History.
3. Merchant marine—Great Britain. 4. Shipping—Great Britain.
5. Cunard, Samuel, Sir, 1787–1865. I. Title.
HE745 .B87 2001
387.5′0973—dc21   2001025251

Printed in the United States of America on acid-free paper that
meets the American National Standards Institute z39-48 Standard.

Cover illustration: Port of New York, 1858.
Courtesy of The Mariners' Museum.
Frontispiece: Boston Packets Advertisement. Courtesy of
The Bostonian Society/Old State House.

Brassey's, Inc.
22841 Quicksilver Drive
Dulles, Virginia 20166

FIRST EDITION

10 9 8 7 6 5 4 3 2 1

For STEPHANIE, firstborn, cherished 24/7

Contents

Illustrations

MAPS

Preface

HISTORY REFERS to the economic changes of the mid-1800s as the Industrial Revolution. More precisely they constituted a striking cultural shift brought on by what the world came to know as technology. Born in England with the development of the steam engine, the Industrial Revolution abruptly altered the structure of the British workforce. Business owners and the laborers on whom they depended formed new relationships as serfdom died. Women put aside their spinning wheels and distaffs to work at powered looms and thought that they were freed from a major portion of domestic servitude by a grand increase in individual production. Social change seemed always to move westward. By the time that the new tools of labor reached the United States, the revolutionary aspect had been refined to an orderly separation of industrial and agrarian economies. Although overseas slave trading was nearing its end, slave ownership continued unabated in the agricultural communities of the American South. Increased objection to the odious practice emerged from the more enlightened, power-equipped industrial centers. Political discord highlighted the opposing factions of North and South as they faced issues focusing on slavery and the rights of individual states under broad federal jurisdiction.

The very issue of states' rights was clarified as a direct result of the development of steam navigation on inland waters. Frictions generated by those diverse interests finally ignited into civil war. In this ferment, companies operating newly designed sailing ships and steam-propelled vessels vied for commercial control of the sea lanes. Meanwhile, the forces of manufacturing and agriculture—production of ironwork and textiles, cotton and grain—bound the United States and its European neighbors along trade routes that stretched in a north-curving arc—a segment of a great circle—on the waters between them.

The Great Circle—the shortest distance across the Atlantic Ocean between the New World and the Old World, roughly a 3,000-mile arc—connected New York and Boston to Bristol and Liverpool. A stormy route, it was ice infested for four to six months of the year as it curved into high latitudes. Mastery of that risky passage—getting a grip on the Great Circle—would provide terminals for American commerce within the seaports of the British Isles, Glasgow to Portsmouth. From there, trade could be extended to the European continent's channel ports, the countries of the North Sea, and departure points from there into the Baltic. American shippers were no strangers to those shores, but their visits were scattered until the industrial surge encouraged increased frequency. From a British perspective, the Great Circle reaching westward away from England's long-established East Indian routes gave it a chance to extend royal hegemony in a firm connection with the United States and the British colonies in the Western Hemisphere.

Nineteenth-century voyages on the transatlantic passage did not, as some historians would suggest, constitute battles between sail and steam. Such battles were rare and conducted more for publicity and color than for conquest. The question was not whether or when but how steam power would enable domination of foreign trade. The answer would be found after achieving control of the pathways by whatever means suited the contenders. A new breed of powerful industrialists sought recognition on one of the world's richest trade routes through both sail and steam vessels that steadily improved in efficiency, opulence, and speed. Profits, commonly achieved by early packet and steamboat operators, became secondary to control for those who sought possession of the Great Circle. A profitable return might be had, but it proved elusive. As Princeton historian Robert Greenhalgh Albion (1896–1983) astutely observed, the "levelheaded businessmen of South Street do not seem to have been particularly concerned, either, that red ink would be used in large quantities in the ledger accounts of those glorious fast craft."

To understand the struggle for the Great Circle, one must appreciate the people involved—their backgrounds, personalities, genius, and flaws. Six skilled men and their unique contributions to the Industrial Revolution stood in public view as these men sent their ships across the ocean in the chase for glory. They aimed to attain that goal through dominance of the long-established commercial routes between New York, Boston, and Halifax on one side of the Atlantic and Liverpool, Bristol, and Southampton on the other side. Connection to ports on the European continent was of lesser importance, for political reasons more than for lack of trade. Control meant the ability to select the cargoes; to set the rates; to draw a thriving revenue-producing class of passengers; and, in achieving widespread recognition, ultimately to pocket the profits. Such control would provide certain testimony to the authority and influence that these men were driven to achieve. Many others competed for it. Fourteen separate steamship lines, American and European, carried transatlantic mail between 1840 and 1860. Some lasted no more than a year or two; only three mail-carrying lines based in the United States remained in operation for more than four years.

The lines of sailing packets are harder to track. They changed names, merged, and converted their fleets to steamships. Their mail-transport activity was limited, lacked government financing, and finally was legally prohibited. Of a dozen American packet lines, two stand out for their longevity in confrontation with overwhelming steamship activity. The combined effect of the packet lines, however, was to keep windjammers active well beyond their technical obsolescence. That alone was a remarkable tribute to the design of their ships and the hardiness of the men that sailed them.

For a half century, as sail and steam sought primacy in ocean transport, the outcome of their efforts remained unclear. Of the three who led the way, Samuel Cunard served as a goad for the American rivalries of Edward Knight Collins and Cornelius Vanderbilt. Intent on claiming supremacy in the territory of the Atlantic, each of them introduced elegant, regularly scheduled steamships into the waters of New York. Two other Americans, Enoch Train and Donald McKay, gambled that, through their combined efforts, they could maintain a lifetime of leadership with the most exquisite sailing vessels ever built. Steam power did not attract them until its superiority went virtually unchallenged. Even after most commercial sailing fleets withdrew from the sea, Samuel Samuels kept the tall ships before those people with the adventurous spirit to voyage in them or to thrill to their passage while they lingered on the sidelines.

The selection of these six men of sail and steam might be challenged as unrepresentative of the broad shipping industry. Why, for instance, choose Train's White Star Line in lieu of the famous Black Ball Line, the originator of packet service that survived for sixty years, well into the age of steam? Why select the maverick Samuels, when so many other well-known sea captains drew a loyal following of passengers? What of Cunard's competitors Brunel and Inman in his home territory? Train's bold gamble in association with McKay, the talented designer of tall ships, separated those two from the crowd. The canny founders of the Black Ball Line get credit for their pioneering venture, but their motivations, as developed in Chapters 3 and 9, excluded them from the intense contest that followed their courageous beginnings. If longevity in sail were the measure, Black Ball, under its third owner, Charles Marshall, deserves full honors. Among the last champions of sail, Samuels stood apart as he sailed a failing company's single vessel through the steamship fleets in testimony to the power and durability of the windjammers.

The British Cunard and the American Collins occupied center stage for ten years as they dueled for possession of the Great Circle. Others, lurking on the periphery once the reach for power became evident, were content to be followers satisfied with the leavings. Vanderbilt, for all his competitive spirit, did little more than roil up the waters, yet he cannot be ignored. The results would have been markedly different had he joined with one of the active shipping companies or turned earlier to the railroads that gained him a second reputation in his old age.

The Atlantic maritime affairs of the United States in the mid-nineteenth century were well documented by Albion (1896–1983). The story can be found in two of Albion's publications, *Square-Riggers on Schedule* and *The Rise of New York Port, 1815–1860*. His texts, bolstered by detailed appendices to each volume, constitute a definitive history of the fifty-year period during which steam power eased into leadership over sail in scheduled transatlantic trade. It would be difficult to improve or expand on Albion's work, even presumptuous to try. There is, however, more to be said about the men who pointed the way across the seas. The stories of their lives present valuable object lessons in high-risk ventures. One could marvel that the risks were taken at all, but we see in them examples that could apply as well today in the field of high technology. Although this term was not known in the nineteenth century, their efforts involved the high technology of their times, along with the accompanying jeopardy of investment in precarious experiments. Although its main stage is the ocean, this book is more than a seafaring yarn. It is the story of those who strove through politics, finance, and foreign affiliations for efficient ocean transport and their extraordinary resiliency in attempting to master the routes across the perilous North Atlantic. In the order of things, they were preeminent as businesspeople. Only Samuels remained a dedicated mariner throughout the period. McKay never navigated the waters on which he launched his ships. He was more artist than entrepreneur, an artist who understood the sea far better than he grasped the Atlantic trade routes that his ships pursued. Vanderbilt started his career on the water but stood at the helm only when it suited his immediate goals. Foremost, they were intent on the business of shipping rather than its direct conduct.

The lives of these men have not been well documented. A century elapsed before a definitive biography of Samuel Cunard was produced. Even then, Francis Hyde's text, *Cunard and the North Atlantic,* was as much a history of the Cunard Line as a recap of Cunard's life through his business dealings. No formal biography of Edward Collins exists. Beyond routine and sometimes startling newspaper reports, little was written about his two transatlantic shipping lines. Despite the wealth, accomplishments, and tragedies that attended Enoch Train's life, he died obscurely. The *Boston Transcript,* daily reading matter of the local Brahmins, gave him no obituary. The principal source of information about him is in *My Life in Many States and Foreign Lands,* the memoirs of his second cousin and employee, George Francis Train, which he published at age seventy-three. Consequently, the recollections of this ever-eccentric writer concerning his youthful period in the offices of the White Diamond Line are understandably flawed in some details. Other books, including Arthur Train's twentieth-century account of the several Train generations in America, *Puritan's Progress,* seem to have drawn thinly on George Francis Train's autobiography. A partial biography of Donald McKay is imbedded in his grandson's history of the McKay ships. Richard C. McKay's, *Donald McKay and His Famous Sailing Ships,* also draws on Train's recollections. Samuel Samuels's memoirs, *From the Forecastle to the Cabin,* concern only his seagoing affairs. He fails even to mention the names of his wife and children, although they frequently voyaged with him. Some of his adventures are so bizarre as to challenge credibility; possibly they amount to no more than the imaginative renderings of an audacious mariner. One can almost sense the raised eyebrows of those who have read them, yet after a century of analysis and review the tales have not been refuted. His story is worthy of another look for what it added to the grappling for the Great Circle.

The struggles of these men were infrequently with each other as they mutually accepted the sometimes deadly hazards of the sea but mostly with the books of account as they strove for territory and treasure. Shipping in any form is a high-stakes gamble with limited promise. While steamship managers plotted among themselves, Americans dedicated to sail worked intensely to drive their ships around Cape Horn and across the North Atlantic as they tracked the two routes that financed the burgeoning nineteenth-century American merchant marine. A Chinese sage once wrote that a single successful voyage would make a shipowner wealthy, two would make him very wealthy, and three would make him wealthy beyond belief. Reflecting the probabilities of continued success in such costly ventures, the rewards hinted at the sometimes deadly odds that mariners faced.

The shift to steam was neither easy nor fully welcome until the champions of sail, as close to perfection in their designs as ever would be achieved, capitulated to modern technology. The transition brought out both good and evil in men, tragedies occurred, and great fortunes were earned and lost. The principal participants in this reach for commercial control of the Atlantic, America's most valuable sea route, have been misunderstood or forgotten by history. Perhaps this tale can set the record straight.

Among the many colorful adventurers during the years from 1810 to 1860 were artist, arms designer, and civil engineer Robert Fulton and his partner, Robert Livingston, a wealthy patriot and politician, whom history has largely ignored; feisty Robert Gibbons, aided by Cornelius Vanderbilt in his bitter rivalry with the Fulton enterprise; megalomaniac William Walker, Vanderbilt's nemesis who died before a firing squad; the sanctimonious conniver Daniel Drew, plunderer of Vanderbilt's millions, who died as a broken and despised old man; Junius Smith, the luckless father of commercial transatlantic steam navigation; George Francis Train, McKay's capricious sponsor; and Newburyport's little-known team of William Currier and James Townsend, builders of what became known as the "Wild Boat of the Atlantic," Samuels's fastest ship. Even showman Phineas T. Barnum and writer Charles Dickens make contributing appearances in the panorama.

Most of the vessels that I name played significant roles in the evolution of the territory of the Atlantic and its adjoining waters. On first mention, where possible, I differentiate among them by class—wind-driven ship without designation, powered vessel with designator "steamboat" or "steam yacht," steamship (SS), or Royal British mail steamer (RMS).

The task of assembling the facts about this diverse collection and threading stories together as they might have appeared during the crucial two decades, 1840 to 1860, of social and technological change was, at once, frustrating and fulfilling. Old texts had to be evaluated for authenticity on detailed matters, which required days of searching through microfilms of newspapers printed 150 years ago. A surprising number of newspapers were published during the mid–nineteenth century—in Boston and its environs alone, twelve dailies, supplemented by numerous local weeklies. My task was made easier by Henry Scannell, newsprint archivist of the Boston Public Library, to whom I'm grateful for his knowledgeable and patient guidance. Retired naval officer, philatelist, and author Richard Winter led me to his own coauthored stamp collectors' book that chronicles all transatlantic mail transport during the period under study. My work in this field was done for me.

An even more complex maze of facts lies in the U.S. Patent Office. Jim Miller, a University of Maryland reference librarian, patiently helped me search that forest of files. I gathered portraits and prints with the help of Karen Shafts, Boston Public Library; Heather Shanks, Peabody Essex Museum; Robin Christiansen, Bostonian Society; and Claudia Jew, The Mariners' Museum, Newport News, Virginia. Judith Doolin Spikes of the Larchmont Historical Society provided information about the estate of Edward Knight Collins. Newburyport resident George Duffy supplied little-known facts about the Currier & Townsend shipbuilding firm. From the bridge of Dick McCarthy's trawler *Spirit,* I gained a mariner's perspective of Navesink, Sandy Hook, the Battery, the South Street docks, and the convoluted waters of New Jersey and New York, all critical to steam's early history. Stan Crapo advised me on the wear and tear of nineteenth-century steam engines. Bob Birmingham and Skid Schermerhorn provided little-known details on the Civil War's maritime edge. Lars Bruzelius, whose encyclopedic knowledge is evident in his Maritime History [Internet] Virtual Archives, added precision to some obscure but useful details. The Internet maritime history exchange supported by the Marine Museum of the Great Lakes with a worldwide subscriber list was often a source of useful information. Through comanagers Maurice D. Smith, curator at the museum, and Walter Lewis, marine historian at the Georgetown, Ontario, Public Library, my thanks go to an unnamed score who responded readily to my queries.

Architectural artist Steve Terrell, although distant from nautical geography of the eighteenth century, was quick to understand my needs and nicely illustrated the challenges of land and sea presented by the broad Atlantic.

Brassey's publisher Don McKeon and editors David Arthur and Jeanne Hickman possess the ability to be concurrently encouraging, cooperative, and demanding. For such an approach in polishing my work, I extend thanks.

Above all, thanks to my spouse, Elinor, for her patience with my hours at the computer, tasteful judgment when requested, and care always.

I

Origins

There is a tide in the affairs of men,
Which, taken at the flood, leads on to fortune;
Omitted, all the voyage of their life
Is bound in shallows and in miseries.

WILLIAM SHAKESPEARE

1

Steam

LEADEN CLOUDS hung over the Hudson Valley as a bitter northwest wind swept downriver in a race with the ebbing tide. On the Hudson's eastern shore, a schooner lay tied to a pier, its bow to the wind and loosely furled sails whipping in the gusts. Half its score of passengers huddled in the lee of the cabin or impatiently paced the deck. Others strode ashore with their satchels and parcels to negotiate a dirt pathway leading to the post road some miles to the east in the hope of obtaining seats on the next Albany-bound stage. How else could they get to the state's new capital until the wind shifted or at least moderated at the turn of the tide? Even then, the schooner faced a tedious upstream passage and endless tacking across the wide river to gain a mile where a league along the shore was to be treasured. Such adverse conditions were blessedly infrequent. On most days, the prevailing winds, fair or foul, angling across the river were buffeted by high cliffs on one side or the other. Upriver progress of the broad-beamed, heavily sparred Hudson River ferries was rarely impeded, but it was always slow. Traveling unvexed meant becoming accustomed to stop-and-go movement and accepting an unhurried pace as part of the process, a disposition hardly in the nature of American entrepreneurs.

In such conditions for the better part of the eighteenth century, men stood on riverbanks and pondered how they might move upstream regardless of the wind. Canals and mule power, meager replacements for patience, were unsuited to the steady increase in commercial traffic between Manhattan and the old deepwater trading post and newly established state government at Albany. There was talk of steam power in Europe, but few of its proponents ventured to project how or when it would assist sailing vessels in the New World.

Then, before the century ended, something happened that turned people's customary disdain for matters *philosophic*—the common term for *scientific*—toward enthusiastic support of science's practical application. The meddlesome tinkerer Ben Franklin considered himself a philosopher. Bifocals, the rocking chair, and a remarkably accurate plot of the Gulf Stream were products of his philosophical studies. The Industrial Revolution propelled the tenets of science on a path aimed at the achievement of broad commercial goals. The arcane studies of physics, chemistry, and mathematics, soon referred to as technology and later put to work as engineering, absorbed urban activities on both sides of the Atlantic.

Within a few decades, the world changed as strikingly as had not occurred in five thousand years, not since ancient civilizations first herded cattle, formed cities, and invented writing. Nineteenth-century technology bettered the farmer's lot with plentiful irrigation, even while improved transport encouraged his migration from farm to factory. Technology brought about machine shops and railroads. It increased the production of clothing for the commoner and cannons for the soldier, which incidentally raised warfare to higher levels of destruction. Technology rushed travelers on routes to the western gold fields, enhanced the delivery of mail, sent thought along copper cables, introduced photography, and generated the need for public schools. It separated the merchant from those transporting his goods, thereby changing the nature of foreign trade. Key to that change was the adoption of waterborne steam power, hastened on rivers and estuaries once it was successfully demonstrated but reluctantly accomplished at sea, so splendid had ocean sailing vessels become.

The first noisy stirrings of industrial development were just being heard when Albany became the capital of New York—thumping pile drivers and slopping water pumps, the squeal of derricks, and the infrequent clang of hammers on cast-iron spikes and beams. Steam power was not then considered an alternate force to the wind; no valid comparison could be made of one to the other. Industrial change in transportation was certain—viaducts, locked canals, iron bridges, mule-drawn railcars contributing—but the outlook on steam's application remained obscure. There was scant motivation behind the burst of new technology. Potential investors were reluctant to adopt unproved approaches or even to experiment with them, there being ample profitable ventures in the new nation's wide-open Western Territory beyond the Appalachians. Steam power built on itself, one minor development on another. Meanwhile, commerce, propelled by the shifting wind, inched upriver.

Since humans had first cooked food in a covered cauldron, men were aware that mechanical energy could be drawn from fire by way of steam. The cover of a boiling stew pot simply lifted off as it balanced between the swirling steam pressure within the pot and the pressure of the outside air. As the contents cooled, the cover fell back as it was pushed into place by the surrounding atmosphere. Somehow, it seemed that work might be accomplished with little human effort. The law describing the physics of confined steam, first defined in the eighteenth century, is simple enough. The pressure of an enclosed gas against its container varies up or down with its temperature.

The Greeks of classical times toyed with a hollow metal sphere fixed on a free-turning axis. Perpendicular to the axis, a tube curving like a belt around the sphere's equator permitted an in-and-out flow of gas. When the container was partially filled with water and its axis suspended in a yoke positioned over a flame, the sphere spun furiously as a jet of steam escaped from the tube. The amusing device, the first steam turbine, was of no practical value in converting heat to motion because it was useless when the water boiled away. Engaging that release of energy in a consistent fashion was another matter, and it was far from simple.

Two years prior to the end of the seventeenth century, before the law of nature was defined for the process, Englishman Thomas Savery produced what he called an "atmospheric" engine by harnessing the motion of an enclosed cauldron. He fashioned a piston on a rod and fitted it within an iron cylinder—cover and pot—and used the pressure of steam expanding into the cylinder to push the piston toward the opposite end. Water injected into the cylinder cooled the steam, reduced the pressure, and allowed the atmosphere to press with greater energy on the piston, thus restoring it to its base. Then the cycle was repeated. Although fascinating to watch, the process did little work. In 1711, improving on Savery's design, Thomas Newcomen succeeded in building enough pressure to engage a machine in pumping water. Soon after, the two men shared an English patent on the first practical steam engine.

Early engines, useful as lifting devices for coal and water, burned immense quantities of fuel and wasted much of the steam. Yet, they eased the mining of coal, and foundries had cheaper fuel. Iron implements came forth and gave rise to metalworking shops and boiler works. Iron workers and mechanics bootstrapped themselves into the development of ever-new equipment and gathered broader-based, productive industries around them. Industrial change sputtered from hope to reality.

A half century elapsed. In 1769, at Matthew Boulton's Soho Foundry in Birmingham, England, James Watt carried the Newcomen engine into new territory. He wrapped the copper boiler and cast-iron piping with felt and plaster to hold the heat and boosted the engine's efficiency. He attached an air pump driven by the engine itself to pack more hot gas into the cylinder, increasing the energy budget. When he attached a separate condensing chamber to recirculate the deenergized steam, the machine could run longer with less waste. The iron piston was 5 feet in diameter, its weight about the limit of what a pair of humans could lift. When steam pressure boosted the disk through an 18-inch stroke, that was enough to power a variety of tasks. A crank and wheel arrangement converted the piston's reciprocal action to rotary motion, and the engine chuffed irregularly at its connected task.

By 1782, Watt had replaced the crank with a system of "sun-and-planet" gears driven by a rigid link between the piston rod and an oscillating beam. Rotary motion drove a sliding valve within the engine that directed steam in alternate strokes to one side of the piston or the other.

1–1. *James Watt (1736–1819) made the steam engine practical.*
The Mariners' Museum, Newport News, Virginia

Engine size was a troublesome obstacle to practical use before Watt and Boulton fashioned a smaller engine that nearly doubled the power output of its predecessor. Today, one can still find a relic steam locomotive—they are still in operation—circuiting cranberry bogs, hauling timber, climbing mountain paths to silver mines, or perhaps performing on a museum's short length of railroad track. When it starts, the engine produces the sounds of Watt's steam plant—sh-h-h-h-h-chuff, sh-h-chuff-chuff, chuff-chuff-chuff-chuff—as its well-oiled parts roll into action. Chuffs blend into a fast-paced accompaniment to the machinery's clanking rhythms. As the engine builds speed, it gasps for breath only when steam pressure drops. Finally, it snorts into idleness and sighs, hot water dripping from its joints and seams. The basic mechanism has changed little in more than two centuries.

The double-acting steam engine propelled locomotives, brought running water into hilltop cities, ginned and baled cotton, powered looms and millstones, helped to dig canals, and drove pilings to support piers and bridges. It opened the doors to the booming industrial age. Steam power's most notable application was the beam engine that shifted the motion to the machinery's side and was compact enough to be installed experimentally in riverboats. On July 15, 1783, Marquis Claude de Jouffroy d'Abbans's *Pyroscaphe* ran for fifteen minutes against the current in the River Saone, France. Its double-acting steam cylinder, connected to a ratchet drive and side paddles, drove the first working steamboat. Although the experiment was considered to be a failure, word of the trial crossed the Atlantic and soon provoked the interest of American inventors. Some day, perhaps travelers could ignore the wind and Albany could be brought closer to Manhattan.

2

The Hudson River Monopoly

EUROPE'S ACCEPTANCE, even envy, of the newly formed United States magnified the fresh ideas and energies emerging from it as the nineteenth century loomed. Commerce, domestic and foreign—ever the principal driving force—shaped the American vision of democracy. Following the Revolution, trade between agriculture and industry increased along newly paved roads connecting flourishing communities to the seaports that fed them. Commerce, dependent on steam power, provided one of the earliest tests of the system of government designed by the Founding Fathers. Divisiveness among the former colonies was spawned by a national zest for independence and largely nurtured by business interests. A critical issue concerning commercial navigation arose among the fractious states and was noisy enough to require resolution by the federal government. The result was a landmark decision with enduring consequences. History gives only token credit to the early steamboat trials that occasioned the affair. The characters in the drama were famed for other adventures.

After a long period of experimentation, much needed breakthroughs brightened the promise of water transportation. Could technology apply steam power to augment the wind's unreliable force? The vague hope became reality only after several would-be innovators stumbled on the way, and then it took a half century for men and materials to arrive at full acceptance.

One of the first steam power enthusiasts, James Rumsey was a shiftless dreamer whose visions often lacked focus. He was a mill operator in Maryland during the Revolutionary War. Then moving to Bath (now Berkeley Springs, West Virginia), he worked as a builder and operated a general store. As he switched interests from one fanciful idea to another, he decided at some point to be the first person in America to produce a mechanically propelled boat. If his goal stopped at the steamboat itself, it did not explain his determined secretiveness. While he guardedly worked on a prototype, it is likely that he sensed the commercial potential of steam-powered watercraft. He might have seen himself as a toll collector on such waters as the James and Potomac Rivers that crossed and paralleled overland commercial routes. Needing money for further development but unwilling to make his work public, he presented a theoretical description of his concept before the Virginia House of Delegates. The delegates were encouraging but not to the extent of financing the continuation of his work, which, at that stage, was more talk than fulfillment. Lurking in Rumsey's shadow was a reputation for shoddy business conduct, widely enough known to have influenced the hedged response.

George Washington, while still commander of the victorious Continental Army, was seeking a place to keep his horses. When he arrived in Bath, he found James Rumsey and engaged him to build a barn.

"General," Rumsey might have balked, "while I'm building this barn, you don't expect me to stop work on my mechanical boat, do you?" He had his priorities, but steady work was not one of them.

The man's description of a steam-driven boat caught Washington's attention. When Rumsey asked him for assistance, the general, fascinated by what seemed like a workable idea, gave him a carefully worded certificate of support. It cost him nothing more than the paper on which it was written. Rumsey built the general's barn and pressed forward, still unfunded, but he was now more anxious than ever to put his plans into reality without disclosure.

Returning in November 1784 to the Virginia government, he pleaded desperately for more specific backing. The compromise that he negotiated turned out to have unexpected long-term ramifications. Rumsey perhaps saw a way to elicit money from other sources, and his subsequent action supports such a plan. It is also possible that the legislature's response was a means to send the applicant away without having to disburse a dollar. It granted him exclusive rights to build his boat and navigate it on Virginia's waters. Two months later, with that permission in hand, Rumsey went to Annapolis and extracted the same license from the Maryland legislature. Small sums of money dribbled his way, but the inventor's debts continued to grow.

The faltering steamboat project obsessed Rumsey, and he began to neglect his family and business. By summer, his reputation in the community was so bad that he had no choice but to forsake his independence and seek employment. He was engaged for a while as a superintendent of Washington's Potomac Navigation Company, then occupied in planning for the Chesapeake and Ohio (C&O) Canal. By then, Rumsey's written endorsement from George Washington must have been well tattered. He was unhappy with what he earned from the canal work and resigned the position within a year. Convinced that he could turn his steamboat notion into a profitable venture, the frustrated and secretive loner decided in 1787 to devote himself exclusively to the perfection of that dream.

UNKNOWN TO Rumsey, another eccentric, John Fitch, had encountered similar rebuffs in Pennsylvania while he was seeking capital to support his own steamboat plans. Fitch was raised, after a fashion, in colonial Connecticut, the fifth child of a dysfunctional family. The distressed youth shipped out on a coastwise sailing vessel and, before long, engaged in a conflict with the mate and was discharged. Several more halting apprenticeships followed. Finally, he found a measure of success after establishing his own brass and clockwork shop. It went well until he invested his accumulated profits in a potash production business, an operation about which he knew nothing. The investment failed, and he lost everything, this while in the midst of an unhappy marriage. The deeply discouraged Fitch left wife and children behind and moved from Connecticut to New Jersey for a fresh start.

John Fitch was not without initiative and talent despite his failed beginnings. Once settled in Trenton, he profitably set himself up as a brass and silversmith. Meanwhile, North America's troubled British colonies moved closer to conflict with the mother country. For seven years, Fitch drew a tidy income from the business, only to see it ruined during the Revolutionary War. Redcoats and the ragtag battlers for independence seemed to be everywhere. Fitch recovered financially by selling tobacco and beer to the Continental Army. His mechanical skills came to his aid when, in 1780, he gained a commission as surveyor to plot land along the Ohio River. Not long afterward, he acquired some 1,600 acres of property in Kentucky, but fortune smiled only briefly on him. While traveling through the wilds of the western lands, he was captured by a band of Indians, probably provoked by the British, and delivered to Canada for imprisonment.

When Fitch was set free after the war, land bordering on the Great Lakes, then called the Northwest Territory, beckoned. He attempted to assemble a number of surveying projects into another new business, but it failed through no fault of his own. Under federal legislation the land was carved into gridlike parcels, which eliminated much of the need for surveys. By then, Fitch had produced an engraved map of the area that was useful enough to give him a sustaining income.

There is no record of how Fitch first became attracted to steamboat development, but by 1785, after he moved to Bucks County, Pennsylvania, the project absorbed all of his energy. Like James Rumsey, he found it to be a costly enterprise and went forth to seek capital. At first ignoring the local agencies, he approached the Continental Congress for financial aid. It is not surprising that, in the new nation trying to get on its feet, his request fell on deaf ears. Undiscouraged, he went next to the state legislatures, and with some success in capturing their attention, his situation improved during the next two years. New Jersey, later New York, then Pennsylvania, Delaware, and finally Virginia gave him exclusive rights to build and operate steamboats on all their waters. Rumsey had delivered nothing on his 1784 grant from Virginia, and, in 1787, unmindful of that withering agreement, the Virginia authorities recognized John Fitch's request. Bolstered by five fourteen-year monopolies and continued earnings from the sale of his map of the Western Territories, Fitch produced models based on his steamboat designs and took them to Philadelphia to present his request for money.

2–1. *Fitch demonstrates his steamboat to the Continental Congress.*
Prints and Photographs Division, Library of Congress

Philadelphia was the American center of scientific interests when Fitch spoke to multiple authorities on what he called "philosophical matters." He met a number of prominent citizens, among them Robert Livingston and Livingston's brother-in-law, Col. John Stevens. Both men, themselves enterprising experimenters, were fascinated by the prospect of steamboat operation. What came directly out of that meeting is unknown, but Fitch's fortunes improved when he was able to raise the funds needed to complete his project. He turned to watchmaker Henry Voight for help in the mechanics of engine construction. On August 22, 1787, they launched an ungainly 45-foot boat, powered by steam and propelled like a South Seas war canoe with six vertical oars on each side. Few passengers could sit among the levers and belts that drove the system. As the strange-looking craft puffed and stroked its way about the Delaware River, members of the Constitutional Convention meeting in Philadelphia gathered on a wharf to marvel at the accomplishment. The publicity fired Fitch's zeal. It eclipsed any understanding that he might have gained of the cost to produce and run a vessel of limited practical use, but it was a start for the inventor of the first American steamboat.

Meanwhile, James Rumsey was making progress. George Washington and other interested observers following his continuing efforts urged him to forsake his secrecy and demonstrate his work. On December 3, 1787, swayed by their encouragement, Rumsey stood proudly at the helm of his boat and navigated her against the river's current at Shepherdstown, Virginia (now West Virginia). He did it again a week later with ample witnesses along the shore to wave him along on each occasion. An atmospheric steam engine propelled the vessel by jets of water pumped from the stern with sufficient force to move the vessel, laden with 2 to 3 tons of ballast, at three miles per hour.

Rumsey and Fitch soon learned of the other's feat achieved within four months of each other. Thereafter, Rumsey made some imprecise claims to priority. In 1788, he published two pamphlets on his position, *A Plan Wherein the Power of Steam Is Fully Shown* and *A Short Treatise on the Application of Steam.* He had thought of a steam-powered boat in 1783, he stated, but not before 1785 did he actually experiment with an engine. Fitch countered with a pamphlet of his own. That extended the controversy but enabled Fitch to keep his monopoly and continue his experimental work. Was it Rumsey's idea to monopolize the inland waters, or was it born of the Virginia legislature? Could it have been Rumsey and Fitch that provoked the other states to establish similar licensing? States' rights were not clearly defined in the new nation. Where individual states' waters swirled into each other's territories, a potential cloud of controversy hovered over the strange new craft exploiting them.

Although Rumsey was credited with the invention of an improved steam boiler, a plan for use of a steam engine to raise water, and two applications of steam power to mills, he derived little income from them. His funds were exhausted. Like Fitch, he went to Philadelphia to plead his case before the scientific authorities. In May 1788, he made a presentation to the American Philosophical Society, founded by Benjamin Franklin. The elderly statesman and scientist had suffered from a severe fall in January, and it is likely that he heard of Rumsey's plea only secondhand unless, as later happened on a regular basis, the meeting was held in Franklin's home. Franklin's interest in scientific matters never waned. At any rate, Rumsey found the society's members eager to help him. To circumvent Fitch's public support, they sent him to England for patents and English capital. In nearly all steamboat developments, money and control combined to form a catalyst, the driving force more powerful in its own way than the few steam engines being produced.

With Rumsey on his way to England, John Fitch plodded about Philadelphia where he was met with public indifference. In July, he launched a 60-foot, steam-driven paddle wheeler, a vessel able to carry up to thirty passengers. For him, it was an exciting step forward. He started an irregular round-trip service on the Delaware River that ran between Burlington, New Jersey, and Philadelphia. Even a twenty-mile upstream trip at an average speed of more than six miles an hour drew little attention. Only shipwrights, mechanics, and a handful of investors, all workers in his own company, showed interest, just enough, as it happened, for Fitch to accumulate funding for an even larger boat in 1790. He put it into regularly scheduled service on the Delaware and advertised daily in the Philadelphia papers. The accomplishment won him a United States patent in 1791 and similar recognition later from France, but it gave him little in the way of personal income. Again aided by company members, he started work on his fourth boat, the aptly named *Perseverance*. Before completion, the vessel was destroyed in a violent storm. Fitch's financiers refused to advance him any more money. The discouraged inventor fled with his patents to France, but he found no further help there among those who had been the first to propel a boat by steam.

Impoverished and in poor health, Fitch worked his way to Boston as a deckhand. The brother of his estranged wife met Fitch and took him to East Windsor, Connecticut, his birthplace. Fitch's life seemingly had gone full circle, and he decided to claim his lands in Kentucky. Before doing so, he made one further attempt to eke a living out of the New York monopoly that he still held. On Collect Pond in lower Manhattan, Fitch put a steam engine into a small boat, one able to carry only four passengers, and attached a screw propeller to the stern shaft. The demonstration gained him nothing but deeper debt. Robert Livingston, who kept his distance while following Fitch's work, expressed interest in assuming his monopoly. The discouraged Fitch went on to Bardstown, Kentucky, where he settled down to write his memoirs. Two years elapsed. Then in July 1798, John Fitch, deeply despondent, ended his own life.

James Rumsey was welcomed in England, where he received patents that friends eventually helped him to acquire also in the United States. He stayed abroad to produce a second steamboat, as always delayed by interim failures and a persistent lack of funds. His American backers had withdrawn their support. For four years, Rumsey doggedly pleaded and tinkered. Finally, as the winter of 1792 approached, the end of his effort was in sight, a vessel that he named *Columbia Maid.* Just prior to its completion, on December 20, at the age of forty-nine, James Rumsey died. His English friends buried him in an unmarked grave in the churchyard of St. Margaret's, Westminster.

ALREADY A budding inventor at age thirteen, Robert Fulton produced a skyrocket for use on the 1778 Independence Day. The town council of Lancaster, Pennsylvania, forbad the use of his invention and told him that it was wasteful of candles, which were in short supply. The following year, Fulton designed and built a foot-operated paddleboat, but it was art, not invention, that had been his primary interest since he was ten years old. Lancaster was a major gun-producing center, and, as Fulton came of age, he became an expert gunsmith. Many of his drawings tested successfully on a local shooting range. At age seventeen, he went to Philadelphia, where he supported himself by painting portraits and landscapes. In his varied activities, the young man developed into America's answer to Leonardo da Vinci. During his four years in Philadelphia, Fulton made enough money at art to purchase a small farm for his widowed mother but jeopardized his own health in the process. Relatives made arrangements for him to go to London and live with an old family friend, and, in 1786, the year that James Rumsey turned from canal construction to steamboats, Robert Fulton left for England. He would not return to his homeland for twenty years.

Two disciplines now drew Fulton's interest: art and the technology of canals, mechanical equipment, and steam engines. His art supported him, and through his patron, Benjamin West, he established contacts with the English aristocracy. Here, at last, was a tinkerer unhampered by lack of funds. Through friendships with Lord Stanhope and the Duke of Bridgewater, he became involved in several engineering projects; by 1793, he was painting only for his own pleasure. Fulton received British patents for a device that raised and lowered canal boats and for machines to cut marble, to twist hemp into rope, and to spin flax. At that point, no doubt aware of the French experiment with the *Pyroscaphe,* he talked with Matthew Boulton and James Watt about his interest in having their firm build a compact steam engine for boat propulsion. Canal systems drew much of his attention as he produced inventions for cutting and dredging channels. In 1796, when John Fitch gave up his nautical efforts and moved inland to his final home, Fulton published *A Treatise on the Improvement of Canal Navigation,* illustrated with his mechanical designs. He signed it "Robert Fulton, Civil Engineer," the first declaration of his new profession. George Washington, an active proponent of the anticipated C&O Canal, received a copy. Fulton, the artist turned civil engineer, assumed what was to become an important role in the Industrial Revolution.

Fulton did successful design work in England and later in the United States on the building of cast-iron bridges and aqueducts. Then, in 1797, he turned his genius almost exclusively to submarine warfare. Because such costly experiments were beyond his means, he went to Paris in the hope of eliciting the support of the French government. An essay that he wrote on the use of mines and torpedoes gained no recognition from the Directory, France's increasingly powerless executive body, but Fulton was fortunate in meeting Joel Barlow, an American citizen who was then a resident of Paris. Barlow became interested at once in Fulton's project and provided much of its financing. Later to gain fame as a poet, statesman, and liberal philosopher, he spoke of the Fulton vessel as the "plunging boat." The torpedo experiments at Brest proved unsuccessful, and without further capital, Fulton resumed painting to do a portrait of Barlow. His major work, a panorama titled "The Burning of Moscow," was the first of its kind. By charging admission to see it, he was able to support himself and return to his submarine investigations.

By 1800, Napolean had become interested in the Fulton plans and appointed a commission to study them. A demonstration of the diving boat *Nautilus* in Havre was surprisingly successful. Four people were able to remain submerged for four and a half hours at depths up to 25 feet. Supplied with compressed air, propelled mechanically, and directed by compass, the unique vessel was used in demonstrations for five years. The British became interested when the device was used to blow up a brig in Deal, England, but, in the end, neither England nor France accepted it. Throughout his varied efforts, Fulton was always careful to keep the U.S. government officially informed. Ultimately, he caught the attention of conservative statesman and marine enthusiast Robert Livingston.

Livingston, a prominent New Yorker with substantial influence in political matters, had served on multiple congressional committees between 1779 and 1781. On August 10, 1781, he became the nation's first secretary of foreign affairs, with an interest focusing on the United States' longtime ally, France. With his departure from office, Livingston returned to Clermont, his estate on the Hudson River. There, while keeping a hand in New York politics, he revived the interest in steamboat development that he had first expressed to John Fitch. During his third term in Congress, 1784–85, Livingston was much concerned with Great Britain's activity at the beginning of the Industrial Age. As New York Chancellor, he administered the oath of office to President Washington in 1789. Washington offered him the ministry to France in 1794. He declined because he planned to run for the office of governor of New York the following year.

2–2. *Robert Livingston (1746–1813); statesman and raconteur.*
Library of Congress

After meeting defeat in that effort, Livingston again turned to national politics.

At various times, Livingston explored his navigational interest with John Stevens and separately with John Fitch, from whom he acquired the Hudson River steam navigation rights in 1796. He was also in contact with two other contenders who could lay claim to worthwhile steamboat advances. In October 1798, while Barlow and Fulton were engaged in submarine development in France, Nicholas Roosevelt, founder of the nation's first engine works and one of Livingston's associates, launched the steamboat *Polacca* in Passaic, New Jersey. It achieved three miles per hour in an experimental exercise that was taken no further.

By far, the most colorful and perhaps pivotal steamboat inventor was Samuel Morey of Orford, Connecticut. In 1793, after experimenting for three years with steamboats, Morey devised a small craft with a steam engine mounted in the bow and successfully operated it at five miles per hour on the Connecticut River. There is also indication that he might have produced other steamboats about this time. It is certain that he was issued patents for a rotary steam engine and a steam pump on March 25, 1797. Seeking financial aid, Morey built a side-wheel steamboat in Bordentown, New Jersey, that he demonstrated on the Delaware River. Although that venture was unsuccessful, it was probably what brought him to Livingston's attention, albeit at an inappropriate time. Livingston's hold on the Hudson River steam navigation rights did not last; without anything to make use of them, he lost his rights in 1798 for failure to perform.

In 1801, Livingston's New York chancellorship expired. After declining an offer of secretary of the navy—there was little navy to oversee—he accepted an appointment as minister to France. He sailed for Havre in October. During the following year in Paris, he participated in the negotiations for the Louisiana Purchase.

Livingston's enthusiastic interest in steam propulsion brought Fulton to his attention. Their first meeting set the evolution of the steamboat on an entirely different course. Initially, Fulton was unwilling to give up his underwater experiments, which were showing increasing potential. It was Livingston's evident political influence in New York State, coupled with a generous financial arrangement, that persuaded Fulton to work on producing a New York steamboat. As he saw it, the project would enable him to exploit some of his canal plans that had taken second place to the diving boat. Livingston, hopeful that he could introduce commercially successful steam-powered transport on the river flowing by his Clermont home, was pleased to have found a stable, well-rounded engineer with firmly established credentials. On October 10, 1802, the two men entered into formal agreement to construct a steamboat for navigating the Hudson River. Livingston immediately sought to renew his monopoly. He regained it in 1803. It was issued in the joint interest of Fulton and Livingston and was extended for twenty years.

That spring, an auspicious failure gave Robert Fulton the lesson that was ultimately the key to his success. A boat launched on the Seine River in France broke in two under the weight of a heavy engine. It became clear that wooden hulls must be accommodated to available engines, and engines must be designed to smaller specifications than typical stationary steam plants. The problem of matching the two criteria would plague steamboat engineers for decades to come. Barlow and Fulton found a stouter hull and fitted it with Barlow's steam boiler and Watt's engine. On August 9, 1803, before a committee of the French National Academy and dozens of onlookers, they drove the boat successfully against a 4½-knot current.

Following that accomplishment, Fulton decided that he was ready to experiment in New York. He placed an order with Boulton & Watt for a steam engine to be delivered to a New York dockyard, where he would have a boat designed and built specifically for the engine. He had to acquire export permits, and, in the meantime, he intended to undertake further study of both French and English experiments with steam propulsion. Lingering always in his mind was the work that he wanted to do in America on canal development. Robert Fulton had a full plate, and he was in no hurry to clear it. Two more years passed before he returned home.

Meanwhile, Livingston's brother-in-law, John Stevens, in 1803 launched the first practical screw-propelled steamboat in Hoboken, New Jersey. The *Little Juliana,* equipped with an overhead beam driving twin

2–3. *Robert Fulton (1765–1815), artist and engineer.*
The Mariners' Museum

screws, was considered experimental and was not put into commercial use. Livingston, with a view to witnessing firsthand the steam navigation developments, resigned from the ministry in the fall of 1804. Until Fulton started his experiments, Livingston, too, was unhurried in his return to the hilltop estate. He visited London and traveled on the continent for several months, while he warmed up to the leisurely life of a retired statesman, collected art, studied agriculture and paleontology, and maintained continuing correspondence with George Washington and Thomas Jefferson. Livingston's arrival in the United States preceded Fulton's by a year. Finally, raconteur and engineer were reunited in New York in December 1806, in time for Fulton to take delivery of the Boulton & Watt steam engine.

Not long afterward, Samuel Morey met with Fulton to show him a model of his own steamboat and persuade him to adopt it. Morey had patented a steam-engine improvement in 1803 and was hopeful that the two of them could do something jointly. It might have been the influential Livingston who put the two men in touch, but, even if so, Morey bowed to Fulton's views without protest. Fulton had his own ideas, now being implemented in Charles Brown's yard, and he rejected Morey's proposition. Once Fulton's project was seen to be fruitful, Morey would claim that Fulton stole his ideas.

While work continued on the steamboat through the spring and summer of 1807, Fulton turned back to his submarine designs. On July 20, he demonstrated his torpedo by blowing up a brig in New York Harbor. For whatever fame that gained him, it did not deflect him from what had now become his major effort. Brown launched the steamboat, and, after a few weeks of fitting out and testing, it was ready to poke its way up the Hudson River.

The vessel was 133 feet long, with an 18-foot beam and 7-foot draft. It was decked over for short distances at both bow and stern. Midships, two uprights and a crossbar formed a frame that provided leverage to raise masts in the forward and after portions of the hull. As ungainly as the rig appeared, it was a masterful design in its practicality. The masts could be lowered for passage under bridges or the sails, square-rigged forward and gaff-headed aft, put to use in the event of engine failure. An enclosed deckhouse near the stern protected passengers from the elements and the machinery's sooty fallout. The Barlow boiler, 20 feet tall and set with its firebox in brick, was housed aft of the midships framework. Forty cords of hardwood filled the fuel bunkers. The Watt engine in the forward half of the hull was open to view. A canvas tent was suspended from a cable that ran from the foredeck to the top of the aftermast. Smoke and steam were carried away through a tall stack rising over the engine. Nonfeathering paddle wheels were positioned amidship on each side.

2–4. *Fulton's* Clermont, *the first steamboat to reap profits.*
The Mariners' Museum

Unnamed, Fulton's vessel was originally referred to simply as "the steamboat," later more formally called *North River Steamboat,* and destined to go down in history as the *Clermont.* Its famous voyage from New York to Albany, completed on August 17, 1807, gave Fulton an unearned reputation as inventor of the steamboat. More appropriately, he was the first to turn its development into a commercial success and to envision the outcome of this revolutionary step in transportation.

The North River Steamboat Company, with Livingston and Fulton now in control of a renewed New York waterways monopoly, charged an immoderate $7 for regularly scheduled one-way passages between New York and Albany. Livingston turned his earnings back into the business, and Fulton continued to produce more boats based on the prototype with ambitious plans to exploit the inland waters of the United States.

The monopoly was challenged almost at once and widely ignored on the Great Lakes and other New York waterways. The rights granted in 1803 and 1807 were renewed under supplementary laws in 1808.

In 1811, Aaron Ogden, briefly a senator and governor of New Jersey, turned from politics and the practice of law to steamboat operation. He built the *Sea Horse* with a Dod engine for a run between Elizabethtown Point, New Jersey, and New York City. The New York legislature had granted Livingston and Fulton exclusive rights to the route into New Jersey. In opposing the monopoly, Ogden, backed by the New Jersey legislature, failed to break the partners' control. Deeply committed to his venture, he arranged a supplemental agreement and, at substantial expense, bought a ten-year right to operate on the route. Taking shape was the precedent that the first common carrier to operate between defined ports thenceforth owned the route.

Undeterred by tests of their control, Fulton and Livingston continued to expand their operations. The first New York canal commission was formed, and Livingston, never a reluctant politician, was appointed to it. Fulton shelved his canal theories as he found himself fully occupied in the construction and operation of steamboats. The two partners were joined by Nicholas Roosevelt and Livingston's brother Edward of New Orleans in establishing a similar monopoly in the newly admitted state of Louisiana. On March 17, 1811, the *New Orleans* was launched on the Monongahela River for operation on the Mississippi, the next step in a plan to encompass all American intracoastal waters. During the following January, it was the first steamboat to call at the port for which it was named and began operations between there and Natchez. The 270-ton vessel

cost the partners close to $40,000 to build and carried a crew of three offi-
cers and six men. Although the opening of the War of 1812 forced cancel-
lation of the nationwide plan, North River Steamboat Company kept the
New Orleans running on the Mississippi and launched the *Fulton* in 1813
to run in Long Island Sound. Under Fulton's leadership, steamboating
had gone beyond an exploratory venture on the Hudson to become an
attractive commercial undertaking.

Robert Livingston died that year. His heirs, including son John, con-
tinued to hold with Robert Fulton the rights that were routinely renewed.
When Fulton died in 1815, his heirs joined with Livingston's to keep
North River Steamboat in tight control.

Meanwhile, Samuel Morey continued his work and grumbled all the
while at the Fulton "thievery." He received another patent for a steam
engine improvement in 1815 and, on April 1, obtained an early American
patent for a "vapor engine" on which he had worked quietly for years. In
place of firewood, water, and steam, it used naphtha, within a single
cylinder, fired from a spark coil—an early version of the first internal
combustion engine. For some time, Morey puttered his *Aunt Sally*, powered by his unique device, around Fairlee Pond (today known as Lake
Morey) in Fairlee, Vermont. The invention generated little interest, however, and, in a state of pique, he sank the boat in the middle of the lake
and withdrew from the struggle for recognition.

Next to muddy the waters around Manhattan was opportunist Thomas
Gibbons, a lawyer and politician from Savannah, Georgia. During the
Revolution, he had split politically with his patriot family, thereby saving
the Gibbons family plantation during the British occupation. After the
peace, Gibbons expanded his Georgian law practice and added some
$15,000 to the plantation income. Legal work led to his being assigned as
campaign manager for Anthony Wayne, who successfully unseated the
representative from Georgia's First District. The election was under sus-
picion, and the losing James Jackson instigated a congressional investigation. He stated that Gibbons's "life has been a scene of political corrup-
tion," which offended the cantankerous Gibbons, and he challenged
Jackson to a duel. Either the two men could not have been serious or they
both had miserable aim; no one was injured after several shots were fired.

Gibbons became mayor of Savannah for three separate terms between 1791 and 1801 and then a federal judge for the Georgia district. In 1810, he moved north and purchased an estate in Elizabethtown (now Elizabeth), New Jersey, on the Raritan River.

In 1817, Gibbons's interests turned to steamboating when he acquired a ferry, the *Stoudinger,* that ran west of Staten Island between Elizabethtown Point and New Brunswick, more or less along the state line. By arrangement, it connected at Elizabethtown with Aaron Ogden's steamers. Ogden's ferry line operated on the north side of Staten Island, under the costly Hudson monopoly license between Elizabethtown Point and New York City, and crossed the Upper Bay above the Narrows.

New York Harbor at the confluence of the Hudson and East Rivers, around Staten Island, and out to the Narrows was laced winter and summer with ferry routes. Most vessels were small and sail powered, their designs harking back to the harbor craft of northern Europe. If the wind

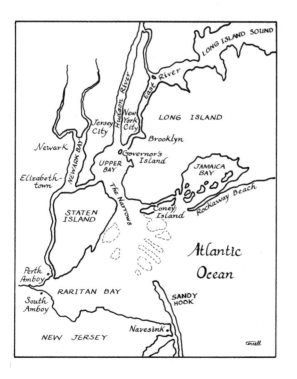

*Hudson River
at New York Harbor*

was fair, the passage from Staten Island's Port Richmond to the ferry pier at the foot of Broadway took about two hours and three hours to tack against it on the return route. On a good day, an eager young skipper from Staten Island, Cornelius Vanderbilt, could handle two round-trips with his piragua and brook little delay in waiting for passengers. On an early morning run, he hauled island produce to Manhattan and came back with a load of fish from the market. He and Thomas Gibbons had similar feisty temperaments. Later, they allied themselves, and the association enabled Gibbons to compete successfully with the Fulton-Livingston combine.

Rumsey, Fitch, and Fulton proved the feasibility of steam propulsion and fostered the Hudson River monopoly that set an example for exploitation of marine commerce. Fulton, the most farsighted, sensed the likely consequences of steam navigation as a vital element in American sea power. During his lifetime, no one was interested in the threatening deep waters of the Atlantic. It was freshwater steamboating that motivated the early adapters to throw their chips on technology's table. Through it, they learned that hull design and sturdy materials were vital to operational success and a viselike grip on the waterways to profits. Decades later, the cold glint of freight and passenger fees would capture the interest of those who would strive at almost any cost to replace sail in the tortuous crossing to Europe. Before that time, wind-driven shuttle service had to create the demand.

3

Deep Waters

AFTER TWO HUNDRED years of woolen cloth production in Yorkshire, England's northernmost county flourished with the advent of steam-powered looms. A ready market for woolen textiles had been found in the former American colonies, which, even better, produced a plentiful supply of cotton for English mills. Isaac Wright and son William migrated to Long Island to take up the importation of goods from their native land. Son-in-law Francis Thompson remained briefly in the Yorkshire cloth trade and then hastened to join the Wrights in 1798. Thompson's nephew, Jeremiah Thompson, age fifteen or sixteen at the time, crossed the Atlantic three years later. The members of this Quaker family were as close-knit as the bolts of cloth that they produced. A tightly bound partnership, they were determined to build a successful textile business in the New World. Manchester mill operator Benjamin Marshall assured them that he would take all the bales of American cotton that they could ship. By the time of Jeremiah's arrival, Francis and the Wrights were spending most of the winter in the Georgia cotton market in an attempt to satisfy Benjamin Marshall's needs at favorable prices. In New York, trade-oriented Jeremiah managed the exchange of raw cotton from the southern states for English-made woolens.

Simple as the process was, there were impediments. In 1803, when Marshall started to export his cotton fabrics to the United States, he found an imbalance between demand for the English mill products and the seasonal output of American agricultural communities. Without equivalent eastbound cargoes, ships waited at their Manhattan piers to fill their holds while exchange goods sat idle in Liverpool warehouses awaiting shipment to New York.

Francis Thompson proposed that the partnership could improve the situation and balance trade by shipping cotton in its own vessel, along with barrels of apples from New England orchards, ashes, flour, tobacco, and perhaps rum, as well as passengers. There was money to be made in the business of shipping, and the family put their efforts into the new venture. Thompson and Isaac Wright located a 384-ton vessel under construction in New York.

In 1807, Thompson and Wright acquired the brig *Pacific* and put it to work, under Captain John Stanton, in hauling bales of cotton from Charleston, South Carolina, and Savannah to New York. They topped off the holds with products from local markets and sent the goods to Liverpool in exchange for fine Lowestoft and Staffordshire china and the plentiful textiles that they knew so well. The firm prospered. In 1815, when the disagreements between England and the United States had been settled, Benjamin Marshall, who had married Captain Stanton's daughter, joined the enterprise. By then, business manager Jeremiah Thompson's name was listed in the New York directory of import/export agents.

Firmly scheduled departures from American seaports in intracoastal trade were customary. Packet lines had thrived on the Hudson River since 1810. Lines sailing from New York to Richmond, Philadelphia, and Baltimore followed. A company in Baltimore sailed routinely to New Orleans. Jeremiah proposed to his partners that they could do the same thing in foreign trade and support the consignment of goods to their names. That would ease the problem of fluctuating seasonal cargoes and draw income from regular transport of goods for others.

In softly spoken Quaker style, the partners weighed the risks against the opportunities and kept the textile trade high in their priorities. More than one ship would be needed to offer a reliable timetable; three should do it or perhaps four. Adroitly, they placed the first additional ship, the *Amity,* into regular service. Benjamin Marshall and Jeremiah Thompson, with a New York office at 273 Pearl Street, presented themselves as textile merchant-shippers. The Wrights and Francis Thompson were shipping operators.

In 1816, the five partners bought shares in a jointly held business named the Old Line; spread the ownership of the *Pacific,* coupled with the *Amity* of nearly equal tonnage; and sent the two ships on regular voyages between New York and Liverpool. The following year, they put the *Courier* into transatlantic service. Finally, their largest vessel, built to their specifications, was named *James Monroe* in honor of the president of the United States. Within two decades, the English businessmen, by evolution or design, had become prosperous Americans.

On October 24, 1817, advertisements in the *New York Commercial Advertiser* and *Evening Post* announced the Old Line's monthly scheduled packet service between New York and Liverpool.

> The ships have all been built in New York, of the best materials, and are coppered and copper fastened. They are known to be remarkably fast sailers, and their accommodations for passengers are uncommonly extensive and commodious.
>
> The commanders of them are all men of great experience and activity; and they will do all in their power to render these packets eligible conveyances for passengers. It is also thought that the regularity of their times of sailing, and the excellent condition in which they deliver their cargoes, will make them very desirable opportunities for the conveyance of goods.

The vessels were pledged to sail on scheduled dates, "full or not full," a new departure for transatlantic service. It would start with the *Courier* departing from Liverpool on January 1 and the *James Monroe* from New York on January 5, followed in February by the well-known *Pacific* and *Amity.* Each vessel would make three full voyages per year.

In Liverpool, Captain William Bowne was delayed in getting the *Courier* into the wintry seas. He sailed on January 4 with eight passengers and a good cargo of textiles, mail, specie, and fine freight. On the snowy morning of the *Monroe*'s scheduled New York departure, Captain James Watkinson eased the ship away from its wharf promptly at the appointed hour. The cargo was light—barrels of apples and ashes, a few miscellaneous packages, and a mail bag, and it carried seven passengers in the cabin. When its fore-topsail was unfurled, the skeptical onlookers on the New York piers were presented with the symbol of the innovative new service, a large black disk stitched to the center of the sail. Bookings were meager during the first several months, but the business gradually grew as firm schedules were seen to be a reality. The Old Line also drew bookings from competing shipping companies before, of necessity, they joined in offering similar monthly service.

"Packet service" came to mean scheduled transport of passengers and multiple consignments of cargo. The Old Line's fresh approach to transatlantic shipping also marked the blossoming of business studies focusing on maritime operations. One precept was evident, even if it had not been fully articulated—merchant ships earn profit only while moving, preferably with full holds. A vessel in its berth is a maelstrom of money—even a reduced crew must be fed and paid, gear replaced, supplies loaded, dockside watchmen and longshoremen hired. Send the ship off to sea and it does what its owners intend for it to do—transport goods. Although largely idle while goods are loading, a crew under way continues maintenance, topmast to waterline, while the moving cargo earns its keep. Skepticism that initially accompanied the striking departure from conventional shipping practices withered. After a slow start, the Old Line prospered. The trademark on each ship's fore-topsail earned it the common name Black Ball Line. Lack of revenue was not a concern for long. The company's efficiency was enough that, within three years, its slim passenger lists lengthened and its ships operated with mostly full cargoes. New Black Ball ships became larger and faster as competition increased. Growth in size and speed—that was the key to leadership on the ocean. Even with packet ship proliferation, the line continued to be profitable because of the increasing demand for regular service. Within four years, Black Ball, unperturbed by the competition, doubled the frequency of its sailings.

Francis and Jeremiah Thompson continued to focus on shipping operations, and Jeremiah crossed the Atlantic as needed to attend to the Liverpool agency. Marshall, like the Wrights, was more interested in the textile business supported by the ships. In 1824, when heavy American tariffs were imposed on foreign cotton manufactures, Marshall turned his activities from shipping to the production and printing of domestic cottons in Utica, New York.

Jeremiah continued to increase both his maritime and textile investments and took positions in two other lines, one running out of New York to Greenock, Scotland, and Belfast, Ireland, and the other between Philadelphia and Liverpool. By 1827, when Black Ball was nine years old, he was thought to be the most extensive shipowner in the country. He was also recognized as the world's foremost cotton dealer, buying 150,000 bales annually in the United States.

There is money in expanding the textile business in America, Jeremiah told a brother and partner who managed the Thompsons' English business. There seemed to be no end to the demand, but the ticklish part was transporting goods across the Atlantic and paying for them with return cargoes.

During the year that followed, as it faced shifts in the volume of transatlantic business once thought to be as consistent as thread spun from a bobbin, the warp and woof of international textile business became snagged in a mesh of international finance. The news came from overseas that Jeremiah was critically overextended to the point that English banks were refusing him credit. In 1828, Jeremiah and Francis found that they were both insolvent and were forced to sell their interests in the shipping line. Uncle and nephew had taken their exploits too far, too fast. New York's stringent bankruptcy laws did not stop crafty Jeremiah from attempting to form another packet line within the same year, but that lone endeavor soon expired and he was forced to look for other opportunities. There's money in transporting emigrants, Jeremiah told a cousin, Samuel Thompson, who once had been partnered with Francis. The renewed effort helped the resourceful Quakers to recover financially, although their contribution to American progress on the Atlantic had reached its zenith.

For nearly a decade, Benjamin Marshall's preoccupation in cotton cloth exceeded his interest in timely ships. In 1833, he sold his shares in the packet line, now consisting of eight sailing vessels of impressive size, to his brother Joseph. Both Marshalls were deeply engaged in cotton printing. Within a year, Joseph sold out to join Benjamin in establishing the Hudson Print Works in what would become Stockton, New York, and the Black Ball Line passed entirely from the hands of its founders. For the rest of the century, its fame as the originator of packet service would surpass its more remarkable reputation for longevity as it competed with steadily improving steamship transport.

The spirit of adventure prevailing in America following the War of 1812 had encouraged the assembly of the first Black Ball fleet. From the ripples of industrial revolution swelling from Europe across the ocean waters, there emerged the nation's first sense of manifest destiny. The attraction of free trade drew a surge of courageous mariners from the protection of coastal waters to the newly opened seas. Ample work opportunites were available in the construction and maintenance of sail-driven vessels sturdy enough to brave the Atlantic crossing on a regular basis and in the repairs required after the beatings they took during three seasons of the year. Unconcerned about the iron men manning their wooden ships, shipping operators deferred long periods of dockyard overhaul by ordering routine repairs "between wind and water" while the ships were under way. Always, despite the optimism inherent in American enterprise, operators continued to worry about the availability of ample cargo to fill their bottoms. At the time, by custom more than by tight-fisted necessity, mercantile trade and ship operations were vested in the same individuals. The innovations introduced by the Black Ball packets divided the interests. Transport of consigned cargoes, mail, and specie to settle commercial trades took on increasing importance.

DEPARTURES of the earliest American mail carriers from New York were typically set for the first Thursday of each month if a ship was available. The packet operators promised sailings on fixed calendar dates, regardless of the day of the week. A difficulty arose when sailors adamantly refused to begin a voyage on Friday because, according to seamen's superstition, it was to bring certain disaster. Punctuality was preserved and a compromise reached by pulling away from the berth on the day before a scheduled Friday date and anchoring for the night inside Sandy Hook, where steamboats delivered passengers and the last mail an hour or two before the vessel set out for the open sea. By later standards, the packet ships followed remarkably casual schedules. The primary challenge, as it had been for two centuries, was to complete the crossing intact. After 1840, when British mail steamers customarily sailed from Boston on alternate Wednesdays, and later when they added New York to their schedules, they interchanged weekly Wednesday departures between the two ports. When American mail steamers came on the scene in 1851, Saturday was set as the New York departure day, a standard for all lines. The result was that overseas mail correspondence was well served, regardless of individual shipping line capabilities.

Dead reckoning on the timber route between the Canadian Maritimes and the British Isles was long known to ocean navigators. They adhered to it for the familiar land perspectives that it presented on departure and landfall, the vague sense of timing associated with the behavior of the winds in those climes, the "feel" of the sea, and a perception of control in dealing with the well-defined Gulf Stream, both in and out of it. Its rich, blue waters, practically a navigational mark, were there to be skirted or joined. There were no interim beacons, nothing but an area with the shifting presence of icebergs from January to June. The danger of an ice encounter was limited to the western waters, which covered a third of the passage. Bergs of threatening size could be seen during the day in most circumstances and their proximity often felt in advance—a glint on the horizon, a strange brightening of the gray sky, a sudden drop in air and water temperatures, all signals for seamen to keep sharper lookouts and to proceed with caution. At nightfall, prudent British mariners reduced sail and lowered their topmasts as they adjusted speed in proportion to visibility. They deemed it unwise to send men aloft into the darkness unless the vessel's immediate safety dictated such action. The bolder Americans took greater risks, which were justified, in their view, by quicker passages. Few records were kept of broken spars, blown-out topsails, and men lost overboard. These events were considered to be routine hazards of the sea.

The British Isles

A transatlantic voyage to England brought a ship from New York northeastward past Cape Cod, crossing Massachusetts Bay for Cape Race on Newfoundland's southeastern tip, the last reach of land on the American continent. On the second or third day out, the vessel approached the Grand Banks, frequented by fishing schooners and often enshrouded in fog—wispy windblown veils in winter, dense blankets during early summer. To avoid such conditions, all but the reckless took their departure on more southern and lengthier latitudes. In any event, skippers were inclined to hold a steady compass course to make landfall on Ireland's Cape Clear and off-lying Fastnet Rock. The variation in compass direction from true north to the magnetic pole was well known. Early in the nineteenth century, British explorer Matthew Flinders observed a further variable deviation. Without fully understanding it, he was able to devise a way to reduce or eliminate shipboard compass error by careful positioning of iron objects nearby. It is remarkable that, until midcentury, mariners generally made accurate landfalls based on poorly adjusted compasses and imprecise knowledge of true directions. Some claimed that, if brought blindfolded to any part of the routes they followed, they could identify within a 50-mile radius where they were "just from the look of things."

Circling the southern Irish coast on soundings, navigators looked next for Tuskar Rock, from which a direct run across the Irish Sea brought them to the pilot station at the mouth of England's Mersey River. After a half day's run on the flood tide, anxious crews dropped anchor at the port of Liverpool, among the busiest ports in the world and much savored by American seamen.

Thousands of ships from around the globe might be visiting Liverpool at any one time. Tides of 20 feet flowed past long barriers of brick and stone lining miles of the Mersey's shores, where ships hovered in wait for the opening of the sea gates. Within, floating at the level of neap tide, the

3–1. *Liverpool, England's gateway to the world, at mid–nineteenth century.*
The Mariners' Museum, Newport News, Virginia

vessels rafted in groups. Packed like herrings in a crate, they were secured one to another until shifted into dockside position for the transfer of cargo. Forests of masts rigged with hemp and tar stood above the dense assembly of wooden hulls. Fire presented an enormous risk and was not permitted in any form within the dock area. Even sailors' pipes went unlit. Galley fires being forbidden, coffee and shipboard meals were served cold. American seamen enjoyed an advantage over those from the less affluent nations in that most shipping companies sent their crews ashore twice a day for hot meals at contracted boarding houses.

For both the pleasure of a change of fare and the customary entice-ments of the waterfront, Americans relished a long stay in Liverpool. Port time sometimes lasted for four or more weeks while stevedores discharged and loaded cargoes. These were easy days with reduced watch schedules. Seamen's pay continued for shipboard duties, which were assigned as much to keep the men occupied as for routine ship's husbandry. Prince's Dock was a haven for American packets and cotton ships, beyond which, night and day, lurked hawkers of cheap clothing, trinket hucksters, tavern runners, beggars, crimps, doxies, footpads, pickpockets—all scrambling for the American dollar. No port in Europe could keep a sailor busy and broke better than Liverpool.

Ships crossing from America to Havre and London laid out tracks to make landfall on Bishop Rock, westernmost of the lonely Scilly Islands. From that approach to the English Channel, they either steered directly through the Chops of the Channel to the continental coast and the mouth of the Seine or hopped, beacon to beacon, past treacherous Good-win Sands and crossed the Greenwich meridian to proceed into Ports-mouth Harbor or to round Dover's white cliffs before entering the Thames Estuary.

In midocean, the packets cruised in or at the edge of the Gulf Stream, both eastbound and westbound, the former for the two-knot lift that it gave and the latter for atmospheric warming despite the adverse current. The voyage to America against prevailing westerlies was longer, on aver-age, by some 500 miles, with the ship tacking across the winds and hover-ing, watch by watch, at alternating angles to the desired course.

Cartographer Gerardus Mercator flattened the globe to make its populated, middle latitudes more presentable on paper. At the price of increasing geographical distortion of charted land approaching the poles, ocean navigation was reduced to following a line of fixed direction that, on a globe, parallels of latitude excluded, forms a loxodrome. Crossing all meridians at the same angle, extended loxodromes spiral around the earth, ever to approach but never to reach the nearer pole.

During the first half of the nineteenth century, Atlantic navigators were accustomed to monthlong ocean crossings on routes influenced by the vagaries of currents and winds. They were content to follow rhumb lines, segments of loxodromes, guided by a single compass point to the latitude of their destination. Given reasonably clear skies and a sharp horizon, precise latitudes could be determined with ease three times per day, if needed. Captains took their departure from a known promontory on one side of the ocean and set a direct course for a corresponding landfall on the other. Then following it as closely as winds and currents permitted, they deviated from the rhumb line only to close in on the landfall's latitude as the final days approached. From there, it was a matter of steering due east or west to the desired point. Identifying local longitude, on the other hand, was a baffling procedure fraught with error. In mid-ocean, the sum of the daily runs, based on estimated speed until verified by an observed longitude, often gave them as much data as they needed to know. Thereafter, it was a case of estimating the remaining distance until the vessel came on soundings, found with a deep-sea lead only hours before a landfall. Such was generally the case in the passages between North America and Europe until voyage duration became competitively critical. Then, in the urgency to take the shortest route, a portion of a great circle, the chronometer became an essential tool for finding a ship's position along the curve arcing toward the nearer pole.

Mathematicians have known the principle of traveling on a sphere since the fifteenth century. Columbus was aware of it, but he did not consider that it contributed to the exploration of unknown waters on his shrunken version of the globe. When a string is stretched between any two points on a sphere, its path marks a segment of a great circle, the shortest distance between all positions underlying the cord. The equator is a great circle; any pole-to-pole line of longitude is half of one. Unless a

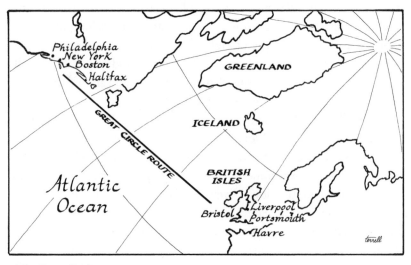

The Great Circle

route lies along the equator or on a line of longitude, it does not hold to a fixed compass point; rather, in its easterly or westerly direction, its arc bends gracefully into colder latitudes. If one constructs a chart, with either pole at its center, on which the longitudinal lines radiate outward over perhaps a third of the globe, every great-circle course can be drawn on it as a straight line. The compass directions of great-circle paths not congruent with longitudes or the equator must be computed at intervals by the complex formulas of spherical trigonometry.

Not until the nineteenth century, when the vast Pacific opened to regular trade routes, did navigators consider great-circle sailing of any importance. Hundreds of miles could be saved in ocean passages between continents by following a great-circle route rather than tracking one-directional rhumb lines. Distance reduction meant conservation of food and water, more important to seamen on long routes than the time spent between ports. Bound to the ship, they wanted none of starvation and thirst. For the captains who spent hours at the mathematics involved in determining their daily course adjustments, it was time well invested when a passage shortened by as little as a fraction of a day gained them fame on arrival at the destination.

The North Atlantic routes were well traveled. After the Revolutionary War, it was uncommon not to sight other vessels during a crossing, a situation as comforting to those waiting at either end as to those on board. "Speaking" a vessel—the practice of logging details of midocean meetings to be reported on arrival at the next port—helped to track the passage of ships during periods when they were normally out of touch. Seaport newspapers carried "Ships Spoken" reports, along with listings of arrivals and departures. Those who had bade a ship farewell two or three weeks earlier checked the shipping news to follow its progress and sometimes learned of its arrival at the destination in advance of routinely returned correspondence from the remote port. Newspapers, mail, and gossip were exchanged at sea or in port as opportunity allowed. Important shipping news, which usually traveled across the Atlantic in five or six weeks, was known to arrive in much less time to the comfort of relatives, insurers, and shippers.

THE WAR OF 1812 was a boon for privateers. Covetous sea chases after plodding British merchantmen taught the plucky Americans that the low, narrow hulls sailed by Chesapeake Bay watermen bought speed at the small cost of reduced carrying capacity. Thereafter, ocean vessels shed their beak heads and high fore and stern castles, raked their masts for efficiency in sail handling, and began moving cargo at an improved "clip." That term, along with their leaping bowsprits and sharp, sloping stems, earned them the designation of clipper. During its early stages, the design was not popular in the Atlantic. A small percentage of increased speed was more suited to long hauls around Cape Horn and east to the Indies. Only the persistent cry for faster passage brought clipper rigs onto the Great Circle of the Atlantic. Still, the ships faced occasional calms and, on the westward crossing, the countercurrents of the Gulf Stream.

The fast-turning paddle wheels of inland waters suggested a compromise solution—spread the sail for a stiff breeze blowing from aft and use steam power in the face of an adverse wind or current. In the southern port of Savannah in 1819, a group of speculators, intent on proving steam's advantage in long-distance passenger transport, arranged the building of a 300-ton brig with auxiliary steam power. The vessel was constructed in New York, and the engine's builder, Moses Rogers, took command. Although stern propulsion was more suited to mastering the currents of shallow and usually placid inland waters, a pair of side wheels provided the power and maneuverability needed for rolling seas.

Named *Savannah,* the ship sputtered up and down the East Coast but gained little attention. Although the vessel seemed sturdy enough for an ocean crossing, the prospect of a long voyage on a smokey paddler proved unappealing to Europe-bound travelers. Loaded with a moderate supply of firewood, a meager cargo, and no passengers, the *Savannah* ran its engine for barely ninety hours during the monthlong crossing from Georgia to England. There, after a shocking arrival—it was thought at first to be a ship afire—it was considered to be no more than an amusing curiosity. Hopeful of arousing the interests of the usually advanced Europeans, the investors scheduled demonstrations in the English Channel and at ports of the North Sea and the Baltic. The *Savannah* was offered for sale to the Russians, but they were uninterested. Nautically, the voyage was no failure, but although it proved that oceangoing steamships might be feasible, it clearly demonstrated that they were uneconomical. When the *Savannah* returned to the United States, the owners removed the steam plant and put the ship to work as a sail-powered cargo carrier.

The *Savannah* was premature by twenty years, even as it gave notice to the world that the Industrial Age, well under way in Europe, was not far behind in America and would eventually find its way to deep ocean waters. Meanwhile, steam tugs, wedging into maritime commerce, were widely used in the British Isles and America's seaports to tow barges and push the cumbersome square-riggers in and out of their berths. Steam puffed over calm water wherever there was a ready supply of fuel, but routes were extended only when vessels grew large enough to support ample bunker space and more efficient machinery.

On both sides of the ocean, zealous steamship advocates stood poised to exploit any advancement in technology. Connecticut native, Yale graduate, lawyer, and temporary expatriate Junius Smith was a well-placed businessman with connections on both continents. He settled in England in 1805 to take up transatlantic trading. Some years later, after a grueling voyage of fifty-four days on a British sailing vessel to visit his agent-nephew in New York and possibly inspired by the successful elements of the *Savannah*'s performance, Smith dedicated his energy to drawing public favor to steamship development. It was a challenging task. He received no support in New York and returned to London, where his ideas were again scorned. His persistent enthusiasm finally made headway after he published a prospectus describing the potential of ocean steamships.

Smith called specifically for the investment of £1 million to bring a development scheme into reality, and, by 1835, he had raised enough to form the British & American Steam Navigation Company. That ignited wider interest, and he was immediately faced with stiff competition. Prodded by engineer Isambard Kingdom Brunel, the Great Western Railway, then running from London to Bristol, looked to steamships as the means to extend its transportation service fully across the Atlantic. In Liverpool, where investors were projecting the Transatlantic Steamship Company, Smith joined with MacGregor Laird of the Birkenhead, England, shipbuilding firm, and they hastened to accomplish their own plans. The race was on, literally, when each company strove to claim ownership of England's first deepwater steamship that would arrive in New York.

Brunel was a man with grandiose ideas as large as his towering stovepipe hat. Immensity attracted him. A year into construction, the 1,320-ton *Great Western* was launched in July 1837, but it required another nine months to fit out. The four-masted schooner had a 750-horsepower, two-cylinder side-lever engine, much like that of a railroad locomotive. The piston, more than 6 feet in diameter, was able to drive the 236-foot hull at nine knots.

Smith and Laird ordered an even larger steamship, 1,700 tons, only to see their skeptical contractor walk away and leave the ship unfinished shortly before the *Great Western*'s trial run. The resolute Smith found a sturdy little coastal steamer, the 700-ton *Sirius,* which he hastily chartered for the scheduled race. He was unconcerned that the vessels were mismatched. The *Sirius* was about the size of a typical New York sailing packet, half that of the *Great Western.* It was one of the first vessels equipped with an important innovation, a circulating freshwater cooling system that eliminated the need to scrape caked salt from the boiler's interior. Smith's primary purpose was to demonstrate the value of oceangoing steam power, not to engage in a race for fame, and he negotiated a four-day lead for the *Sirius*. In April 1838, the seagoing tortoise-and-hare race took place, with both vessels commanded by lieutenants of the Royal Navy.

On the night of April 22, nineteen days after its departure from Cork, Ireland, the little *Sirius* arrived first at the Sandy Hook pilot station. Its bunkers nearly depleted, it was allegedly burning some of the wooden furnishings to complete the passage. The next day, it steamed into the Upper Bay just minutes ahead of its rival. The *Great Western,* bucking the Gulf Stream on its route, had completed the passage from Bristol in fourteen and a half days. Overtaking the *Sirius* while the two side-wheelers traded signals, the *Great Western* headed into its East River anchorage. Thus ended the first in a continuous series of Atlantic steam shuttle runs, the desires of Junius Smith fulfilled.

In one of history's interesting sidelights, the little 32-ton steam tug *Robert F. Stockton,* crossing on the same route in April 1839, arrived one year almost to the day after the *Sirius*. The first American commercial propeller-driven ship, the *Stockton* was also the first iron-hulled vessel to cross the Atlantic. After its pioneering voyage, it was turned over to the U.S. Navy for experimental work before laboring for some thirty years on the Delaware and Raritan Canal.

Despite the disappointing accomplishment of his substitute steamship, Smith did not give up. The *Sirius* continued in operation, and eventually Smith's first planned vessel, the great *British Queen,* was completed and put into service. The opposing Transatlantic Steamship Company never was a contender. Within a year, it withdrew its ships from service, and Brunel's *Great Western* ruled the route. Theorists proposed that steamships could squeeze in six full voyages a year, twice the frequency of the sailing packets. Size was critical for both cargo- and fuel-carrying capacity and important to sustain the extra weight and pounding forces of the iron machinery.

In 1840, Smith added the 2,000-ton, superbly outfitted *President,* the largest steamship afloat, to his fleet and hired as its civilian captain the man who had first brought across the *Sirius*. On its second voyage in

March 1841, the *President*, with 136 people on board, became engulfed in
gale winds. A sailing packet later reported having seen the ship laboring
in tremendous seas somewhere between the Grand Banks and Nantucket,
where it vanished without a trace. From the description of the lone sighting and no subsequent evidence of flotsam, the conclusion was that the
ship fell victim to a design shortcoming that had plagued steamships and
steamboats since Robert Fulton's first launching in France. Excessive

3–2. *Last voyage of the SS* President.
Library of Congress

machinery weight in the midships section caused the hull to sag, which put undue stress on its longitudinal plating. Consecutive wave crests lifting bow and stern could then crack the midsection, possibly wide enough to split the hull. The *President* probably broke in two and went down in minutes.

The great *British Queen* remained in operation, but the life of the British & American Steam Navigation Company, from Smith's proposal to the *President* disaster, eerily foreshadowed similar events of a decade later. Junius Smith, unsung enthusiast of steam power, must be credited as the first accomplished steamship promoter on either end of the Great Circle. The loss of the *President* drove Smith out of direct management of the steamship business. He returned to the United States to resume trading activity and continued to lobby an obdurate government for support of transatlantic steamship operations.

Factories and mills joined plantations and farms to build trade between the continents. The courageous scheduling of sailing ships strengthened it. The hope of steam power energized it. Thus was the Atlantic Kingdom formed. Both size and speed, the demands of its voyaging denizens, compelled hasty advances in technology. It would take astute business managers to contain the menacing costs of such opposing forces.

4

The Means

T HE WAR BETWEEN the United States and Great Britain that curbed the Fulton-Livingston expansion dragged on for nearly three years. During the summer of the first year, the Americans won two decisive battles with the great wood-hulled *Constitution*, built after the Revolution and privately funded for the new clash. In 1814, British warships terrorized the citizenry on the Potomac River and Chesapeake Bay until they were stopped during their approach to Baltimore's Fort McHenry. Lacking an adequate naval defense force to hold back the invaders, the federal government encouraged citizen shipowners to go forth privately and cut the supply lines by open confrontation with the long-experienced British merchantmen; the captures were theirs to keep. Chesapeake watermen eagerly armed and sailed forth in their uniquely shaped vessels, crafted for rushing to market with their catches after days spent harvesting the Bay.

Maritime designers had long held that the ideal underwater shape of a commercial vessel's hull was that of a cod's head combined with a mackerel tail—a rounded bow with the broadest beam no more than a third of the way aft and gradually tapering to a square stern. To fit well into the sea, it should never exceed 500 registered tons. For centuries, merchantmen, whether or not they were armed, were short and beamy, and carrying capacity had priority over speed. Fast-moving American vessels were first seen in deep water when the Chesapeake sharpies sailed along the mid-Atlantic coast as privateers in search of richly loaded prizes. What could have brought a striking and broad improvement in commercial maritime performance was eclipsed by an application of the design to legalized piracy. Refashioned oyster dredges and net haulers were found to be predictably faster than bulky British transports. But adoption of the fishermen's privateer design for commercial shipping use would not occur for twenty years, while the practice of privateering had been raised to the level of a fine, pernicious art that took nearly forty more years to outlaw.

From earliest colonial times, commercial vessels had been heavily rigged, with wide hatches built into broad decks, and designed for profitable, safe long-distance transport. Goods destined for foreign ports accumulated in dockside warehouses until the assigned vessel could depart with full holds. Loosely scheduled sailings were often deferred during winter months. The Black Ball Line's American-built barks, the first rigidly

4–1. *Steerage, emigrants at dinner.*
Peabody-Essex Museum

scheduled packets, were square-rigged on fore and main with a sloop-rigged mizzen, the *James Monroe* being the largest of four at 424 tons. The design presented no radical departure from traditional shipping. Within its 121-foot length, the *Monroe* carried both first-class and steerage passengers, the latter crowded into a combined dormitory and eating space buried in the 'tween decks, aft near the waterline. Typically, the first-class saloon was a long, central room below the main deck, illuminated by a skylight and whale oil lanterns, and furnished with refectory tables and benches fixed on both sides and upholstered in leather and horsehair. Passengers spent most of their days here during inclement weather. Six or seven doors on each side of the saloon gave direct access to snug first-class cabins that berthed a total of twenty-five to thirty people.

Eastbound crossings took about three and one-half weeks, New York to Liverpool, and four to seven weeks for the return in contrary winds and currents. The first schedules appear to have been worked up with little sense of urgency, with each ship assigned three complete voyages per year. Packet skippers were inclined to handle crossings in either direction with haste in order to extend port time before the next fixed departure date and better ensure a full bottom for the return. Because captains generally took 5 percent of freight charges and a percentage of passenger fares, it benefited them to sail with full capacity. Based on that early perspective, speed was to gain time in port for collecting bookings, not to win recognition for faster transport of passengers and cargo.

Alexis de Tocqueville, a penetrating observer of American life, wrote in 1848:

> The European navigator is prudent about venturing out to sea; he only does so when the weather is suitable; if any unexpected accident happens, he returns to port; at night he furls some of his sails; and when the whitening billows indicate the approach of land, he checks his course and takes an observation of the sun.
>
> The American, neglecting such precautions, braves these dangers; he sets sail while the storm is still rumbling; by night as well as by day he spreads full sails to the wind; he repairs storm damage as he goes; and when at last he draws near the end of his voyage, he flies toward the coast as if he could already see the port.

The American is often shipwrecked, but no other sailor crosses the sea as fast as he. Doing what others do but in less time, he can do it at less expense.

In the course of a long voyage the European navigator will touch at several ports. He loses precious time in seeking a port to rest in or in waiting for a chance to leave it, and every day he is paying for the right to stay there. . . . I cannot express my thoughts better than saying that the Americans put something heroic into their way of trading. . . . This same spirit applied to maritime commerce makes the American cross the sea faster and sell his goods cheaper than any other trader in the whole world.

As long as American sailors keep these intellectual advantages and the practical superiority derived from them, they will not only continue to provide for the needs of producers and consumers in their own country, but they will increasingly tend to become, like the English, the commercial agents of other nations.

Shipping companies generally looked tidier from a distance than they might appear upon close examination of their records. By mid–nineteenth century, individual ships were apt to be owned by a half dozen or more investors and assembled in a fleet of three to a dozen vessels operating under the aegis of a shipping line. Each vessel, in effect, was a small company in itself and the line a conglomerate. The captain often held a share in the ship that he commanded, and his partners were typically the builders, a few bankers, and a representative of the shipping line listed as registered owner. Except for the captain, investors had no more say in the operation or management of the ship than do stockholders in companies whose shares they own.

Share owners entrusted shipping operations to "the company" as nominal owner. When a voyage did well, profits were attained as much through speculation in the cargo as through freight charges on consigned goods. The vessel's individual share owners could hold their shares for continued return, trade them, or use them as collateral to invest in other ships. Dissection of a typical shipping company would have shown a mixed group of capitalists who spread the risk for the company itself while narrowing it, ship by ship, for the investors. Vessels famed for performance attracted those investors willing to pay a premium for superior returns. Shares in a fast and profitable ship made good collateral, even as the ship itself aged and newer, more capable vessels came down the ways. Pyramiding of funds by borrowing on one ship to underwrite another promised generous returns, but it was correspondingly fraught with danger for share owners.

Demand for cargoes shifted frequently on all but the most stable trade routes. The discontinued service of one vessel because of age, accident, or temporary lack of cargo might have small effect on a company with a large fleet but impoverish an investor who had unwisely confined his assets to the single bottom. The larger the fleet, as long as its vessels remained engaged, the less was the overall risk for the company. Marine insurance, usually purchased by the company from several underwriters who each took a portion of the risk on an individual vessel and its cargo, might aid recovery in a disaster. However, as profits diminished in competitive markets and companies cut costs, insurance premiums were among the first expenses to be reduced. Shipping company management became calloused toward individual losses due to shipwrecks or storms and ruthless in the expansion of their fleets during periods of high returns.

THE ACTIVITIES of trade and transport separated upon the advent of packet lines. The smaller ships allowed merchants to take advantage of more frequent departures and to ship smaller consignments of goods on individual vessels. The use of packets lowered the risks of cargo loss, damage, and sharp price fluctuations. Shipowners' capital, formerly invested in import and export cargoes, could now be diverted to building larger ships with greater passenger capacity. Gradually, operator and merchant went separate but closely allied ways. Shipowners increased their interest in passenger transport and divided the services offered according to ability to pay. For the 2 or 3 percent of ocean travelers who could afford them, fares of about $150 bought moderately comfortable berthing immediately below the weather deck, three substantial meals per day, and bathing facilities that varied widely—the last not a high priority during the nineteenth century.

Holds deep in the hull with limited earning capacity alternated according to demand between the transport of cargo and of passengers, the latter more routine on westbound routes. Commonly known as steerage, a fare of about $20 provided berthing in crowded dormitory quarters, shared cooking facilities on an open deck, and legally required frugal rations of food distributed on at least a weekly basis.

Masters became famous in their own right. Shipping lines sought the best and routinely associated their captains' names with the ships that they commanded. As a captain's reputation grew, the print of his name became bolder on the shipping cards and his vessel was booked earlier in advance of sailing dates. Transatlantic captains, beyond being capable seamen, possessed chameleonlike personalities. At the head of the gangway, a hearty smile from first greeting to final handshake confirmed that the voyage would be or was the best that the captain's well-known skills could deliver. At the saloon table, with a full seating of first-class passengers, a favorite captain oozed confidence and charm. Alone on the quarterdeck—territory forbidden to all except those on official duty—he stood somberly for hours with all thought apparently concentrated on the welfare of the ship. Shifting his eyes from the horizon toward a malingering seaman, a captain's withering glance commanded more respect than the bosun's rope ends. Just a word or two passed to a mate precipitated the slack sailor's assignment to odious duty at the pumps in the bowels of the ship or on his knees with holystone and brush. Clad in sou'wester and oilskins at the height of a storm, the skipper spiced his orders with strings of earthy phrases, emerging from lungs with the acoustics of a cannon, that could propel a pirate into prayer. The captain's will alone generated alacrity; the ship itself heard and obeyed.

During the nineteenth century, it was not uncommon for their families to travel with captains of merchant sailing vessels. It was recorded in 1852 that Captain Josiah Cummings of the Train Line's *George Washington* took his daughter and a distant cousin on board and placed both young ladies under the care of the ship's stewardess. Once he had achieved command, the adventurous Samuel Samuels was accompanied for some years by his wife and daughters, and at least one daughter was born on board ship. The practice was not widely observed on the packets, and, on steamships, only rare exceptions were made to the prohibition of captains' families accompanying them.

Passengers had little of importance to occupy them during the long voyages, but idleness rarely troubled them. Every day during the crossing was twenty-four hours in length, or more precisely, forty-eight turns of the sandglass. Time was adjusted to the sun by lengthening or shortening the forenoon watch, with the captain calling out, "Make it noon," as the sun reached its height above the meridian. Noon it became, and a fresh glass was turned over. It was convenient and often the practice at sea to turn the calendar over to the new date at the same time. Not until after 1837 were ships commonly equipped with accurate timepieces, and each day commenced at midnight. Within a dozen years, each crossing duration was fine-tuned to a fraction of the hour by carefully noted chronometer observations.

As land slipped under the horizon astern, passengers who had never crossed before were routinely and involuntarily initiated to the ocean's rigors. They were virtually certain to vow that the first crossing would also be the last. People spent time either at the rail or carefully avoiding green-visaged individuals headed in that direction. The cook curtailed rations; sea biscuit and water were the easiest to keep down. In the poorly ventilated lower quarters, nausea spread in epidemic proportions. The wise steerage traveler stayed on deck, day and night, more comfortable in cold, wet wind than sprawled out only a foot or two above fetid bilges. In time, most people gained their sea legs and adjusted readily to the ways of the ship. Steerage space was aired out, and after a few days passengers indulgently accepted the leisurely life of being under way. A typical cabin-class midday meal consisted of soup; fish chowder; roast turkey, perhaps alternated with chicken stew; pasta and fresh bread; beer or porter; and pudding swimming in molasses. Wise captains, aware that long postprandial naps kept them out of the way below decks, fed their cabin-class clients well. In midocean, the cook began to reduce the barnyard population. The early morning squeal of a pig or shrieks of a half dozen hens being put to the chopping block tipped his hand as to the day's menu. On many ships, ardent spirits and wine were available for purchase throughout most of the day.

Music being part of everyday life, saloons were often furnished with an organ or a spinet. Steerage passengers were certain to include someone with a fiddle or a flute. Only rarely would some form of music, interspersed with recitations or readings, not echo through the passenger space from midmorning until after sunset—harmony, hymn, lieder, or love-song to buoy the spirit. Some ships provided gaming equipment. "Shovelboard" is believed to have been a shipboard invention. Reading occupied great lengths of time, as did charades or games that were often frivolous among people living in close quarters for so long. Men gambled, and the ladies dithered at whist. There is something about separation from the land that loosens civilization's ties and releases the lacings of longstanding cultural constraints. The rules of day-to-day life are left on shore, and with them accountability, to be taken up again at the other end of the journey. People share their deprivations and thrills and bind themselves together, if for no other reason than to curb potential boredom. Even the austere are apt to lower their guard to join in frippery and adopt mannerisms that will be shed the moment they walk down the gangway.

Eighteen months after British steamships established regular schedules, Charles Dickens voyaged to America on Cunard's flagship *Britannia* and returned on Train's sailing packet *George Washington*. If he bore any national prejudice, one should think it would have been toward his homeland's shipping line. He chose January, the worst month of the year, to steam westward and June, perhaps the best, to sail home. Conceding that imbalance, his observations still provide insight on the differences between the two modes of travel.

On *Britannia*'s accommodations:

> Before descending into the bowels of the ship, we had passed from the deck into a long narrow apartment, not unlike a gigantic hearse with windows in the sides; having at the upper end a melancholy stove, at which three or four chilly stewards were warming their hands; while on either side, extending down its whole dreary length, was a long, long table, over each of which a rack, fixed to the low roof, and stuck full of drinking-glasses and cruet stands, hinted dismally at rolling seas and heavy weather. . . . I observed that one of our friends, who had made the arrangements for our voyage, turned pale on entering. . . . He recovered himself, however, by a great effort, and, after a preparatory cough or two, cried, with a ghastly smile which is still before me, looking at the same time round the walls, "Ha! the breakfast-room, steward, eh?" We all foresaw what the answer

must be: we knew the agony he suffered. He had often spoken of *the saloon;* had taken in and lived upon the pictorial idea; had usually given us to understand, at home, that to form a just conception of it, it would be necessary to multiply the size and furniture of an ordinary drawing-room by seven, then fall short of the reality. When the man in reply avowed the truth: the blunt, remorseless, naked truth: "This is the saloon, sir"—he actually reeled beneath the blow.

The stateroom engaged for "Charles Dickens, Esquire, and Lady," identified by the inscription pinned "on a very flat quilt, covering a very thin mattress, spread like a surgical plaster on a most inaccessible shelf," the occupant describes as an utterly impracticable, thoroughly hopeless, and profoundly preposterous box. There he sat on a horsehair slab to consider his situation while friends twisted themselves into all manner of shapes to squeeze themselves into the room through the small doorway. The writer's detailed description could well have been the source for a Marx Brothers scenario filmed ninety years later.

On life at sea:

Now every plank and timber creaked, as if the ship were made of wicker-work; and now crackled like an enormous fire of the dryest twigs. There was nothing for it but bed; so I went to bed. . . . I read in bed (but to this hour I don't know what) a good deal; and reeled on deck a little; drank cold brandy and water with an unspeakable disgust, and ate hard biscuit perseveringly: not ill, but going to be. . . .

In a storm:

The laboring of the ship in the troubled sea on this night I shall never forget. "Will it ever be worse than this?" was a question I had often heard asked, when everything was sliding and bumping about, and when it certainly did seem difficult to comprehend the possibility of anything afloat being more disturbed without toppling over and going down. But what the agitation of a steam-vessel is, on a bad winter's night in the wild Atlantic, it is impossible for the most vivid imagination to conceive. To say that she is flung down on her side in the waves, with her masts dipping into them, and that, springing up again, she rolls over on the other side, until a heavy sea strikes her with the noise of a hundred great guns, and hurls her back—

. . . that every plank has its groan, every nail its shriek, and every drop of water in the great ocean its howling voice—is nothing. Words cannot express it. Thoughts cannot convey it. Only a dream can call it up again in all its fury, rage and passion.

When the gale, described by a grimly attentive steward as "rather a heavy sea on, sir, and a head wind," passed, they found the lifeboat dangling in the air, crushed like a walnut shell. The planking of the paddle boxes had been torn away, wheels exposed and bare. The "chimney" was white with crusted salt, topmasts struck and storm sails set; "a gloomier picture it would be hard to look upon." The chief engineer reported that there never was such weather before, four hands given in, dead beat. The ship's cook, found drunk, was hosed down until sober. All the stewards, having fallen downstairs at various meals, went about with plasters affixed. The baker was ill and so too the pastry cook. The voyage was concluded, amid rockets and signal guns, by a grounding on a mudbank, the ship brought to that embarrassment by a confused pilot in a fog, and fortunately soon lifted off by a friendly tide.

By comparison, Dickens describes his return passage, through squally weather and calm, on the packet *George Washington:*

> We breakfasted at eight, lunched at twelve, dined at three, and took our tea at half-past seven. We had an abundance of amusements, and dinner was not the least among them: firstly, for its own sake; secondly, because of its extraordinary length: its duration, inclusive of all the long pauses between courses, being seldom less than two hours and a half; which was the subject of never-failing entertainment. . . . In all weathers, fair or foul, calm or windy, we were every one on deck, walking up and down in pairs, lying in the boats, leaning over the side, or chatting in lazy groups together.

Dickens does not confine himself to the comforts of the fifteen gentry living in the aftercabin. He chats with several of the hundred or so steerage passengers returning to their homeland, disillusioned and starving after failing to find a welcome in America. "The whole system of shipping and conveying these unfortunate persons," states the champion of the poor and downtrodden, "is one that stands in need of thorough revision. . . . The law is bound, at least upon the English side, to see that too many of them are not put on board one ship: and that their accommodations are decent: not demoralizing and profligate. . . . It is bound to provide, or to require that there be provided, a medical attendant; whereas in these ships there are none, though sickness of adults, and deaths of children, on the passage are matters of the very commonest concern."

Dickens's work supports the fact that the ocean, even in its placid moods, is rarely boring. Porpoises frolic in the bow wave. Careful observers might sight pods of whales or sharks feeding in frenzy on the galley's trash. Bloody sawdust and the residue of slaughter were tickets to an aquarian parade staged in the receding wake. Other ships were apt to pass in the course of a Great Circle crossing, always causing a stir on deck, and sometimes resulting in a half hour's gam, as they hove to at close quarters to trade the news.

Matters of hygiene always required attention. Just getting through the weeks with moderately clean clothing took work. Bathing facilities were practically nil until the advent of the American steamships. Fresh water was not plentiful. Cologne, cigars, heavy outer clothing, and reduced nasal sensitivity helped to defer the task that most faced before the eventual landfall—scrubbing out a few articles with yellow soap in a wooden bucket, rinsing them with warm water from the galley stove, and stringing them to dry near the passenger's berth. Laundry was not a service provided with passage. A generous tip to one of the stewards might have helped to acquire it.

So the days passed until the scent of distant forests blew across the deck. Then excitement rose, and anxiety to be among the first to see something solid on the forward horizon underlined the sluggish pace of the tubby barks. Never did a packet sailing schedule promise an arrival date. Always, it seemed to impatient travelers that something should be done to advance it.

In contrast with the early packets, the hulls of the fast-sailing privateers were eventually adopted to meet that need. Because they were low on the water with a straight keel and reduced freeboard, a portion of customary cargo space was sacrificed for speed. For commercial use, the faster packets had to be built larger than their prototypes. Taller masts could be carried, with more sail, which offset, to some extent, the comparative reduction in hull capacity. Whereas Chesapeake watermen needed a low, level deck to work their dredges, sheer was introduced into the passenger and cargo hulls to keep deck space drier. A knifelike stem sloping aft to the waterline justified the "clipper" name. It became an architectural term, characterizing a vessel that sacrificed cargo space in a narrower hull, convex above the waterline and concave below, and was stepped with taller rigging capable of raising a spread of sail designed for speed. After further development, for good reason they also became known as "tall ships."

BALTIMORE's Kennard & Williamson shipyard built an early clipper for Isaac McKim in 1833. At 494 tons, it was at the commonly accepted practical size limit, with enlarged lines based on the Chesapeake sharpies stretching out generously to a length of 143 feet. Named for the owner's wife, the *Ann McKim*, at the time, was the largest or, at any rate, the longest ship in the American commercial fleet, and its radical design was soon adopted by subsequent builders. The beam of just over 27 feet was less than most vessels of similar tonnage and narrowed from near midships to a long above-water afterdrag and a wedge-shaped stern. The slightly raked masts and five courses of sail added to the standard of what became known as the clipper style. A straight, level keel and 14-foot draft gave the ship ample carrying capacity, and the bluff bow seemed not to interfere with the potential for speed. Concave bows, for which clippers would become known, had yet to be introduced. Later held to be one of the first true clippers, the *Ann McKim* became famous under its first owner during the four years that he commanded it. After Isaac McKim died, the vessel was sold to Howland & Aspinwall of New York. From there, it sailed routinely to India, once in a swift round-trip of seventy-nine days, and continued in service under multiple owners for eighteen years.

This ship design was an abrupt breakthrough after hundreds of years of evolutionary change. It reached its culmination by the middle of the nineteenth century with the development of extreme clippers that capped some forty years of steadily refined designs. Their foremost architect and builder, idealist Donald McKay, would not have agreed, but there was not much that could be improved on them. Their lines had a significant sheer, straight keel, sharp concave entrance under a leaping bow leading to a long hollow run, and rounded stern. As clippers grew in elegance, their cutwaters often bore carvings of busty, full-blown women; an angel with golden trumpet; or a bearded, sea-soaked Neptune blowing on a conch shell; and, flowing aft, a gilded scroll bearing the ship's name extending like a pennant from beneath the figurehead around the hawseholes. The clipper hulls were works of art beneath sails forming glorious cathedrals of canvas, the combination forming the acme of marine architecture.

TALL MASTS and complex rigging set apart the extreme clippers from the original packet ships. Fully rigged, a clipper carried three or four masts, each with six or more sails one above the other and, in light airs, parallel square sails stretching sideways over the water. Only the bowsprit, forestays, a diagonal stay between masts, and the aftermost mast supported fore-and-aft canvas; all other sails, twenty or more, were suspended from crossed wooden yards, some over 100 feet in length. On each mast, a dozen or more men might be sent aloft to furl sail. Bending over a yard and pushing their legs against wire footropes, they bundled canvas—in icy weather, hardly more flexible than sheet metal—on three tiers of spars. The clippers were exquisite ships, but as they increased in size, their construction costs soared to the point that the investments matched those of established steamships. As for the men who had the stamina to serve above or below decks, they were ever in short supply, not for lack of courage but because of the meager pay. Yet, once under articles, nothing deterred the "packet rats" if they were amply fed and treated with justice, no matter how roughly.

There was a large measure of overlap in the two modes of ocean travel, with the earliest packet lines reaching their highest level of perfection long after the novelty of steamships had turned to practicality. In the British Isles, steam-tugboats plied the Thames, Clyde, and Mersey from the middle of the 1820s. In Glasgow, engineer Robert Napier produced side-lever engines for shipwright John Wood's sturdy hulls and paddle wheel packets for coastal and Isle of Man trade and the waterways extending to the Channel ports and to the North Sea.

Windjammers and steamers strove voyage by voyage for top honors in passenger service. The rise in performance and popularity of the clippers closely paralleled that of the foremost steamships, while passengers contrasted the shortcomings and advantages of both. Inevitably, comparisons were made of the accomplishments of the two most newsworthy vessels, the steamship *Pacific* and the clipper *Flying Cloud,* but they were futile. The two vessels did not even use common ocean paths. Steamers avoided the beam seas that brought on a rolling motion, but windjammers sought the same winds that generated those seas. Adverse winds into which steamships readily thrashed closed off a quarter of the compass to the sailers.

The split between old and new cultures brought on by the Industrial Revolution was well delineated in the seaports of the United States. In colonial times, American dockyards were famed for delivering sturdy vessels at low cost. That reputation continued for several decades into the nineteenth century until comfort and speed became the critical measures of operational success. Similarly, Scots iron and engineering works held an early reputation for top-quality steam plant production. As oceangoing steamers increased in number and gradually in onboard conveniences, sailing vessels became larger, faster, and incidentally dependent on steam tugs for movement in and out of their berths. Size meant speed. A steamship owner, because of the higher cost of labor and fuel required for ocean voyages and longer in-port periods of maintenance, had to reduce average ocean-crossing time by more than two or three days to justify the use and associated passenger discomforts of the vessel. Elapsed time of passage, the most visible measure of performance, became a significant standard of comparison in the struggle for recognition.

Shipowners cared little for the technicalities, as long as speed was attained with small loss of canvas and cordage or without waste of coal. It was a challenge to determine whether sail or steam was more efficient in transporting goods and people. Ton for ton of displacement, square-riggers could carry more cargo than paddle-propelled steamers with their dusty coal bunkers and heavy machinery. Coal was cheap when it was delivered alongside in lighters or stacked on the piers in burlap bags, but its cost ran higher when it was stowed in space otherwise used for cargo. Yet, it was difficult to weigh its price against the cost of cordage and an occasional topsail blown out of its bolt ropes. Thrashing paddles enabled close steering into contrary winds and easier adjustment to ocean currents. Year by year, the vagaries of the Gulf Stream were better plotted and more predictable. Generally dissociated from wind direction, steamships either circumvented the midocean river or used it to advantage.

Steam plants developed haltingly, dependent more on the strength of materials and the technology to shape them than on inherent design. The invention of the double-acting, single-expansion engine in 1819 first encouraged experimentation with steam in ocean crossings. That engine and water-tube boilers, eventually fashioned of rolled iron, enabled the delivery of sufficient power to drive paddle wheels through heavy seas.

FOUR ELEMENTS made up the under-deck engine complex. The furnace, a brick firebox with a cast-iron flue, rose into a metal stack funneling smoke into the rigging. The funnel was sometimes angled and swiveled to lead the black clouds to leeward. That ungainly rig, used properly, saved thousands of dollars in canvas and hemp, which were subject to rot when coated with the chemical fallout of sulphur, carbon, and damp salt air. Over, within, or around the firebox stood the boiler as an integral part, its makeup varying according to its designers. The initial seagoing boilers were made of copper or iron plate, rectangular in cross section, riveted at the seams, and unable to sustain steam pressure of more than twenty pounds per square inch. Fire flared up within tubes passing through water in the sealed boiler, later driven by forced draft, to generate steam. The water-tube boiler was a more efficient alternative in raising steam to the desired pressure, but it was more difficult to maintain. Fireboxes stoked with hotter-burning anthracite fuel, preferred over the softer bituminous coal often used by the British, came into use when iron gratings were made that could hold their shape at the higher temperatures. Pitch pine logs were used to fire up a cold plant, and the cords were often stowed on deck to free bunker space for the primary fuel. Only after rolled iron could be produced in quantity, at the time of the Civil War, did oval or cylindrical boilers—so-called Scotch boilers—enable a generous and, by then, a necessary increase in steam pressure, but steamships had already come into their own.

The agony of working in the fireroom, deep in a poorly ventilated hull, could bring a normal man to the limits of life in a matter of weeks. Gasping coal passers lugged baskets or pushed loaded wheelbarrows from nearby bunkers to the men at the firebox openings, two to three hundred loads per watch. Multiple pairs of side-by-side fireports beckoned for continued attention to the roaring hell within. At one furnace, a sweating stoker shoveled fuel to within inches of the blaze. At the adjacent fireport, a trimmer pushed back the fire; raked out dead clinkers and split larger ones with a heavy iron slice bar; spread the layer of coals evenly to increase the intensity of the flames; and shook down the ash, and scooped it, hot with glowing embers, into buckets. Stoker and trimmer then exchanged duties as the next barrow was trundled into place. Periodically, ash buckets were hoisted by hand lift to the open deck and the ashes dumped over the side, a duty coveted for the escape that it gave into fresh air. With 60, 80, 100, or more tons of coal burned in a day, the heat was so intense that nothing in the fireroom but the filthy slate floor was touchable. Flame at the fireports singed hair off of arms and seared facial flesh. Only under ventilators trimmed to the breeze might a cooling draft of air be felt, but it was pulled from above deck more to fire the furnaces than to relieve the workers. During the course of a watch, it was not uncommon for a man to collapse, either exhausted or stricken with cramps from drinking too much water too hastily in an attempt to slake his thirst. Even the bunkers gave little relief from discomfort. Tight compartmentation to prevent coal from shifting also blocked the circulation of air in the dusty atmosphere.

Above or to one side of the fireroom, the water tender stood on a grating, his attention centered on a vertical glass tube showing the boiler's water level and the arrow of a glass-fronted gauge indicating the pressure of steam being piped to the drive cylinder. An engineer, positioned on an upper platform, spun the horizontal wheel of a valve controlling the engine's pace, a rein on the horsepower of the massive machinery beneath him. It was the water tender's task to balance the opposing forces of firemen and steam engine. If the boiler water fell too low, the pressure rose, with puffs of steam leaking from seams dangerously close to bursting. If the water rose too high or the flames diminished, steam pressure fell and the engine slowed. A brass gong was fixed on a bulkhead near the duty engineer, its lanyard parallel to a voice tube; both led to the bridge. On

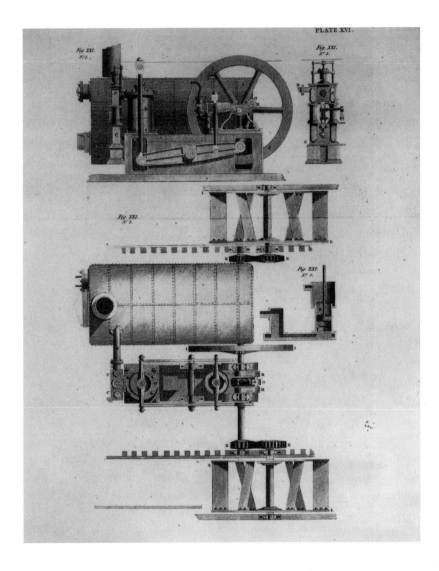

4–2. *Early side-lever steamship engine plans.*
   The Mariners' Museum

voice or bell signal from above, the engineer shouted for more steam or turned down the valve, thereby controlling the engine's speed and hastening the water tender to his double duties.

The machine that set the Industrial Revolution in motion, the single-expansion engine, was double-acting. A sliding valve within the steam line, driven by a portion of the flow, allowed the boiler's major output to enter first one end of a wide cast-iron cylinder, which pushed the piston to the opposite end, and then back to the earlier position. Exhausted steam, its effective energy spent, was recirculated to a nearby condenser, cooled, and returned to the water supply. Before the invention of the cooling condenser, seawater was used. Residue minerals were flushed with more seawater, which inevitably led to caking and corrosion of the tubes and the subsequent need for replacement.

The iron piston, 7 to 8 feet in diameter, with a vertical stroke as much or more in length, was connected by a rod to an oscillating beam. British and American engineers differed in their methods of coupling the beam to the paddle wheel's driveshaft. The British preferred a geared linkage in their oceangoing vessels; the American approach, stemming from the earlier riverboats, was to drive the paddle shaft directly from the overhead beam. The machinery's height was such that the beam, visible above decks, could be seen rocking in synchronization with the turning paddles. The walking beam resembled a giant, grasping metal insect. Although the engine room's open shaft allowed escape of excessive heat, it exposed those below to the vagaries of weather and turbulent seas. Considered by most engineers to be impractical for Atlantic crossings, the beam engine nevertheless was used well after midcentury by one of the major entrants in the Great Circle competition.

The side-lever engine was the preferred alternative solution. The piston moved vertically and was attached to a crosshead with connecting rods that reached down to mechanisms near the engine's base that, in turn, drove the paddle shaft. Somewhat more complex than the walking beam, the side-lever engine was adopted by the leading American competitor on the Atlantic. Horizontal cylinder arrangements were tried without much success. They were troublesome to work on; parts wore out more frequently; and, until John Ericsson's development of direct drives for screw propulsion prior to 1839, they could not supply the steamships with adequate power and speed.

Limited steam pressure kept the paddle wheelers operating long after the screw propeller proved to be a superior form of propulsion. There was no good way to build the higher pressure needed to achieve suitably fast propeller shaft revolutions. Early oceangoing side-wheelers were slow—at five knots, they were easily outrun by the fast clippers—and drastically uneconomical until means were devised to increase fuel efficiency and steam pressure. The answer, introduced around 1852, was the compound, or double-expansion, engine, which was not used until contention for the Great Circle was close to resolution. A second, larger cylinder received the first cylinder's exhausted steam and extracted more energy from it, thereby improving fuel efficiency. To drive the two cylinders, steam pressure was tripled, which required stronger and tighter boilers that could be formed only from rolled iron plate. It was the production of rolled iron in quantity that guaranteed steamships the lead in ocean transportation.

One more design feature became necessary—the shift from wooden to iron hulls. As steam plants became bigger and heavier and required sturdier underpinnings, wooden vessels tended to sag, which stretched the hull planking below water and caused it to leak. One corrective technique was the installation of a pair of unsightly iron bridgelike arcs stretching fore and aft, one running along each side of the main deck and stiff enough to prevent bow and stern from twisting upward. The effect of the hogging beams, so called because the shape resembled the curve of a hog's back, was to offset the machinery's midships strain on the hull. Hogging beams were seen frequently on riverboats, but they were unsuitable where sails hovered low over the decks. The solution for oceangoing steamships came finally with the development of iron framework, the hulls at first sheathed with wood and then with riveted iron plates.

The opposing forces of sail and machine propulsion lay as much in design and material availability as they did in wind and steam. The Cunard Line was slow to convert to iron hulls. It was prevented from doing so by a British Admiralty contract that subsidized only those vessels suitable for warship conversion. Convinced that iron was more liable to permanent fracture in battle—wood could absorb cannon shot better and offered the possibility of underway repair—the Admiralty insisted on wooden construction for ships under mail contracts. Not until the French introduced the explosive shell, capable of rendering damage on impact by blast, fragmentation, and fire, did the Admiralty modify its view and then slowly. The Americans, behind the British in iron plate production, tended to follow their lead in choice of materials. The costs of advancing technology would be such that commercial shipping using it could not survive without the fostering funds of government. Iron plate introduced a radical twist in the commercial reformation under way.

There was a marked difference in the financial structures of sailing packet operators and steamship companies. Until the Black Ball Line made consignment of small lots a common practice, sailing packets and most of their cargo were owned by individuals or groups. The practice was a holdover from privateering days, when merchant princes were more interested in the cargoes than in the vessels, considering the latter to be only the means to an end. Operating under the umbrella of a shipping company, a shipping firm provided dockage to the shipowners while attending to much of the financing and freight booking, usually centralized at the shipping line's office, but this process became too cumbersome and costly with the advent of steamships. Governments expected to deal with more tangible and tightly organized entities as they began to consider shipping subsidies. Stock companies were formed, and steamship owners and operators turned over their financial interests in cargoes to the planters, manufacturers, and merchants who traded in them. The focus of steamship operations shifted to the steady business of passenger trade, whereas cargo transport was taken for granted.

The Americans outshone the British in passenger service. American operators offered more comfortable accommodations and a more varied bill of fare to draw travelers to their ships, whether sail or steam. If the ambience cost more, they felt that speed would make up the difference, keep the fares competitive, and add the advantage of quicker passage. The British shipping companies, led by Cunard, put safety first and waited for such prudence to be justified. When the competing nations met on the Great Circle, Tocqueville's perceptions came sharply into focus. The Americans did indeed put something heroic into their way of trading.

II

The Contenders

. . . *the harder the conflict, the more glorious the triumph. What we obtain too cheap, we esteem too lightly; 'tis dearness only that gives everything its value.*

THOMAS PAINE

5

The Forerunner, Samuel Cunard

TWENTIETH-CENTURY European travelers associated the name Cunard with Harrod's, Rolls-Royce, and Sotheby's. During the 1930s, the name conjured up visions of ermine-wrapped celebrities walking pampered poodles on a promenade deck, famed actors waving white caps to their fans, and smiling sportsmen, nattily outfitted in argyle sweaters and flannels, leaning on the rails while above them towered the steamer's black-topped, clay-red stacks, symbols of safe, stable transport between New York and London. By 1950, the Cunard name became synonymous with elegance in transatlantic voyages as the line adopted the opulence that had been introduced by an American entrepreneur a full century earlier. If someone mentioned taking a Cunard liner to Europe, the response might have been, "Getting there is half the fun." So it had been during the Victorian era for passengers traveling on American ships. Ambience was not then a hallmark of the Cunard Line.

The line's founder, Samuel Cunard, was born in 1787, the eldest of five sons of Abraham and Margaret Cunard. At the close of the Revolution, the loyalist pair had migrated with their slaves to Nova Scotia, Abraham from New York and Margaret Murphy from Charleston. Both Quakers and apparently well off financially, they married shortly after their arrival in Halifax and settled into the community.

When Samuel was about fifteen years old, Abraham, a master carpenter, realized that his eldest son's penchant for commercial matters offset his displeasure with school, so he sent him to Boston for three years as an apprentice shipbroker. The lad was warmly welcomed by the businessmen of the New England port, then America's largest. Samuel found challenging work on the Boston waterfront and reciprocated with a lifetime allegiance to the city. During the colonies' breakaway war, 30 percent of the British merchant fleet had been American built. Early in the nineteenth century, the skilled craftsmen of Massachusetts dockyards were producing sturdy vessels for the open market at less than two thirds of the cost of

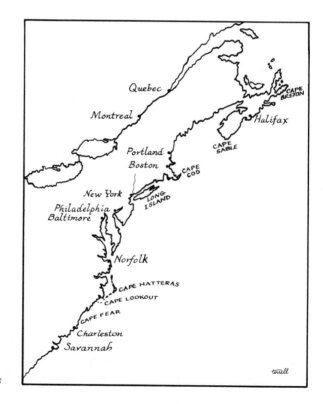

North America
and the Maritimes

vessels from English yards. Lumber was cheap, and labor was plentiful. Halifax, where Samuel's brother Joseph took up lumbering, was little different, and it was considered in England to be North America's most important seaport.

Returning to Halifax where his shipwright father was engaged in building a small fleet of whalers, Samuel worked as an import-export merchant. He was twenty-five years old when issues of free trade and sailors' rights brought on war between England and the untested United States. The British colony of Nova Scotia was not in direct contention with the new nation. Equally in favor of free trade, its citizens were eager to maintain good relations across the Bay of Fundy. Samuel was quick to determine what foreign goods might be needed by those in commerce and government. Adept at identifying the means to acquire them, he received permission from Nova Scotia's lieutenant governor to carry on trade between that colony and any port in the United States. With £200 in capital, Samuel joined his father and brothers and formed the trading firm of Abraham Cunard & Son after they dispatched the father's whalers to the Pacific. In 1813, the company purchased a British prize of war, the sailing vessel *White Oak*, and put it into transatlantic service out of Halifax. A lone cargo ship being likely prey for privateers, the Cunards astutely arranged for it to sail in company with English men-of-war.

In 1814, at age twenty-seven, Samuel married Susan Duffus, a local unpretentious young lady. He became active in local government while continuing to manage his family's financial affairs. By 1825, under his guidance, the firm had partial or full interest in as many as forty vessels and shipped cargoes among the Maritimes, New England, Bermuda, and the West Indies. Capitalizing on its success, the firm built Cunard's Wharf in Halifax to accommodate the fleet's comings and goings.

Joseph, with as much drive as his older brother, added a steam-powered sawmill to his lumberyard, took up shipbuilding, and formed J. Cunard & Company. Expanding into the diverse activities of brickmaking and fisheries, he soon found himself overextended. Loaded with debt and unable to meet his commitments, Joseph watched his business fail. It mattered to Quaker-raised Samuel that family honor be preserved, and he took up settlement of the debts. That worrisome experience conditioned

Samuel for a lifetime of narrowly conservative financial control in business and personal matters, a trait that would endear him to the canny Scotsmen with whom he later associated. Brother Henry withdrew from the family business to go into farming, while Samuel and father, Abraham, became the mainstays of a growing family fortune.

Commerce and communications never withered entirely between the warring nations. When hostilities ended, the Cunards were poised to take up commercial mail transport among Halifax, Newfoundland, Bermuda, and Boston. The activity required the assignment of multiple ships on regular schedules. No delay to top off partially full holds could be tolerated. Managing a fleet of sail-driven vessels did not distract Samuel from keeping an eye on developments southward, where steamboats plied the waters of New England's protected coastlines. Across the sea, the coastal steam packets cruising among the British Isles were doubling in numbers every two to three years. Highly utilitarian steam-powered tugboats appeared in nearly every busy harbor on both sides of the ocean. A paddle wheel connection was the obvious next step. Yet, in 1819, the American steam-assisted brig *Savannah* had gained little notice for its round-trip crossing of the Atlantic. Its one voyage with steam power, unmatched for years, had signaled that paddlers were not ready to extend trade on the high seas.

Abraham retired, and the name of the family shipping line was formally changed to S. Cunard & Company. By then, the firm had become the tea agent in the Maritimes for the powerful East India Company. After Abraham's death, Samuel valued his assets, including his inheritance, at £200,000 ($980,000), while his fine reputation spread as he engaged in both government and mercantile operations. The good life had its setbacks. In January 1828, after nearly thirteen years of marriage, the reserved Susan Cunard died at Halifax and left Samuel, then forty-one years old, with seven daughters and two sons.

In 1831, the three remaining Cunard brothers, Samuel, Henry, and Joseph, purchased an interest in the steamship *Royal William,* a sail-equipped twin-engine paddle wheeler then running between Halifax and Quebec. Two years later, after a successful one-way crossing from England to Nova Scotia by the British sail-steamer *Cape Breton,* the Cunards warily sent the *Royal William* across the Atlantic to London. It is difficult now to sense the slow pace of transatlantic communications during the early nineteenth century. Months could pass before ship mail brought pertinent news from across the sea. Private letter transport by designated ships was customarily an improvement over the rudimentary overseas postal service. The more efficient masters saw their reputations enhanced by the service, their names often specified as carrier on overseas envelopes. Yet, too often, a long delay in response to European mail was explained by word received that a ship possibly carrying messages had "gone missing." One can imagine the anguish that troubled the Cunard brothers as the weeks following the departure of the *Royal William* passed into months. Finally came news reporting its ocean-weary but safe arrival at the River Thames, having limped for ten days on a single engine.

In thinking about packet transport, Samuel was seemingly unimpressed that sailing vessels were doing quite well on the Liverpool routes. Philadelphia's Cope Line had claimed profitable operation since 1807 and New York's Old Line, known widely as the Black Ball Line, since 1817, but only steam power attracted Cunard. Fast steamships, he reasoned, could offer more frequent and reliable regular service. A half-dozen years before regular transatlantic steamship service was proved feasible, Cunard started to explore its possibilities. In January 1838, Samuel, brother Joseph, and Samuel's twelve-year-old son sailed to England, where they met with steamship enthusiast Judge Joseph Howe of Halifax. When news of the April race between the paddle steamers *Great Western* and *Sirius* was posted, several commercial shippers took notice. Howe's excitement over having sighted the little *Sirius* during its westbound passage aroused his interest in expanding and modernizing the existing British packet service. The conservative Cunards, receptive to the concept but without a specific plan of action, let prudence temper Judge Howe's exuberance.

THE STEAMSHIP race sparked the attention of authorities at Whitehall, home of the British Admiralty. The Admiralty's interest was aroused in great part by a radical program of reform in postal service initiated during the prior year. Until 1837, mail service in Great Britain and generally throughout the world had been disorganized and complex and its cost out of all proportion to benefits. The British government looked on postal charges as a troublesome source of tax revenue that, while necessary, was not self-supporting. Most of the stiff fees were collected from mail recipients upon delivery; addressees were free to refuse letters sent to them and to ignore the charges. The combination of exorbitant fees and payment on delivery led to widespread abuse of the service, especially in overseas mail. Travelers would agree with their families and friends to send pre-planned "safe-arrival" letters upon reaching their destination. An intentional misspelling or code mark in familiar handwriting on the cover might signal that additional information was within and the envelope should be accepted. Otherwise, on examining the hand-stamped cover, the recipient refused to accept or pay for the letter, awareness of the letter's existence being adequate to the purpose. Thousands of rejected letters collected in post offices and added to the costs that underlay the heavy postal rates.

English educator Rowland Hill made a detailed study of the postal service to discover that the typical domestic mail fee of one shilling and one penny was thirty-six times the actual cost of transport. His report with statistics and conclusions, published in the pamphlet *Post Office Reform; Its Importance and Practicability,* was widely read. Hill's recommendations were eagerly accepted and resulted in a drastic reduction of postage rates in Great Britain and a complete turnabout in the method of collecting charges.

Hill suggested that the intricate mileage calculations then in use should be discontinued, and that postage should be prepaid by the sender at a uniform rate based on weight. Hill was the originator of the adhesive postage stamp. In lieu of hand stamping to show payment, he recommended that the government sell a gummed "bit of paper just large enough to bear the stamp." The proposals became effective on January 10, 1840, with prepaid rates of two pence per ounce for any distance within the United Kingdom. Worldwide postal reform followed. A number of international mail service treaties officially replaced the antiquated method of transporting private "ship letters" via individual sea captains, although the practice continued until prohibited by law. Skippers had little objection to the ban, for the new arrangement generally compensated them with the full amount of the overseas portion of the fees.

It was not until 1847, following careful study of the British system, that the United States government issued its first adhesive stamps, taking action after several other nations. Prepayment was optional until 1855; then nine months later the use of government-printed stamps became compulsory. Appropriately, the portrait of the long-deceased postmaster general, Benjamin Franklin, appeared on the initial American issues, a symbol that lasted on envelopes for more than a century.

In the capacity of administering contracts for British overseas postal transport, the Admiralty gave notice in the fall of 1838 that it sought tenders for monthly service between England and Halifax. The specification called for steam vessels of no less than 300 horsepower to operate from one of five listed English ports. Samuel Cunard was in Halifax in November when he first saw the specifications. Attracted by the prospect of fixed funding for transatlantic mail conveyance, a new concept in maritime affairs, he booked passage on the packet *Reindeer* and sailed to England early in 1839. By now a man of substantial wealth, Cunard carried noteworthy credentials. Except for his tardiness in responding to the Admiralty's notice, he was well qualified to meet its requirements.

Cunard was short in stature, but he had a stately bearing. His high brow, tight mouth, and narrow jaw fostered the impression of innate intelligence and strong will. He was a gentle person, with a natural energetic enthusiasm that led some to think him impetuous. Cosmopolitan Londoners saw the quiet man from the Maritimes as rustic and even shy, traits that well could have enhanced his negotiating ability. His past service as lighthouse commissioner in North America and as a colonel in the local militia, as well as being a continuing Honorable Member of the Halifax Legislature, gained him a ready welcome among government authorities. Commercially, it helped his cause that the Cunard firm was the Nova Scotian agent for the East India Company. East India's secretary, James Melvill, well fixed with the Lords Commissioners of the Admiralty, became Samuel Cunard's London advisor and intermediary. "You cannot do better," Melvill wrote to Cunard, "than to go to Robert

5–1. *Robert Napier (1791–1876), Cunard's counselor.*
The Mariners' Museum

Napier for your ships." The Glasgow firm of Wood and Napier was also under contract to East India.

As early as 1833, Napier had looked into the possibility of steam-powered transatlantic passenger service. He sent his analysis of contemporary ocean traffic to a potential investor in the Clyde Trust—Patrick Wallace of London: "Besides the regular Packet ships, about 170 sailing vessels averaging 400 tons each have left Liverpool for New York from March 1st 1832 to the 1st of March 1833 and in the same time about ninety vessels about the same burden have left Liverpool for New Orleans, which all carry more or less passengers, a number of whom no doubt would go by steam once it is fairly established." Wallace and his fellow London financiers found Napier's ideas of steamship management much too advanced when he advocated the inclusion of low-cost arrangements for emigrants in addition to space for the customary cabin passengers. They failed to sense that the few elite travelers in the upper decks would be a lesser source of profit than the volume of commoners willing to accept minimal accommodations below. Napier would have to wait until he found more farsighted capitalists.

Cunard's interest found Napier eager to collaborate. The proposal for low-cost passenger trade was put aside. At best, the proposal merged into the concept of a single-cabin class of accomodations for all travelers. He was impressed by the initial specifications for two steamships of 300 horsepower and about 800 tons burden that Cunard delivered through Glasgow agents, William Kidston and Sons. "I shall want these vessels to be of the very best description and to pass a thorough inspection and examination by the Admiralty. I want a plain and comfortable boat, not the least unnecessary expense for show. I prefer plain work in the cabin and it will save a large amount in the cost," Cunard wrote Napier. The words were predictable of Samuel Cunard's ultimate style of operation: safe, plain, and economical vessels for the cabin class. In time, that policy, to which he held firmly, would be sharply at odds with his American competitors.

At their initial meeting in March 1839, the two men agreed to the building of three wooden paddle wheel steamships, at least 200 feet in length with 32 feet between paddles. It is possible that Cunard never intended the pact as anything more than an indication of his good intentions. At any rate, the ships were never built. Napier, having second thoughts, suggested that the ships were too small for their purpose and urged him to increase the size. Troubled by the added cost, Cunard stalled. Napier was eager to proceed and proposed that he himself would pay for the enlargements. Overcome by the offer, Cunard weakened and on March 18 the two men signed a contract. Each of three Glasgow-built vessels displacing 960 tons and equipped with two 375-horsepower engines would cost £32,000 ($156,000, circa 1850). Napier wrote to Melvill, "I have given him the vessels cheap, and I am certain they will be good and very strong ships."

Cunard's association with naval officer Edward Parry, formerly stationed at Halifax and now Admiralty Comptroller of Steam Machinery and Packet Service, might have been the source of an inside lead. At least, Parry hinted at the extent of the Admiralty's interest when Cunard approached George Burns, Napier's associate, to explore Burns's interest in the Admiralty's needs. An agent for the Glasgow Steam-Packet Company, a coastal trading firm, the religious Burns was also a ship operator. Each of his vessels carried a clergyman as a standard member of the crew. Appalled at the extent of the transatlantic project, Burns turned the Admiralty proposition down cold. Unaware of the rejection, Cunard took a coach from Scotland to England, construction contract in hand, and soon wrote to Napier from London, "The Admiralty and Treasury were highly pleased with the size of the boats." Everyone, it seemed, was pleased, except Burns and perhaps the English shipbuilders who had lost to their Scots competitors.

The size of the proposed ships continued to nag at Napier. "Your boats are too small," he again told Cunard, who resisted further change. Melvill supported Napier by reporting to his headstrong client, "The adoption of Napier's views is imperative. He is the great authority on steam navigation and knows much more about the subject than the Admiralty." Cunard, torn by the possibility of a greater investment and making slow progress on raising the necessary funds, faced a dilemma that, with Melvill's advice, he put squarely before Napier.

Meanwhile, competition stiffened when both the St. George Steam Packet Company, from which Junius Smith had chartered the *Sirius*, and the Great Western Steamship Company, which was planning improvements on the *Great Western,* submitted bids. Both failed to meet specifications, and their separate tenders were declined. Everything now centered on the well-connected Robert Napier.

Lest all progress to date should become unraveled, early in 1839 Napier arranged a dinner to introduce his Nova Scotian client to a group of moneyed Scots businessmen, some of whom Cunard had already met. They listened without comment as the soft-spoken Cunard described his presentation to the Admiralty. After answering their questions, he tactfully polled them on their reactions.

Cotton broker James Donaldson accepted that the Sea Lords were as sensitive as the Civil Lords to the need for sound overseas postal service. He needed convincing, however, that conditions were right for an overseas investment and that money could be raised to finance the venture.

George Burns, also a close associate of Donaldson's and as penny-tending as any Scotsman, conceded that, since he had talked with Parry, he was leaning in a more positive direction. At the least, he was now ambivalent.

Glasgow merchant David MacIver was firmly opposed to the proposal because he could not balance the required sum of money against the risks of such a hazardous project.

Napier focused on the risks. He pointed out that they hinged largely on matters of safety and could be contained by astute selection of seamen and large enough vessels that were carefully operated.

MacIver circled and prodded at the financial requirements and was joined by his brother Charles in levering the original estimate higher. George Burns was joined by brother James in hinting at a regretful withdrawal.

Cunard saw that he was getting nowhere and fretted over the lack of proper funding. He sensed that he had aroused interest, but he feared that further delay would result in the all-important Admiralty losing interest. "We must make no decisions tonight," he declared and suggested that they meet the next day to resume the discussion.

The next morning, George Burns deftly brought them together. Between Glasgow and London, he counseled, the group ought to be able to find a few friends to join them in the venture. Cunard encouraged George and James Burns to invest by offering them the Glasgow agency for his ships. With Napier's help, he won the MacIvers over by offering them the select Liverpool agency. Contracts in the two busiest ports of the British Isles were certain to be valuable if Cunard's fleet performed as he had outlined. For the four men, that substantially modified the financial risk. Cunard agreed to allow a month's delay. By the end of the day, the diverse group was off in search of additional subscribers.

Within a week, thirty-two men from Glasgow and Liverpool had joined the group, which helped to achieve a subscription of £270,000. Cunard himself underwrote the largest portion of £55,000. Among the initial investors was William Brown, a former member of Parliament and then a partner in the Liverpool banking firm of Brown, Shipley, Ltd. The connection was an important one that would last for decades, with Brown, Shipley serving as the firm's financial agent. An agreement was drawn up in the names of Samuel Cunard, George Burns, and the once recalcitrant David MacIver as co-partners for the formation and management of a transatlantic steamship company to operate under the cumbersome but descriptive name British and North American Royal Mail Steam Packet Company. Known later as The Cunard Steam Ship Co., Ltd., its ships would carry the designation RMS, royal mail steamship, and the company's name was less formally and unofficially reduced to Cunard Line. Cunard went at once to Whitehall and submitted his tender to the Admiralty for the conveyance, once a fortnight, of Her Majesty's mails among Liverpool, Halifax, and Boston. The latter port was Cunard's own extension of the original posted terms.

Enthusiasm tempered by careful planning, an astute eye for finances, and a substantial reputation among the aristocrats of commerce had brought Cunard this far. He had met socially at least two of the Lords Commissioners of the Admiralty who were introduced by a widow who might well have had her eye on the eligible widower, according to the gossipy memoirs of the beauteous, well-known English actress Fanny Kemble. Discretely, Cunard separated any such meetings from the formal deliberations of the crusty Admiralty ministers, seasoned bureaucrats who brooked few objections to their own hidebound ideas on mail transport. Several burdensome conditions were associated with the subsidy. In the small print, it was closer to a financial settlement for work completed. The Admiralty insisted on the right to requisition the ships on demand for transporting British soldiers and sailors to any part of the world. Such a conversion of commercial vessels required taking them off their routes to strip them of their few luxuries and clutter the decks with minimal armament. The nettlesome practice of issuing letters of marque to eager privateers would continue in the event of hostilities, but that did nothing to relieve the pressure on those intent on government-sponsored, scheduled mail transport.

How could one plan a transatlantic passenger service with the threat of requisition hanging over the schedule? Tactfully, Cunard narrowed the specification to troopship conversion only in time of war. The ships were routinely to carry naval officers on board in order to assure Whitehall of their constant state of readiness. It was unclear what other duties they would have on board, although the sharp distinctions in training and assignments of naval and merchant personnel did not then exist as it would in the twentieth century. Reluctantly, Cunard accepted the onerous requirement. He offered to provide additional service to Quebec during the periods when the St. Lawrence was ice-free by using smaller vessels running out of Pictou on Nova Scotia's north coast, which attracted the commissioners. It also might have distracted them from Cunard's insertion of a clause stating that any changes to construction and machinery be made "as the advanced state of science may suggest." Latitude for the incorporation of new developments in steamship technology was thereby assured for the vessels whose construction details remained unspecified.

In May 1839, Samuel Cunard signed the overseas mail-carrying contract with the British government, the agreement to last for seven years. Service among Liverpool, Halifax, and Boston would begin in 1840, for which Cunard would receive £55,000 ($269,500) annually. This was the first major instance of any government subsidizing the operations of a private, profit-oriented enterprise. Negotiations continued as both Cunard and the Admiralty added new amendments and modifications. Increasing the subsidy to £60,000, the Admiralty called for four ships and the inclusion of specific sailing dates in the contract. A penalty

5–2. *Samuel Cunard (1787–1865), founder of 160-year dynasty.*
  Peabody-Essex Museum

applied to lapses from the named dates, a proviso that had troubled the port agents from its first mention after Cunard's initial Admiralty meeting. They calculated that if their ships averaged but one day's delay on each sailing, the revenue from the subsidy would be absorbed in fines and concluded that the engines would be key to regular, timely passages. The Napier designs were altered in both power and size. The first ships would displace 1,135 tons and have single-class cabin space for 115 passengers. Against these more demanding specifications, Cunard succeeded in getting the subsidy raised to £80,000 ($392,000) as of September 1, 1841, following several months of service.

On the basis of the increased subsidy, the British and North American Royal Mail Steam Packet Company was formed. The founders went their separate ways—Cunard to London to establish the firm's headquarters, Burns remaining in Glasgow to oversee planning for the ships and progress in the shipyard, and the MacIver brothers to Liverpool to attend to the practical matters of steamship operations. It was no simple task to make arrangements for a steamship terminal. Coal-bunkering services, a convenient machine shop and dockyard for repairs, and passenger and freight facilities had to be arranged, all at substantial cost. Because most of these facilities were already available in Halifax, Cunard's original plan called for the vessels to make a direct run to Halifax, where they would join with a Boston-Halifax feeder service.

When Boston merchants learned of the plan, they took exception, being unwilling to be second to anything as potentially lucrative as this commercial connection. They conceded that it made sense for the ships to arrive at Halifax for refueling and discharging or boarding passengers—the penultimate westbound stop on the Great Circle—but insisted that the new steam packets should run a through service from Liverpool to Boston. That avoided prohibitive transshipment costs and reduced the potential of discontinuance. To gain the benefits of full service, a group of major Boston merchants and bankers assembled and resolved that "a suitable Pier and Dock should be provided for a term of two years, for the reception of the Liverpool steam packets to this port, where they may receive and discharge their lading, free from expense to the owners of the steamers, and that such other facilities be afforded as the importance of the subject may require." In his most ambitious dreams, Cunard could not have imagined anything as generous. He took the proposal to his new friends at the Admiralty and obtained their support and affirmation of the increased subsidy. His work in London done, he sailed for New York on the *Great Western*, thence to Boston and Halifax to bring his plans into reality.

LONG AFTER the Romans occupied the islands they named for their leader Britannicus, the appellation Britannia became a poetic term for Great Britain. In 1740, British playwright James Thomson attributed the isles' freedom charter to their guardian angels and reaffirmed the name in the words "Rule, Britannia, rule the waves; Britons never will be slaves." Cunard selected the name *Britannia* for his flagship, the first in a long line of Royal Mail steamships with names ending in "ia."

As the summer of 1840 approached, Cunard returned to Liverpool in time to sail with his daughter Ann and Ann's companion, Judge Haliburton's daughter Laura, on the *Britannia*'s maiden voyage. The flagship's funnel colors were taken from Napier's coastal vessels, black band above, clay-red below. The Cunard Line's small auxiliary steam vessel *Unicorn* preceded the *Britannia* by several days to complete dockage arrangements in East Boston and then join it in Halifax.

On July 4, 1840, huge crowds collected along the Liverpool waterfront. Gaily decorated small craft darted through the harbor and along the main channel of the River Mersey as they tried to accompany the new 1,135-ton *Britannia* departing on its first voyage to America. Most of the brig's 115 passengers gathered on deck and positioned themselves about its three masts and single stack as they waved farewells. Some of them climbed atop the paddle boxes, below which beat the vessel's major means of propulsion. The prospect was good for a pleasant voyage; the agents had promised fine accommodations and splendid service. The spirits bar would be opened daily at 6 A.M. and the staterooms swept and slops emptied every morning while the occupants tippled a bracer or took a turn on deck. Bedding would be changed in midvoyage and again after sixteen days if the voyage should exceed that time. That was long enough to go without a hot bath. Bathing facilities were nonexistent. There was a plentiful supply of livestock on board to supply fresh milk, eggs, roasted chicken, and perhaps some chops and a leg of lamb.

The *Britannia* was the first of Cunard's four planned ships. The sister ships *Acadia, Caledonia,* and *Columbia,* similar in size and power, were to follow, one per month, into the fall. The contest for control of the Atlantic had begun—fifty-one-year-old Samuel Cunard was the forerunner, and his four new steamships were the vessels to challenge.

6

The Challenger,
Edward Knight Collins

For nearly ten years, Cunard's shipping line had the North Atlantic steamship path nearly to itself as it left in its wake only the *British Queen* and the sail packets. The *Queen* was showing its age before Cunard Line vessels faced any serious test of their tight grip on the commercial route. What words best describe the man who boldly dared to wrest control—visionary, pioneer, showman? He was all of those, as well as a spirited and well-intentioned schemer, traits that came together to make him a most significant agent of change at a time when change was much needed in the American maritime world.

Straddling the sandy forearm of Cape Cod, the village of Truro, Massachusetts, was a dedicated fishing community. To the east burst the Atlantic's high surf. A mile or two to the west lapped the protected waters of Massachusetts Bay. A lad growing up in that environment during the early part of the nineteenth century, like it or not, could hardly ignore the call to a seafaring life. Edward Knight Collins was born in Truro on August 5, 1802. His mother, Mary Ann (Knight) Collins, died within six months of his birth. His father, Israel Gross Collins, whose Irish ancestors were long involved in American seagoing ventures and himself an active master of sailing ships, turned to nearby relatives to take Edward as their ward. Israel's young brother John, just eight years older than his newly arrived nephew, also lived with the relatives. John was perhaps only fifteen years old when he left home to go to sea as a foremast hand but not before he and young Edward had become companions. During the War of 1812, John served on a privateer, advanced to mate, and eventually joined brother Israel's shipping company as a captain.

At age fifteen, Edward was sent to a school in New Jersey. Throughout the boy's early years, Israel had worked out of New York in the transatlantic trade, sailed chiefly to England, and eventually became a shipowner and operator while overseeing his son's development as best he could. Edward found that formal schooling lacked luster, a common attitude among youths in society's largely unstructured approach to secondary education. Not motivated to the seafaring life, he went to work as a clerk for South Street commission merchants McCrea & Slidell and found a taste for the world of commerce.

At age nineteen, Edward became his father's assistant. By then, Israel had retired from the sea to conduct a lively overseas trading business. Holding on to a thin Spanish and Portuguese trade, chiefly lemons and salt, his firm opened new routes to the Caribbean and sent vessels to Cuba for the rich cargoes of sugar, molasses, mahogany, hides, coffee, and cigars. Israel remained in the counting house, while Captain John took ships loaded with cotton to Ireland and returned with goods from the British Isles, the North Sea, and the Mediterranean. Fanning ships widely over the Atlantic in search of high-return cargoes, the Collins enterprise prospered.

Edward, shorter than average height but assertive in nature, took to wearing a stovepipe hat in public to enhance his stature. Although he had little taste for a career at sea, he sailed at intervals on coastal ships between New England and Pensacola, Florida. In a joint venture with John F. Delaplaine involving multiple ships traveling to Florida and Cuba, he signed on as supercargo, work more to his liking. It proved beneficial that he became familiar with these risk-laden routes, populated by pirates and edged by the Florida Keys, barrier islands that separated the Atlantic from the Gulf of Mexico, both geographically and commercially. Marine geographer Matthew Fontaine Maury—his massive study of ocean currents and winds would earn him the title "Pathfinder of the Seas"—wrote in the eighth edition of his *Sailing Directions,* "The Gulf Stream, with its eddies and counter currents, renders the navigation of the Florida pass one of the most dangerous in the world. Those currents have strewn the Florida reefs with carcasses of ships and men, and have caused the loss of many millions worth of property." Marine insurers charged a quarter percent more on the coastal lanes from New York to New Orleans than on the longer ocean routes to London or Havre.

Edward's talent lay in analyzing the figures and managing the movements of the schooners, brigs, and ships operated by the I. G. Collins firm, in booking its cargoes, and in participating financially in its ventures. When Edward was twenty-two years old, the Collins office at Burling Slip on South Street put up a sign indicating that the company's name had changed to Israel G. Collins & Son. By 1827, the Collins pair shifted their operation from transient trading to a line of packets sailing monthly between New York and Vera Cruz, Mexico. Newly independent Latin America was opening to world trade and generated a rush for Mexican silver. Collins capitalized on that as he invested in both shipping and trading goods through the Vera Cruz Line.

Within a year of becoming his father's partner, Edward justified the honor by combining his zest for a good bargain with the ability to run a fast ship and to keep the European trade active. Their ship *Canada* was engaged in the English cotton market when word circulated among New York merchants that the cost of southern cotton was expected to soar. At once, several commission agents, intent on buying as much as they could at a low price, booked passage on the next scheduled New York–Charleston packet. Young Collins chartered a pilot boat and, commanding it himself, departed from New York in the wake of the packet. It was on just such high-risk business activity that Edward Collins thrived. The 630-mile route is no easy voyage past the three North Carolina capes, Hatteras, Lookout, and Fear, particularly if it is made in haste. Circuiting the Gulf Stream's opposing current while keeping the passage short gives little room to maneuver. Rushing under full sail, Collins arrived in

Charleston ahead of his competitors in ample time to buy up all the available cotton, a coup that added substantially to the fortunes of the renamed firm.

Pirates swarmed through the Caribbean during the first three decades of the nineteenth century. Shippers lost cargoes, vessels, and lives to the renegades until the U.S. Navy finally sent out a squadron commanded by Commodore David Porter, who routed most piracy from the area by 1830. During the period, Collins vessels destined for Mexico and the Caribbean islands were advertised as "copper-fastened, coppered and armed, and very fast sailers." Their only brush with the marauders would have been at a distance, for there is no evidence that privateering, which was still legal, affected the Collins coffers through pirate encounters. The Collins firm made its money from shrewd trading investments.

In 1826, Edward married thirteen-year-old Mary Ann Woodruff, the eldest child of Thomas T. Woodruff, a wealthy and influential New York alderman, architect, and contractor. Woodruff had investments in the Collins commission-merchant enterprises. Probably through that connection, the twenty-four-year-old Collins met the girl who became his bride. Well accepted by the Woodruffs, Edward enjoyed the warmth of their large family and remained close to them throughout his marriage.

In 1827, Edward Collins was listed as owner and nominal captain of the New York–built *Virginia,* at 356 tons, the largest of three vessels ordered by the Collins firm. The vessel probably never sailed under his command, for his uncle, Captain John, soon replaced him to take the ship regularly on the run between New York and Vera Cruz. Following his marriage, Edward focused his attention on Gulf Coast ports to develop the Vera Cruz Line into the largest packet operator between New York and Mexico.

Soon after the death of Israel Collins in November 1831, the firm's name was changed to E. K. Collins & Company. Edward started exercising the powerful control that he would not yield for a quarter of a century when he finally turned his back on ocean waters. Shrewd manipulation of shipping company investments, particularly during the early years, was key to his commercial growth.

From 1827 to 1832, the Collins firm lost two schooners and two ships but was quick to replace them. By 1835, it had assembled, through various means, a total of eight vessels. The Vera Cruz Line faced two major competitors on its Caribbean routes, one the nine-year-old Louisiana and New York Line that was experiencing shaky results in its cotton packet operations. The owners of the New Line, its popular name, looked to Edward Collins for help, and he replaced Thomas Servoss as managing agent in 1832. Edward used little finesse in the takeover as he pushed Servoss aside to combine the company's cotton liners with capital culled from other Collins investors and drawn from the Vera Cruz Line. That gave Collins five square-riggers, each over 500 tons and the largest ships in the cotton trade, all capable of matching the established transatlantic packets in both capacity and speed.

The Passes of the Mississippi flowing from New Orleans to the Gulf are laced with shifting sandbars. Broad and flat bottomed with relatively shallow draft, the five ships acquired in 1831–32 were designed to serve the Delta and the ports protected by Central America's barrier islands. Bargelike cargo capacity was not exchanged for speed, as in traditional deep-keeled packets, and these ships would prove to be just as suitable for deepwater transport. Ignoring the skepticism of experienced transatlantic operators, Collins saw merit in the broad hulls. He engaged shipbuilders David Brown and Jacob Bell to build what would become the largest freighters in the American commercial fleet. Collins added the *Mississippi,* 648 tons, and the *Yazoo,* 675 tons, in 1833 and, in 1835, the largest of all, the *Shakespeare,* 748 tons, with John Collins in command. (There is some indication that the line might have used the archaic spelling *Shakspeare;* historians differ.) The refurbished line was first to offer regularly scheduled service between New York and New Orleans. By 1835, its sole remaining competitor, Silas Holmes's Old Line (no connection to the Black Ball Line's official name) withdrew from business.

Two other vessels, the *Congress* and the *Vicksburg,* were added to the line as Collins began looking over his shoulder toward the teeming ports across the Atlantic. Because English looms constantly depended on American supply, cotton was among the more reliable commodities shipped to Europe. With a lock on the Gulf Coast, Collins continued his activities as a general merchant in New York and traded in a wide variety of agricultural goods, most of them transported from New Orleans in his ships.

In return, he shipped manufactured goods, including clothing, building materials, and foreign and domestic wines, to the South and, in both directions, a growing number of passengers. The seasonal nature of the passenger trade had initiated his interest in the transatlantic route. Summer's oppressive heat along the Gulf Coast drove well-to-do passengers onto Collins's northbound ships in the spring as they headed for Europe and the Maritimes. Come fall, the same people fled the chilly climes and hurried south. That suggested an opportunity to shift the routes of his largest vessels and balance the trade between his regular southern routes with the ebbs and peaks of the customary European trade.

NATHANIEL ("NAT") PALMER was a well-known sea captain of long experience. On a voyage around Cape Horn in 1820, he had discovered and plotted a major portion of Antarctica. Edward Collins was acquainted with Palmer and sought his advice about the Atlantic routes. He also consulted with his uncle John to assess the potential of a new line of Collins-operated transatlantic packets. Four scheduled lines were then sailing out of New York for Liverpool or London. They included the originator of packet service, the seventeen-year-old Black Ball Line, which would be formidable competition. Nor was the Cope Line of Philadelphia to be ignored with a stable business that had sent vessels to England in both transient and scheduled trade for more than a quarter of a century. Nevertheless, Collins's advisors were encouraging and believed that the potential for another carrier to load full cargoes existed. The Europeans had not entered into scheduled transatlantic operation, the American fleets were in need of overhaul, and passenger lists were increasing.

Enjoying substantial profits from the cotton trade, Edward Collins proposed to his uncle that he command the *Shakespeare* on a trial voyage to England. John was quick to agree and added that the ship could be cleaned and refurbished there, where labor was cheaper, and then put on display in the Liverpool docks.

The Collins pair were showmen, and they carefully carried out their plan. In 1836, with flags flying fore to aft on the sparkling vessel, Captain John opened the *Shakespeare* to the public for a week of inspection. Meanwhile, he solicited New York–bound cargo, ticketed a full load of passengers, and finally turned away twice the number of applicants before casting off the docking lines. On arrival in New York, the *Shakespeare* recorded the largest single load of cargo ever brought by one ship into that port. With a single voyage, Edward Collins had proved to himself and to the New York community of merchants that he could be a capable transatlantic sailing packet operator.

At once, Collins reinvested the *Shakespeare's* profits into expansion of the fleet. He had already set a style that centered on first-class trade; elegance, capacity, and service were the hallmarks. On September 16, 1836, the New York papers carried advertisements for the "New Line of Liverpool Packets" starting monthly service in six weeks. The *Shakespeare* was permanently shifted from its Caribbean route, and three other square-riggers were assigned to join it in the Atlantic. A literary flair coursed through the Collins blood. Edward named all of his ships for men of the stage—the *Shakespeare* was followed in the same year by the *Garrick,* then the following year by the *Sheridan* and the *Siddons,* of which Nathaniel Palmer was named skipper. Every addition appeared more luxurious than its predecessor, and the accommodations exceeded those of any Collins competitor. Cabin passengers were pleased to find menus listing sumptuous food and select wines. When reporters were invited to examine the facilities, it was inevitable, although never official, that the fleet would be known as The Dramatic Line.

The sobriquet was well chosen. Collins proposed to pit his *Sheridan* against the Black Ball's *Columbus* in a windy eastward crossing during February 1837, with a stake of $10,000 put up by multiple speculators as the reward. Captain De Peyster of the *Columbus* arrived in Liverpool after fourteen days. Although two more days elapsed before the *Sheridan's* Captain Russell hauled into port, Collins was not entirely disappointed with the result. His goal was public recognition of the new line, which was more valuable than the prize. The gauntlet had been put down, and among shipowners speed became the next and frequently the most important qualification for success in gaining control of the Great Circle. Fourteen days became the mark. There were no guarantees; most passages could be expected to take longer. E. K. Collins & Company had set the stage. A vaguely defined speed contest would continue for 115 years. It

6–1. *Edward Knight Collins (1802–1878), mogul of lavish tastes.*
The Mariners' Museum

gave substance to the *Great Western*'s 1838 steamship race along the Great Circle against time for a mythical "Blue Riband," the honor of being the fastest ship to cross the Atlantic. Publicity, not prize money, constituted the ethereal award.

By the time the *Siddons* joined the line, irresponsible banking operations in the Western Territory brought on the abrupt Panic of 1837. It was followed by a financial slump that lingered for five years on both sides of the Atlantic. Collins remained undeterred. In 1838, he introduced the 1,000-ton *Roscius*, the actor's name hearkening back to ancient Rome. New York became a transshipment center for the two separate Collins lines. Gulf Coast agricultural goods, chiefly cotton, were exchanged there for manufactures from England, and, above the holds, passengers sought comfortable voyages of shortest duration. In time, the flashy Dramatic Line boasted a splendid record of reasonably fast, safe voyages. The line's captains won awards for rescues at sea from both England and the United States, while their own safe conduct helped to quell the ever-present public apprehension of ocean crossing. There developed a certain real and expected pleasure for passengers in the undertaking. Travel for its own sake by more than an elect few was a first in maritime annals.

Despite the depression, for Edward Knight Collins, a brusk, portly man, clean-shaven and jowly, these were richly expansive years. With plentiful wealth at age thirty-six, his Dramatic Line period had been formative. The shipping operations blossomed and made Collins one of New York's wealthiest citizens while he achieved a secure reputation as one of the most successful shipowners in the United States.

The New York arrival of the *Sirius* and *Great Western* in 1838 kindled Collins's thoughts about how best to manage the North Atlantic trading route. He was convinced, he told a friend, that steam "must win the day." There was "no longer a chance for enterprise with sail," he said. Still, although he was by then financially capable, personal investment in steam engines was not for him. In a letter to President Martin Van Buren, Collins urged the distribution among merchant shippers of government mail subsidies in support of steam-powered vessels that could be converted to naval use. He received little response from the waning administration. The first president not to have been born a British citizen, Van

Buren was an adept politician who had the misfortune of presiding over the nation's first depression. Some years later, it was reported that Van Buren replied to Collins that the nation needed no navy at all, much less one powered by steam vessels. The president firmly believed that the best government was the least government and that belligerency in the Atlantic was a thing of the past.

The public known brash request, however, caught the attention of Cunard interests that kept an eye on American enterprise. Discussing Collins's efforts, Cunard Line managers scoffed among themselves when they saw a prospectus that mentioned Collins and his desire to operate federally funded steamers. A tinge of jealousy might have provoked their derision. The Dramatic Line's sailing vessels were more comfortable than Cunard's early steamships. Spectacularly appointed in fulfillment of the line's name, they were soon drawing much of the westbound trade out of Liverpool. Passengers on the smooth-riding windjammers felt less of the rigors of the sea. They were unfazed by tales of steam disasters and undisturbed by throbbing engines, gritty decks, and soot-flecked air. The sacrifice of an extra day or two was worth it for the luxury in crossing. Comfort took the edge over speed in the countercurrents of the Great Circle.

Skilled at cultivating public interest, Collins advertised routinely in the *New York Herald* and kept himself in the good graces of publisher James Gordon Bennett. He enjoyed a fine reputation, grand publicity, and an impressive income. With characteristic flamboyance, he bought a 388-acre parcel of land in Westchester County that was situated on the north shore of Long Island Sound. The property and its imposing old mansion became his country seat to which he gave the name Larchmont as he took his place among the gentry of Manhattan-based industrialists.

Cunard's link to New England was but a year old when Georgia Senator Thomas Butler King first spoke out for a federally subsidized steamship fleet, only to have his plea ignored. It was not until 1845 that Congress, influenced by Junius Smith who had withdrawn from shipping and settled in South Carolina, became concerned about the English threat to America's maritime operations. For no compelling reasons that could be addressed and eased, tension increased between the United States and Great Britain. The United Kingdom had abolished slavery in 1833, which weakened America's position among industrial nations. The competitive advantage held by Great Britain's exports, gained through the Industrial Revolution, brought new emphasis on free trade while New England manufacturing plants geared up their production. The idea of entrusting U.S. mails to foreign vessels now seemed objectionable. Several congressmen began to voice concern over the Navy's apparent disinterest in putting steam power to work in its few fighting ships.

Finally, at Smith's instigation, Congress passed a bill to provide a mail subsidy under a ten-year contract to any company that would operate four steamships of about 2,000 tons between New York and any port on the English Channel. As defined, the vessels should be convertible to naval transports on short notice and be able to improve on the performance of the Cunard ships. In October, Postmaster General Cave Johnson solicited tenders for mail services from New York to nine European ports ranging from Hamburg, Germany, to Lisbon, Portugal, and including Liverpool, Bristol, and Southampton, England. Lobbying efforts became intense, with American shipowners nearly crowded out by foreign commercial interests proposing their own ports as the European terminus.

Six ship operators responded, Collins among them. Three failed to meet specifications; Collins was late; and Junius Smith, his interest in shipping revived, was underbid by Edward Mills, a promoter unknown in the shipping world. Mills started by asking for an annual award of $300,000 for regular steam service to Havre. After further negotiation, a five-year contract was defined and the fee raised to $400,000 for fortnightly sailings to Bremen with alternate service to Havre. Four ships were required. The government wisely defined the distribution as $100,000 per vessel rather than a gross amount for the total service. The award was sufficient for Mills to organize the Ocean Steam Navigation Company in May 1846 and to seek subscriptions for $1 million in stock.

Despite public enthusiasm for the project, Mills encountered resistance in raising capital from skeptical New York financial interests. Goaded by Col. A. Dudley Mann, American consul to the German state, Bremen bid for $100,000 in stock and sweetened the pot by offering a free port, liberal trade laws, and tax-free coaling at the mouth of the Weser River. Prussia matched the financial offer, and the German states eventually accumulated $289,000. Along with American subscriptions, total investments reached $600,000. American merchants, seeing a line to Bremen as one that would stir up undesirable competition, voiced their preference for the reliable Cunard Line. In response, Mills included an unspecified English Channel port as part of the through route to Bremen.

Mills's inexperience became evident before he had adequate subscriptions for the first pair of proposed ships. He had to be aided by a new firm formed for the purpose, the New York and Havre Steam Navigation Company. Mills remained involved, although he received only half the proposed subsidy. The Ocean Line, as it would be called, contracted with Westervelt and Mackey, producers of Havre sailing packets, for the 1,700-ton, wooden-hulled, and bark-rigged steam-paddler *Washington*. The Novelty Works, named for the inland-water steamboat for which it had produced an early coal-burning steam plant, delivered the boilers and scant 2,000-horsepower engines. Fueled only by cooler-burning bituminous coal, the *Washington* lacked the power to outrun even Cunard's dowdy old *Britannia*.

As in Great Britain, mail transport was the major issue behind the American subsidy. A sharp rivalry prevailed among the many German states, and Bremen was anxious to gain full control of America's postal arrangements. Selecting Bremen as a European terminus and displaying a good deal of arrogance, Congress insisted that harbor improvements be made on the Weser River, and that a railroad line be established between Hanover and Bremen so that Hanover could set up a post office in Bremerhaven. To oversee the postal contracts associated with these requirements and to complete contracts with Havre, London, and Paris, the assistant postmaster general, Maj. Selah Hobbie, went along on the *Washington*'s maiden voyage. The new steamship departed from New York on June 1, 1847. On that same day, seasoned Atlantic veteran *Britannia* left Boston and arrived in England two days before the *Washington* opened the English Channel port of Southampton to American service. The English gave the line a cool reception. Nevertheless, the Ocean Steam Navigation Company's vessel was met with enthusiasm in Bremen and took the dubious honor of being the first government-subsidized mail carrier to operate in the United States.

Ten months later, the Ocean Line put the *Hermann* into service and, with two steamships, did a good business in fine freight and dry goods shipped from the continent. Despite several alterations to their machinery, the vessels' performance did not stack up to that of the long-established European sailing packets or the Cunarders. Such was the growth of trade with northern Europe and the influx of German immigrants putting behind them the disruptive politics and economic pressures of their native land that the Ocean Line continued profitable for nearly a decade without modifications to its fleet.

After losing the bid, Edward Collins turned back to his opulent sailing vessels and, like Junius Smith, resigned himself to government rejection. Then, Major Hobbie, an associate of the well-connected Collins, returned from the *Washington*'s awkward maiden voyage and unexpectedly informed Collins that Mills did not have exclusive rights to mail transport despite his contract. Hobbie introduced Collins to Postmaster General Johnson and encouraged him to work up a new proposal of his own. It was only then that Collins learned of the extent of the congressional appetite for American dominance on the Atlantic, as expressed on Capitol Hill by Delaware Senator James Asheton Bayard, "I suggest cost not be considered. . . . I suggest, too, that Congress grant a carefully selected American shipping expert a completely free hand to proceed with the absolute conquest of this man Cunard."

Cost not to be considered and a completely free hand—shipping expert Edward Knight Collins knew that he was their man. Hastily, he submitted a proposal to Johnson to carry mail on twenty round-trips annually between New York and Liverpool twice a month but reduced to once a month in midwinter. The cry went forth that he would "sweep the Cunarders from the sea." His earlier negotiations contributed to an improved understanding of the target. He asked for an annual subsidy of $385,000 and proposed that, in return, he would build five steam vessels superior in design and operation to anything else afloat. Experienced steamship operators evaluating the plan might have concluded that it was overly ambitious. Vessel turnaround would leave little time to overhaul anything but the most reliable engines, ones that should be capable of shortening the crossing by days. On the other hand, Postmaster General

Johnson was impressed. In his recommendation to Congress, he stated that he found Collins to be "a gentleman of the highest reputation for his judgment and skill, as well as ability to perform the service he proposes."

It took a year and a half for the Collins offering to wind its way through the hands of more than a dozen congressmen while the shipping expert who could drive the Cunarders out of the transatlantic business waited offstage. The wait proved worthwile when a bill, passed in November 1847, incorporated everything that Collins had requested. Imitating and expanding on the Admiralty's dealings with Cunard, the contract included a specification that the line maintain four passed midshipmen as observers and accommodate voyaging mail agents with subsistence as necessary. In the years before the establishment of the Naval Academy, a man intent on becoming a naval officer was a political appointee who learned his trade at sea. Once tested satisfactorily by a naval board on basic seamanship, he was qualified as a passed midshipman and might continue his service at sea on either naval or merchant vessels.

In the meantime, Collins interested two close associates, bankers James and Stewart Brown, and also Elisha Riggs and W. S. Wetmore in joining him as investors. A brother, William Brown, was the senior partner of Brown, Shipley, Ltd., Liverpool bankers with dual interests in both Collins and Cunard lines. The new steamship line was capitalized at over $1,000,000, with Edward Collins, as director, investing $180,000 and banker James Brown, president, investing $200,000. To support his share, Collins sold his two sailing packet lines in 1848 and gave up the profitable trading activity in the Gulf of Mexico. He now had but one path to follow, a deep one on the Great Circle of the Atlantic. The New York and Liverpool United States Mail Steamship Company was formed in time to enter into a contract signed for the government by Secretary of the Navy John Young Mason. With the mail contract in hand and $385,000 in annual subsidy, Collins called for ships of 2,800 tons, thus displaying his characteristic extravagance when "at least 2,000 tons" was what the contract specified.

Commodore Matthew Perry, Congress's agent on lighthouse service matters and soon to lead an expedition to open trade with Japan, was detailed to oversee the Navy's interests in the Collins ship construction.

The vessels were all to be built in New York by William H. Brown. The first two would be 282 feet in length, 2,856 gross tons, and lavishly equipped to expand on the Dramatic Line's flamboyance. When the plans were laid out before Perry, the straight-stemmed hulls with tubby, rounded sterns were already complete. The fussy commodore regretted that he had not been appointed earlier because, in staunch naval fashion, he would have discouraged some of the showiness. The hulls were ribbed with live oak and sheathed in pine, but until Perry had his say, the method of propulsion, screw or paddle wheel, remained to be determined. The commodore insisted on the latter—highly visible side paddles. Accompanied by the firing of cannons on February 1, 1849, sister ships *Atlantic* and *Pacific,* the first two steamships of what everyone called the Collins Line, were launched. Riding high in the water with the freeboard of an ark, the vessels faced a year of being outfitted with passenger accommodations never before seen on ocean waters and undergoing sea trials before making their marks for the American merchant service.

The ships were twice the tonnage of the *Britannia* and roughly three times more powerful. U.S. naval engineers had studied British advances in propulsion and designed machinery, the size and power of which never had been built in the United States. A pair of two-cylinder side-lever engines, each of 2,000 horsepower, had a 108-inch stroke and were capable of propelling the vessels at thirteen knots. In response, Cunard launched a second set of wooden-hulled steam-paddlers, but they were not projected to approach the ships of the Collins Line in speed or comfort. With an American terminus in the prime location of the burgeoning New York Port, E. K. Collins held a firm grasp on the western portion of the Great Circle. It seemed that a figurative flick of his wrist could toss Cunard's ships off the route and end the ten-year British hegemony.

7

The Traditionalists, Donald McKay and Enoch Train

FOREMOST AMONG those who sent sailing ships boldly into the paths of steamships was Nova Scotian Donald McKay. Lauchlan and Donald, the first two children born to Hugh and Ann McKay of Shelburne County, became recognized throughout the maritime world from England to Australia, as superbly talented designers and builders of sailing ships. Second son Donald was born in 1810 at about the time that Robert Fulton could look back on three successful years of Hudson River steamboat operation. While Thomas Gibbons, aided by Cornelius Vanderbilt, was adding steamers to his own Hudson River fleet, the two McKay brothers emigrated to New York, where, with parental approval, sixteen-year-old Donald was apprenticed to ship carpenter Isaac Webb. The move could well have been an economic necessity, as the elder McKays added fourteen more children to their family. Lauchlan, working off and on with Webb, interspersed his time as carpenter and shipwright with periods of seagoing. Their duties with the shipbuilder started both brothers on a long period of growing fame and good fortune, the more so after meeting with Enoch Train.

Train, a conservative New Englander, was nevertheless not one to take the well-traveled path. He was born in the spring of 1801, probably in Weston, a sylvan community west of Boston. Little is known of his parents, but his uncle, Samuel Train of Medford, was a well-to-do merchant and ship broker. Train family members, some of whom farmed in nearby Waltham, traced their Yankee heritage back to the seventeenth century. Following the War of 1812, Enoch served in the Massachusetts militia. Long after he had become a prominent Boston merchant, he was often addressed as Colonel. From his uncle Samuel, he learned the fundamentals of shipping and foreign trade. In 1823, Enoch married Adeline Dutton, and, the following year, she gave birth to a daughter named for her. Enoch Jr. was born in 1833, shortly before his mother died. Three years later, widower Train married Almira Cheever. The couple and the two children settled in a new home on Boston's Beacon Hill.

Colonel Train and later the McKays routinely associated with the literati of Cambridge and Boston, as well as the elite of the maritime world. Harvard professor and poet Henry Wadsworth Longfellow; essayist and renegade pastor of the Old North Church, Ralph Waldo Emerson; and actress Julia Bennett Barrow were frequent guests at Mount Vernon Street. In 1842, Train built a mansion in Dorchester, originally a summer home that he later made his permanent residence. After shipping operations eclipsed his mercantile trade, his visitors included Adm. David Farragut, when he came north from his home in Norfolk, Virginia; the irascible naval engineer John Ericsson; and, until the Civil War divided them, Lt. Matthew Fontaine Maury.

While still in his twenties, Train had achieved substantial success by trading in South American and Baltic goods. Baltic cotton was shipped in bulky, uncompressed bales that were cumbersome for the traditional Yankee vessels, which seemed to "fit better in the sea" when limited to no more than 500 tons. Train felt that bigger hulls would serve more profitable voyages. In 1839, with the idea of establishing a Boston-Liverpool route still in the future, he joined a Manchester sea captain, Richard

Trask, to produce the largest vessel built in New England at that time. Together, they contracted with the Medford dockyard of Waterman & Ewell for the construction of the *St. Petersburg*, 814 tons register, 160 feet in length, and a 33-foot beam. Its major concessions to the Western Ocean packets sailing out of New York were a square stern and painted ports. Master and part owner Trask took the vessel on its first outward voyage to the Baltic, then turned command over to his chief mate, and returned home via London by steamer. If the contrast of the return voyage favorably impressed Trask, it did nothing to alter Enoch Train's views on the efficiency of sail.

Train Line ships were slow, and the trading firm often lacked for a regular supply of export cargo. To fill the holds, Train sent his vessels south along the coast for cotton. Although the southern leg added to the duration of overseas voyages, an unappealing option for passengers, it gave Train a valuable entry into western European markets. The idea of a line out of Boston that would compete directly with the New York packets began to command his attention. Train's business associates accorded him great respect, but they were dubious about his proposed plan to vie with the well-established North Atlantic shipping companies. By 1844, Samuel Cunard had assembled a firm base at magnificently rebuilt piers across the harbor in East Boston. Every docking of the flagship *Britannia* was greeted by festivities. An ice-fostered love affair that Boston had with Cunard's four-year-old steamship was still fresh in Train's memory. Thomas Cope's line out of Philadelphia and, foremost, the New York–based Black Ball Line dominated the Liverpool sailing packets and achieved substantial profit from nearly every transatlantic voyage. Collins's Dramatic Line had done splendidly since 1836 as the New York Port drew ever-growing amounts of foreign trade.

Train's plan to capture his share of East Coast business by introducing a new line of sailing packets appeared misguided. He would get little public support from his fellow Boston merchants. Fortunately, he maintained his associations with members of the old Yankee financial community who were more open minded about maritime investments. The biggest competitor facing Train's bulky ships was Samuel Cunard's Royal Mail Steam Packet Company running four vessels out of Boston on regular schedules. Black Ball, Dramatic, Cope, Cunard, and other transient ship-pers routinely cruised the Great Circle, with the full assembly having a tight hold on the Liverpool trade.

Train went to England in 1844 to meet with Baring Brothers, potential agents for his proposed line of packets. Aware that he was undertaking an extraordinary gamble, he remained uninterested in steam power. Captain Trask after his westward steamer crossing, as well as Farragut and Erics-son, might have advised him against a major commitment to sail, but Train saw advantages over the thrashing steam-paddlers. He preferred the traditional entrepreneurial method of investment, in which merchant princes joined with financially involved skippers, to the complexities of a corporate enterprise requiring steam plants, coaling ports, and modern dockyards. Sail was safer; it could be faster and more comfortable in the heavy weather that plagued the North Atlantic from September to May; it was more familiar to passengers, many of whom still thought steamers to be a novelty; it was less costly to operate and well suited to voyaging extended distances, particularly interocean transport. No paddle-wheeler could routinely risk the Cape Horn passage.

The route around South America was not part of Train's initial plans, but its existence reduced his financial risk by providing a ready market for his vessels should he find it necessary to withdraw them from European service. Much of the requisite maintenance of sailing ships could be accomplished by the vessel's own crew, contrasted with the longer dock-yard turnarounds of steamships and the scheduled delays that had be-come traditional among New York packets. The North Atlantic passage between the U.S. East Coast and Liverpool was perhaps the most prof-itable trading route in the world; it certainly was the busiest. Passenger bookings were destined to grow—Train intended to open his line to European emigrants. Fast passage at lower than steamship rates would be critical to that trade.

The Boston merchant did not lack connections in high places. In August, while attending chapel at Windsor Castle with Prince Albert and Queen Victoria, Train fell in with fellow American Dennis Condry of Newburyport, Massachusetts. Condry owned the 427-ton *Delia Walker,* a vessel that Donald McKay had finished for John Currier, Jr. Condry was

7–1. *Enoch Train (1801–1868), modest Boston Brahmin.*
    Courtesy of Dover Publications

sufficiently impressed with McKay's work that he urged the young builder to set up a yard in his home port. Condry knew that Train was thinking of shifting his trade routes to England, for which he would need fast sailers to have any chance at success. He challenged Train, "Why go to the added expense and delay of purchasing ships in England when there is a very capable builder in our own commonwealth?" Train's interest was piqued, and he assured his associate that he would visit McKay's yard before entering into any shipbuilding contract.

ISAAC WEBB was a much-admired shipbuilder and a splendid mentor for his apprentices, his eldest son Eckford, John Willis Griffiths, and the McKay brothers. Later, they all would follow similar design principles as they had evolved under Webb but that were often attributed to the vessels that emerged from Chesapeake waters as wartime privateers. Webb-trained designers differed only in minor details—length of a hull's run and the corresponding placement of the wide midsection fore or aft of the midships load line. They were consistent in adopting narrow bows and broad, overhanging sterns, both of which would ultimately characterize the clippers.

Webb's terms for apprenticeship were firm and encompassing. Each lad was taken on "to learn the art, trade and mystery of a ship-carpenter," all the while keeping his master's secrets, serving him, obeying his commands, and caring for his goods. During the period, he was not to marry or play at cards, dice, or other unlawful games nor was he to haunt taverns, dance halls, or playhouses. This was for a pay of $2.50 per week, plus $10 per quarter for room, board, and clothing. The conditions of employment, to last until the apprentice's twenty-first birthday, were not thought to be extreme. Such was the contract that young Donald McKay had signed, and it was quite satisfactory to his stern Methodist father who cosigned the agreement. Fortunately for the spirited youths, an apprentices' boarding house supported by a group of master shipbuilders was not as restrictive as the contract of indenture and afforded them a share of off-hours freedom.

Upon completion, the period of ten- to fifteen-hour daily duties qualified a conscientious apprentice as a shipwright/carpenter. Donald McKay was quick to display ability and industry. By mutual agreement, he was released early from his contract and allowed to take up carpentry work for Jacob Bell of the Brown & Bell shipbuilding firm. The company was engaged at the time in producing America's largest commercial vessels for Edward Collins's expanding line of cotton packets. Some of the planks of those ships, in an ironic twist of history, could have been nailed in place by the man who would later put the world's most famous sailing vessels on the same path as the equally famous Collins steamers.

By age twenty-three, Donald McKay had set aside enough money to marry. Albenia Martha Boole was both daughter and sister of shipbuilders. Her family was affluent, and the couple settled into their own home on New York's East Side, where, in February 1834, their first child, a son, was born. The well-trained Albenia taught her husband how to draft and lay off a vessel's plans as she introduced him to elements of the rudimentary science of marine architecture.

During this period, American builders first studied the principles of hull design and gave structure to rule-of-thumb techniques for sparring sailing vessels. Treatises on marine architecture had been composed in Europe as far back as the eighteenth century, but Donald's older brother Lauchlan would be the first American to put design principles into print. Prior to his 1839 publication of *The Practical Shipbuilder,* a ship was laid out and sparred by a well-practiced eye, the details dependent chiefly on experience gained from earlier hulls. Lauchlan, also a disciple of Isaac Webb, became a naval architect, shipbuilder, and sea captain. Until 1851, his book was the only one on naval architecture that explained the design process.

When the quest for speed began matching in importance the usual requirements of seaworthiness and capacity, architects began to analyze even the shapes of fishes. As the result of the design ideas of draftsman John Griffiths, a formal specification of the clipper ship hull—one having a knifelike entrance and its greatest width a straight deadrise amidships—that flowed to graceful fine lines and a broad overhang aft took shape. McKay maintained his friendship with Griffiths and, when first on his own, emulated his designs. From two Boston sea captains, Robert Bennett Forbes and Frederic Howes, came the labor-easing concept of the

double topsail, rigs that allowed taller masts and more flexible sail-carry-
ing ability.

McKay equated hull size, especially length, to sustained speed. Like
many early designers, he was uncertain or possibly did not care about the
relationship of hull forms to given trades. There were differences in the
trim of vessels loaded with cotton, coal, iron, sugar, or rum. In McKay's
early view, cargoes and routes should require no differences in the basic
configurations. Adjustments would follow from experience as his ships,
laden with mail, cargoes, and passengers wealthy and poor in numbers
small and large, girdled the globe in long and short passages. Sponsors
might have specified hand-carved door frames and polished paneling for
the warmth that they added to cabin decor, but interiors and comforts
were ever secondary to capacity and speed.

While he was working at the Brooklyn Navy Yard, McKay's skill so
impressed the demanding New York shipbuilders that, in 1839, Bell sent
him to Wiscasset, Maine, as a freelance shipwright where a set of vessels
remained to be finished. From there, he went to Newburyport as foreman
charged with finishing a vessel for John Currier Jr. This assignment drew
the attention of Enoch Train's friend, Dennis Condry.

By 1841, the young shipwright settled in Newburyport on the Merrimac River. With a modest investment, he joined William Currier as junior partner in the shipbuilding firm of Currier & McKay. Together, they
produced two vessels, the 323-ton barque *Mary Broughton* and the 449-
ton ship *Ashburton*. They were followed by McKay's first solo production
as designer and builder, the 380-ton ship *Courier*, commissioned as a coffee carrier for the New York–Rio de Janeiro trade. Found to be sea kindly,
reasonably fast, and easily handled, the vessel enhanced McKay's good
reputation.

Currier and McKay did not get along well, and their partnership ended
within a year. After the *Courier* was completed in 1842, Currier learned of
a packet line being organized in New York by David Ogden. He broke
with McKay and persuaded James Townsend, once a fellow Webb
apprentice with McKay, to join him. In going separate ways, the former
partners literally cut their models and molds in half so that both could
make use of them. Meanwhile, as Enoch Train was getting his Boston-

based packet line organized, McKay formed a new business with junior partner William Pickett for construction of the 845-ton *St. George*. The big vessel was to be the flagship of Ogden's newly established Red Cross Line, which would operate in England under the name St. George's Cross Line. The two partnerships spawned from the brief Currier-McKay association became rivals in contention for Ogden's business. Ogden's line was to suffer several setbacks until Currier and Townsend produced the one ship that saved it and eclipsed anything that McKay sent across the Atlantic.

7–2. *The* Joshua Bates, *McKay's first packet for Train.*
The Mariners' Museum

Soon after Train's return to Boston, he took a carriage to Newburyport to pursue Condry's advice to meet with Donald McKay. The pair, builder and operator, struck it off at once in discussing McKay's credentials and Train's ideas for the North Atlantic trade. At the end of an hour, they formally agreed that, within the year, McKay would build a 620-ton packet to be named *Joshua Bates*. At its launching in 1844, Train was so pleased that he stepped out of his austere character, impetuously grasped McKay's hand, and said, "Come to Boston; I want you!" The two then worked out an arrangement whereby Train would finance a shipbuilding operation in East Boston. McKay withdrew from his friendly and profitable partnership with Pickett and left the Merrimac River behind for his own shipyard, 40 miles to the south.

Train concentrated on converting his reorganized line to the Boston-Liverpool run that he had planned from the start for carrying immigrants. Thus far, the Cunard Line had avoided steerage accommodations in its ships. Train felt that by offering low-cost transport, he could fill his holds and gain an economic edge. Lack of coal bunkers, tighter berthing, the reduction of elegant first-class fittings below, and stockyards on deck would result in lower operating costs. He needed only a ready list of applicants that the growing number of emigrants from the British Isles could provide. The *Joshua Bates,* first ship in the new White Diamond Line, was fitted out to make a shakedown run to Mobile, Alabama, for a load of cotton under Captain James Murdoch, one of Enoch Train's longtime associates, before taking up its regular route to Liverpool.

Few readers of maritime history would consider Donald McKay to have been controversial. The typical historian's adulation for the designer seems to be proportional to the chronicler's proximity to East Boston. Perhaps taking their lead from Train, Bostonians revered him. Only in recent decades has there been a more critical look at his work in the full context of the turbulent nineteenth century. McKay was not as versatile as his mentor, Isaac Webb, and some critics would say that his combined talents did not match those of his older brother. His frequent change of partners could give the impression that he was less than adequate as a business manager, yet, until late in life, he never seemed to be troubled by a shortage of funds.

7–3. Donald McKay (1810–1880), perfectionist.
The Mariners' Museum

McKay's new firm was productive from the start with a new ship every year, the third one in 1844 for William Francis Skiddy operating out of New York. At 930 tons, the packet *John R. Skiddy* was his largest ship. When it put to sea, McKay had two vessels operating on the New York–Liverpool packet route, as well as Train's *Joshua Bates* between Boston and Liverpool. Sailing packets were being refined, ship by ship, under the emerging tenets of naval architecture as they continued to outnumber steamers on all scheduled trade routes. The growth of waterborne steam power was slow and narrowly confined, yet difficult for shippers to resist on protected inland and coastal waters. Occasional ocean forays on both sides of the Atlantic, for the most part, were experimental and not overly successful. The Cunarders, plodding in and out of Boston, were the exception.

SOME YEARS before Train and McKay met, Enoch's cousin Walter Train had moved with his family from Waltham to the Gulf Coast. Enoch lost contact with his transplanted relatives after learning that Walter had lost most of his family to disease. Early life was not kind to Walter's surviving son, George Francis Train. Having watched the lad's mother and three sisters die of yellow fever in New Orleans before the boy was thirteen years old, his bereaved father put him alone on board a ship bound for Boston. Walter Train was never heard from again. Young George found his way to Waltham, where he attended school briefly while helping on his grandmother's farm. At age fifteen, objecting to the proposal of a full-time farm apprenticeship, he left home and went to work for a greengrocer in nearby Cambridgeport.

Unaware of his cousin's death, Enoch somehow learned of young George's presence in the Boston area. He found him in Cambridge after inquiring about his welfare. When he saw that the lad was in good health and soundly employed, Enoch mounted his carriage and continued across the river to Boston. The next day and the next again, George Francis went to Train's office at Lewis Wharf to seek better employment.

Enoch balked, "Why, people don't come to a big shipping office like this in that way. You're too young. See me when you are seventeen."

"That's but a year away. I've learned all I can at the grocer's. There's not a reason that I could not start with you at once."

The shipowner shook his head and started to turn away.

"Look, sir," George Francis pressed on, "'twill be a decade before your own son will be groomed to step into your business. Was not your Uncle Samuel your mentor for the mercantile trade? Could you not do the same for a blood relative?"

On the brash lad's second visit, his argument prevailed and he was hired by Train & Company as a shipping clerk. It was a fortunate agreement for both parties. The *Joshua Bates* had been put in commission, and while Enoch was tied up with Captain Murdoch in planning for its Gulf and English cargoes, he put his young kin to work in the warehouse. Considerably younger than either his staunch Yankee cousin or the artistic Donald McKay, George Francis was nevertheless quick to recognize McKay's potential and encouraged Enoch Train to exploit it. He set out to push both men in their separate enterprises to the geographic and economic limits of sail's territory.

7–4. *Boston Harbor at midcentury.*
Boston Public Library

Train announced his line of Liverpool packets in the Boston papers of May 20, 1844. Following the June 8 sailing of the flagship *Dorchester*, "a first class ship will hereafter be dispatched from Boston on the 8th and from Liverpool on the twenty-fourth of each month. The *Dorchester*, 500 tons; *Cairo*, 600 tons; *Governor Davis*, 800 tons; *St. Petersburg*, 800 tons. All first class Medford-built, copper fastened, coppered and fast sailing ships." Lewis Wharf became known as "Liverpool Packet Pier," from which flew the house flag bearing a white diamond on red background.

OVERSEAS, unforeseen events soon enhanced Train & Company's fortunes. For decades, the tenant farmers of Ireland had worked the English-owned ground and sustained themselves scarcely a wagon load beyond starvation. High rents and meager wages kept the sectioned-off harvests scanty, the lots too small to raise livestock for export as wool and meat. Subsistence farming depended on a single crop, row upon row of potatoes growing in rocky soil, to feed families living on landlord-dominated plots. Seasonal famines pushed Parliament to study the problem as the Irish population grew and then, under the pressures of the absentee landlords, repeatedly to ignore it. In 1841, a century after a slow migration had started to the New World, the population peaked at eight million. America welcomed the immigrants with mixed emotions—suspicious of their beliefs, fearful of their influence on wages—yet needing their labor.

Reluctant as the Irish might have been to leave their native land, the ocean crossing provided an escape from starvation. Year by year, farmers and tradesmen turned their backs on their English landlords and sought passage on the small ships sailing out of Galway, Waterford, and Dublin. The troublesome trip to the hated Liverpool, where better bookings might be found, was too costly for most. Then, in 1846, a devastating blight wiped out the potato crop. Acres of rotting potatoes led to wholesale starvation, ignored by those in famine-free England who had the means to alter the situation. The exodus continued in earnest as crops failed in successive years. To the impoverished Irish, the docks of Liverpool looked more attractive than an almshouse in which hunger was not likely to be eased. A few British packet lines stepped into service, the

Cunard Line not among them; the Cunard ships were well booked by the upper class, for whom they were designed.

Changing cargo from dry goods in the holds to humans in steerage required a pitiless, firm resolve and little more than the erection of stacked wooden berths, four high, 33 inches in width, and the installation of a scuttlebutt and a few barrels of fresh water. A stove was secured within a lean-to on a forward hatch for the passengers to cook their food because it would not do to permit fire below. A thousand-ton packet could carry more than four hundred passengers, most packed within the hull's triple decks, with perhaps a dozen willing to pay extra for semiprivate cabins on the main deck. Steerage fare was £3 (about $15 in U.S. currency).

To the docks the Irish came, first to Dublin and then by ferry to Liverpool. The lines at the Dublin Custom House sometimes stretched over a mile. Destitute people shuffled along, some without shoes, as they trundled all their worldly possessions, threadbare clothing, pots and pans, a fiddle or an Irish harp, and perhaps a bundle holding a last-minute purchase of lard and sugar.

The British Passenger Act required emigrant ships to provide a weekly allocation of seven pounds of provisions, which they met with oatmeal (the sailors called it burgoo, almshouse gruel), hard biscuits, rice, and potatoes. American ships sailed under 1819 legislation meant to curb overcrowding in steerage, but the laws were weak and largely unenforced. Nevertheless, they were considered more comfortable ships, being limited to two people for every five registered tons, whereas the British ships carried half as many again. Under such crowded conditions, the outbreak of contagious disease was common. Sometimes in midocean, it became rampant. More than a decade passed before the seaports exercised any effective control. In 1853, the American packet *Washington* arrived in New York with sixty active cases of cholera after a crossing during which one hundred passengers had died of the disease.

GEORGE FRANCIS TRAIN became a manager in his cousin's firm at age eighteen and a partner at twenty, with a munificent wage of $10,000 per year. That year, 1849, according to his memoirs, he "started 40 clippers to

California." Reports of Sacramento gold drew his attention westward. While Enoch concentrated efforts on the Great Circle, George Francis pushed to open a westbound route with McKay's fast-sailing clippers. The lad's business acumen proved a boon to the Train firm, even if, as became apparent, his employer preferred to have him working at a distance. George's precocity lasted a lifetime, while his independent spirit and quirky attitudes set him apart as an eccentric. Meanwhile, the White Diamond Line's business benefited by his touch. Boston's waterfront enjoyed a delicate prosperity, untroubled by the clouds of smoke and steam hovering over the parade of British paddle-wheelers.

8

The Opportunist,
Cornelius Vanderbilt

WHEN HE TURNED from the oceans to the railroads and reflected on nearly seventy years of life, it might have occurred to Cornelius Vanderbilt that he had been a vital part of the sail and steam controversies from beginning to end. While Samuel Morey was grumbling about Fulton's steamboat "thievery," Corneile the boatman was running a wind-driven ferry at a tidy profit. Say what they would later about his steamship fleet, reject him from New York society, or question his ethics, Vanderbilt knew how to pull profit from the water. He might have regretted his arrogant confrontation with Edward Collins when they both faced the odd threat of the fast clippers and the government's withering steamship support, but he doubted that anyone could better him in financial matters—anyone, that is, but Samuel Cunard. In Vanderbilt's zest for a good scrap, he found the give-and-take of conflict to be a routine part of life. Play the cards that you've been dealt straight; change the rules if you can; know when to bet high and when to fold. Lose some, win more. Wasn't that what industrial power was all about? Cunard did not join the game.

The second son of Phebe (Hand) and Cornelius Vander Bilt was born in May 1794 and raised in Port Richmond on Staten Island. The elder Cornelius was a poor farmer and lighterman for whom the sturdy young Corneile worked after leaving school at age eleven. Dutch heritage showed in the boy's blond hair and blue eyes, as well as in his energetic dedication to waterside work. His limited schooling, possibly curbed by a Dutch work ethic, was to curse him throughout his adult years with poor handwriting, dreadful spelling, and the coarse language of the dockside, which moderate efforts to overcome met with little success. He was inconsistent in the spacing of his surname, shifting from occasional use of Van Derbilt to the anglicized Vanderbilt, later insisting that his family use only the latter.

At age sixteen, Cornelius, the given name he answered to as an adult, took a $100 advance from his mother to buy a two-masted, flat-bottomed piragua. Staten Island was a principal source of the sharp-stemmed, sturdy little vessels. Stapleton Pier lies midway between the Narrows and Kill Van Kull, some seven miles across New York's Upper Bay from the Battery. Here, young Vanderbilt started a freight and passenger ferry service between the pier on Staten Island and Whitehall Landing in lower Manhattan. With a fair breeze, the trip would be a nearly two-hour sail, which allowed two round-trips per day or perhaps three if the wind cooperated. Business was good, and Vanderbilt soon became known for reliability in adhering to posted departures. After paying his debt, he bought another piragua and then another, but he took little time to spend the money that his ferry service earned. The youth's ferry enterprise was developmental. He became fiercely independent, adept at doing business in his head, and shrewd in his investments with his quick eye to where financial opportunities could be found. So thoroughly did he enjoy his dealings that decades would pass before he took a respite from work.

On December 19, 1813, at age nineteen, Cornelius married his first cousin and neighbor, Sophia Johnson, and settled in Port Richmond. He was no longer Corneile the boatman. With the War of 1812 in its second year, he procured a short-term government contract to provision the forts around New York Harbor. They had been built after the Revolution and remained untested in this latest fracas with the British. The venture was safe and lucrative arrangement for young Cornelius, and, by war's end, he had several boats under his command. From that base, he began a coastal trade centered on the Hudson River. He had a schooner built for service in Long Island Sound and followed that with two larger ones during the next two years. Vanderbilt took command of the largest and sent the others as cargo carriers and traders along the Hudson and on coastal routes to harbors from New England to Charleston.

After seven years, he had accumulated $9,000 in cash, several piraguas, an interest in coasters, and a ferry, with his total assets amounting to $15,000. Then, abruptly, in 1818, he sold the fleet and took up work as a captain for former Georgian Loyalist Thomas Gibbons, now owner of the Raritan River steam ferry *Stoudinger.* The Raritan was New Jersey's link in the well-traveled New York–Philadelphia route and catered to an ample demand for transport of mail, freight, and passengers. At New Brunswick, the *Stoudinger* connected with Aaron Ogden's steam ferries running between Elizabeth, New Jersey, and New York. Gibbons was over his head and unable to sustain a profit by competing with Fulton's steamboat monopoly. He turned to the inventive Vanderbilt for help.

Rebuild the old *Stoudinger,* he told Gibbons. Meanwhile, he would have a new steam ferry built and procured at a good price. It was to be named *Bellona,* with Vanderbilt as its captain.

Gibbons was drawn to his associate's aggressiveness. By assembling crews of able waterfront toughs and driving them to the limit, Vanderbilt had Gibbons turning a profit within a year.

FORMER New Jersey politician Aaron Ogden had his own difficulties with the Hudson River monopoly. The waters on which the ferries operated split New Jersey and New York. The New York legislature gave exclusive steam navigation rights within the state to Robert Fulton and Robert Livingston in 1803 and renewed them regularly. New Jersey vessels were free to enter New York waters to buy supplies and fuel or for any noncommercial purpose, but the monopoly owners vehemently opposed any commercial operation. The rights between New York and New Brunswick, New Jersey, had been assigned to Livingston's son John, thus extending the monopoly's reach into the latter state. Backed by the New

Jersey legislature, Ogden contested it but failed in the effort. In 1815, at substantial expense, he grudgingly purchased from John Livingston the right to run the ferry *Atalanta* in service between Elizabethtown Point and New York.

Coached by Vanderbilt, Gibbons broke his arrangement with Ogden in 1818 and put his two vessels on the same run. That gave Ogden competition on the route that the Fulton monopoly had granted him exclusive license to operate. Ogden brought suit and secured an injunction against Gibbons from New York Chancellor James Kent. That action, on October 21, 1818, was the first in a long litigation series.

Throughout those years, Vanderbilt freely exercised his zest for conflict. He and Gibbons were kindred spirits, irascible when faced with what they saw as interference with their commercial and civil rights. They differed in that the belligerent Gibbons could be petty, whereas hearty Vanderbilt, charging onward with imagination, believed it better to seek forgiveness than permission. While his employer engaged in the legal side of the battle, Vanderbilt took up the maritime skirmishes and regularly dodged the New York sheriffs when they tried to arrest him for entering their territorial waters. Steaming into New York Harbor, he flew a banner proclaiming "New Jersey Must Be Free!" to inflame the local officials.

After the *Bellona* docked in New York and its passengers were trodding down the gangway, the captain was apt to slip into the ferry's cabin to elude the eyes of a deputy waiting on the pier to arrest him. When the farmers, with their wide-brimmed hats and bulky saddlebags, had debarked, the pursuing deputy, warrant in hand, boarded to find the captain's cap and jacket hanging on a peg. Vanderbilt would have changed into the clothing of a farmer or businessman and be long gone up South Street. The warrant remained unserved. Rumor had it that Vanderbilt had a secret compartment within the steamboat's stowage space that he occupied when arrest seemed imminent. All the while, he helped to expand the Gibbons fleet and splendidly increased its profits.

In appealing the New York chancellor's decision, Gibbons claimed that his federal license for coastwise trade justified his ferry operation, but Kent upheld it. The plaintiff took the matter to the New York Court of Errors and then to a reluctant United States Supreme Court, which declined to accept jurisdiction. Gibbons was furious and spared no expense to resolve the issue. He hired Daniel Webster as his attorney and set aside $40,000 in his will to continue the case should his death precede its settlement. Finally, under highly respected Chief Justice John Marshall, the Supreme Court decided to hear the case of *Gibbons v. Ogden.* In 1824, the verdict was far more than a victory for Thomas Gibbons. It declared the Hudson River monopoly and all others like it null and void and gave Congress the authority to regulate interstate commerce. Ogden was ruined financially, and Gibbons accrued a fortune. Reveling in Gibbons's success, Vanderbilt continued to work for him and moved to New Brunswick, where he took over a seedy roadside tavern that he named Bellona Hall.

Two women were much a part of Vanderbilt's life, his mother Phebe, whom he revered, and his wife, the dutiful Sophia, whom he often treated like chattel. On major matters, he was apt to consult Phebe but rarely considered the opinions of his spouse. The couple had been married five years, and Cornelius was about twenty-four years old when he and Sophia settled in New Brunswick. Together, they renovated Bellona Hall, and Sophia became the innkeeper. It was a convenient stopping place on the road between Philadelphia and New York, and she made it famous for good food and friendly service. Savoring the success of her work, Sophia was happier there with children under foot than living in the shadow of mother Phebe on Staten Island.

Vanderbilt gave eleven years of service to Thomas Gibbons, added seven more steamers to the fleet after the *Bellona,* and extended operations into the Delaware River where it connected with the Delaware-Raritan Canal. By 1819, double-expansion engines and high-pressure water-tube boilers were hesitatingly introduced into steamboats, but their adoption was limited by their greater cost and weight. Shipowners took little notice that year of the *Savannah's* steam-assisted Atlantic crossing (Chapter 3). They were otherwise occupied by the steam-driven tugs and ferries proliferating on inland and coastal waters. While Donald McKay was applying his carpentry to the hulls and masts of schooners being assembled on the East River, Cornelius looked out on the Hudson and determined that his future would be steam. With little notice, he again changed course, a practice that became characteristic of his business activity. In 1829, financed by his own savings and his wife's income from Bellona Hall, he left Gibbons and took over his favorite steamer, the *Bellona,* to reenter the shipping business, this time on his own.

In need of capital, Cornelius sold Bellona Hall over Sophia's objections and moved his family, now numbering eight or nine children, to New York City. Vanderbilt was rarely fortunate in his selection of partners, even his own genial brother Jacob. The two formed the Vanderbilt Line, Cornelius sharing the operation of the *Bellona* with Captain Jake. Following the breakup of the monopoly, the North River Steamboat Company, founded by Robert Fulton and Robert Livingston, went out of business. It was replaced by the Hudson River Association, substantially owned by the John Stevens family, related by marriage to the Livingstons. After its first year of operation, the association distributed a handsome 70 percent dividend. Competition converged on the river, principally the lower section in Putnam County between Manhattan and Peekskill. During the same period, the Vanderbilt brothers extended their operations from the staid old Raritan routes to the moneyed Hudson.

At this stage, sly horse trader and capitalist Daniel Drew entered the picture. A native of Carmel, New York, his sanctimonious Methodism failed to curtail his conniving and unscrupulous practices. Drew was wiry, shifty-eyed, and had a wispy, whining voice. A veteran of the War of 1812, it might be that, while stationed at Fort Gansevoort in Paulus Hook, New Jersey, he had first met Cornelius Vanderbilt, then the fort's supplier. It also has been said that the two met on a bench in lower Manhattan where they swapped stories of their steamboat operations after Drew found his way to the water. He worked first as a cattle drover, collected stock in the Mohawk and Hudson valleys, and reached over the Alleghenies as far as Kentucky and Illinois. Big stockyards were maintained in Manhattan near the Bull's Head Tavern at Twenty-fourth Street, where Drew set up his trading operation. Eventually the money to be made on the Hudson enticed him into forming his own company, the Hudson River Line, around the steam ferry *Water Witch.*

Drew and Vanderbilt might have been social in their park-bench banter, but their Hudson River jousting became vicious. Vanderbilt forced the reduction of Robert Fulton's exorbitant $7 New York–to–Albany fare to $5. That triggered a rate war on the southern leg to Peekskill, which Drew coveted. Vanderbilt set the Peekskill fare on the *Bellona* at $3. Fares between New York and Peekskill dropped to $1, to 50 cents, and once to 12½ cents, the equivalent of the colonial shilling still in circulation. Both operators strove to make up the difference by the sale of spirits and food. At one point, travelers were even offered free passage; they paid only for cabin and board. Drew sent out the first 300-foot vessel, the *Isaac Newton,* and followed that with the *New World.*

Both men knew that they could not sustain the ruinous underbidding indefinitely; one of them had to fade. Only the farmers and drummers of Putnam County were pleased with the situation. Not one to admit defeat, Drew approached Vanderbilt to propose a sellout. The Vanderbilts bought controlling interest in Drew's *Water Witch,* took it off the river, restored the old rates, and sent their antagonist packing but, as it turned out, not far enough. While Cornelius, intent on working the same tactics against the Hudson River Association, headed up the river, Jacob bought out his brother's share of the *Water Witch* to open the Long Island Sound route to Hartford, Connecticut.

Next, Cornelius Vanderbilt built the 230-ton *Westchester* for the thirty-six-hour run to Albany, then added the *Emerald* and ordered another vessel as replacement for the aging *Bellona.* Meanwhile, Daniel Drew boasted to his stockholders of his own adroit management in disposing of the money-losing operation, only to face their wrath when they saw Vanderbilt successfully challenge the Hudson River Association with vessels bought through what they called "blackmail." Drastically slashing fares to drive competitors into resignation and then buying them out at rock-bottom prices was a tactic that both men repeatedly used. In two years' time, the association's profits were so reduced by Vanderbilt's "blackmail" that it paid him to withdraw from the route and stay off it for ten years.

By the time that he was forty years old, Cornelius Vanderbilt had accumulated assets of over a half-million dollars as he continued to invest in large and luxurious steamboats, described often in the media as elegant "floating palaces." A frightening frequency of fires and boiler explosions on steamboats between 1830 and 1838 led to federal legislation requiring, for the first time, the inspection and supervision of passenger steam vessels. Vanderbilt knew his limits and conformed accordingly. By 1840, the *Journal of Commerce* started referring to the steamship owner as "Commodore," a title that he took to at once. Paying little attention to recent transatlantic developments, the Commodore confined his interests to river and sound. His success in the rate wars set the style of his affairs for the rest of his life.

Although he was normally parsimonious in business operations, Vanderbilt's lavish personal activities revealed his resentment toward the New York society that excluded him. Despite his wealth, he completely lacked social graces and his uncouth grammar was well salted with profanity. Moving his family again, he returned to Staten Island, where he built a large mansion. There, Sophia, now the mother of thirteen children, while exhausted with their care, found herself at her happiest. The elder Mrs. Vanderbilt, still the focus of her son's devoted attention but unable to penetrate the army of grandchildren under Sophia's command, stayed in the background. Then, with his wealth approaching the million-dollar mark, Cornelius abruptly announced an intended move to new quarters in Manhattan.

Sophia was shaken, shattered physically, and suffered what could have been a nervous breakdown. Distracted by the construction work on his projected palatial home on Washington Place and looking forward to resumption of operations on the Hudson, Vanderbilt had his wife committed to a private mental asylum in Flushing. It was a flagrantly insensitive move, and after three months, influenced by his mother, he agreed to Sophia's release. Equally heartless with his children, he ignored the girls and was overbearing in his attitude toward the boys. The man was not miserly, yet, as the young men started courting, their father insisted that, upon marriage, they be entirely self-supporting.

In anticipation of a return to Hudson River operations, Vanderbilt launched a grandiose steam vessel, boastfully named for himself, in 1846. The following year, he proposed a race on the river between the *Cornelius Vanderbilt* and George Law's steamboat *Oregon*, with a stake of $1,000 for the winner. On June 1, with the Commodore at the wheel, the race took place on a designated 70-mile course between New York and Sing Sing.

The vessels, evenly matched on the upstream leg, were running so close that they collided on making the turn. That caused the *Vanderbilt* to lose headway and fall into the *Oregon's* wake. By the end of the three-and-a-quarter-hour race, Law had opened a 400-yard gap. Winning the wager could hardly have gratified Law. His coal was exhausted on the return route; rather than lose to the Commodore, he called for the burning of the *Oregon's* furniture and fixtures, a $30,000 investment.

The afternoon's sport was one of Vanderbilt's rare losses. His chagrin was not lessened when Law sold the *Oregon* to Daniel Drew, who put the freshly outfitted vessel to work in his revived Hudson River Line. It joined the well-known steamboat *Knickerbocker*, which had been purchased at bargain price during the rate war squeeze. By then, Drew controlled a steamboat service on Lake Champlain, as well as the route to Stonington on Long Island Sound, thereby pushing Jacob Vanderbilt's inept efforts aside. In 1844, with his usual oily smirk, Drew expanded his interests to Wall Street, where he formed a brokerage and banking house. The two adversaries were still not finished with each other. Only their battles on the water had come to a pause.

In 1848, gold glinted in the west. Demand surged to get to California by any means. There were but two routes, since the transcontinental railroad was not yet fully developed. Vanderbilt was not impressed with the Cape Horn passage. Steamers could not handle the long haul through the stormy waters between coaling ports and necessary repair facilities, and he had no experience with oceangoing windjammers. The formation of separate Atlantic and Pacific shipping lines connected by a Central American land route seemed to him more practical, albeit assembly of a West Coast fleet combined with construction of an overland passage constituted an enormous additional investment. The trans-Isthmian route across Panama was monopolized by the combined Pacific Mail Steamship Company of William H. Aspinwall and United States Mail Steamship Company of George Law. Vanderbilt looked to Nicaragua, an emerging nation plagued by civil strife, political intrigue, and border wars, characteristics that would not have disturbed the quarrelsome and adventurous Commodore.

Steamboat lines on American rivers and sounds were at their peak at

The Central
American Route

midcentury when Vanderbilt set up his agency among the merchants of
South Street. In 1850, the Nicaraguan government had granted him a
charter to form the Accessory Transit Company for the development of a
route across the isthmus. He sought financing in England, where money
was presumably available to extend British navigational interests around
the globe. There, his proposal for the American Atlantic & Pacific Ship
Canal Company met with no success. Resolutely, he arranged financing
on his own and acquired federal government permissions without sup-
porting subsidies for expansion of Accessory Transit's charter to encompass the ocean routes. The effort called for the laying of a macadam road
to Lake Nicaragua, the improvement of the rapid-riven San Juan River,
and the building of port facilities on both coasts. By 1851, Vanderbilt had
assembled eight new steamers running between New York and New
Orleans that would connect with the *Prometheus* at the latter port for the

Gulf and Caribbean passage. In Nicaragua, the travelers would take a rough steam ferry voyage to the opposite coast through rapids and rockbound shallows, where they would meet the steamship *Pacific,* managed by a West Coast agent, for the final leg to California. On July 3, the New York papers carried the announcement of "The New and Independent Line for California, via Nicaragua." It became popularly known as the Vanderbilt Line. Shipping lines' legal names and common usage often differed.

The New York–to–San Francisco route by way of Panama, a country politically more stable than Nicaragua, was 4,992 miles in length. George Law had gained an annual subsidy of $290,000 for his United States Mail Steamship Company to carry intercoastal mail on board the *Ohio* on the Atlantic run to Panama, then via mule and rail to meet with Pacific Mail Steamship Company's *Oregon* for the trip to California. Aspinwall received almost as large a subsidy for the fully independent Pacific portion of the transport.

The shorter 4,531-mile route via Nicaragua enabled the unsubsidized Vanderbilt Line to complete an eastbound voyage, on average, in twenty-five days, including a three-day crossing through the rugged isthmian mountains. That was four days less than the coordinated sailings of the paired Panamanian lines. Even without the subsidy, Vanderbilt, in predictable style, offered to carry the mail for less than Law and Aspinwall. Averaging five to six hundred westbound passengers per voyage and three hundred eastbound, the Vanderbilt Line arranged to lease vessels for the Pacific leg, which substantially increased its profitability. The ships were overcrowded, the food was poor, and the service was shoddy, but such details seemed to matter little to the gold-seekers. The line became known for speed; low fares; and, unfortunately, unsafe operation.

In 1853, Cornelius Vanderbilt estimated his wealth at $11 million, the sum returning him an annual yield of 25 percent. In February, the leased vessel *Independence* hit a reef on the coast of Lower California and caught fire. During the evacuation of crew and passengers, 186 people were drowned in the surf. The leased vessel *Lewis* then grounded near San Francisco without loss of life, but the ship was severely damaged. Both ships were uninsured, in conformance with Vanderbilt's deep-pockets policy, and written off as total losses. A decade would pass before the American Board of Marine Underwriters, plagued by the frequency of beached wrecks on both coasts—thirty-five per month in 1860—began to put salvage on a business-like basis. Meanwhile, insurance companies set premiums with odds in their favor and made a profit. The Commodore saw no reason why, with his ample assets, he should not save the fees and self-insure the ships that he owned or chartered.

As expected, Vanderbilt initiated a price war. First-class passage, introduced at $400, was lowered to $150 and included Nicaraguan transit, to which was irregularly added a $35 surcharge. Law and Aspinwall were forced to match the fares on their longer route.

Into this steamy milieu came a shifty opportunist, William Walker. Not yet twenty-five years old, he had been a doctor, a lawyer, and a journalist when he arrived in San Francisco coincident with the Gold Rush and the emerging importance of Spanish California and the Central American isthmus. Walker first formed a scrubby army to invade lower California on the pretext that he had been requested by the Mexicans to save them from the depredations of the Apache Indians. The expeditionary force landed at La Paz, and Walker proclaimed himself as president of the new and independent Republic of California. The effort failed for lack of supplies, and Walker was charged in U.S. federal court with violation of American neutrality laws. Acquitted by a sympathetic jury and his megalomanic spirit nurtured, his next target was the shaky political state of Nicaragua.

Cornelius Vanderbilt encountered poor relations with the local managers of Accessory Transit. In 1852, he threatened to resign, shift his fleet of seven ships to Panama, and leave the Nicaraguan route without feeder support. Then, resigning his directorship, he offered to sell the fleet to Accessory Transit for $1,350,000, and the offer was accepted. Vanderbilt pocketed the money and was then reappointed as director and president. There were subtle motives behind his actions. The company, he felt, should conform more closely to his intentions. He was tired of bantering with the militaristic leaders of the jungle republic. For the first time in his life, he planned an extended vacation, but not without a deeper purpose. While Vanderbilt was engaged with Nicaraguan affairs, he had been siz-

8–1. *Cornelius Vanderbilt (1794–1877), Midas of transport.*

ing up the steamships then crossing the Atlantic. He commissioned the building of the steam yacht *North Star* and announced that he would take his burgeoning family on a European cruise. The yacht, in fact, was a passenger ship splendidly outfitted with a large satinwood saloon and ten staterooms equipped with plate-glass doors, silk draperies, and berths curtained in lace.

As the vessel approached completion, Vanderbilt hired Asa Eldridge, the top captain of Edward Collins's Dramatic Line, as his skipper. Then, in 1853, Vanderbilt resigned the presidency of Accessory Transit and turned its management over to two directors, Charles Morgan and Cornelius K. Garrison. Joining him on board his yacht were his wife, Sophia, a daughter, two sons, a daughter-in-law, and nineteen associates who included a doctor and his wife, Captain Eldridge's wife, and, as chaplain, the solicitous Reverend John Choules accompanied by his wife. The adventurous cruise of the *North Star* was recorded in a subtly humorous monograph published in 1854 by Reverend Choules. The Commodore, the minister noted, was often heard to invoke the name of the Deity, but it was he, Choules, who was designated to shape it into daily prayer. His work made little mention of Vanderbilt's inquiries, on his arrival at Southampton, into the possibility of starting a transatlantic steamer service.

Ten days after the *North Star*'s fireworks-illuminated departure from Staten Island, Charles Morgan assumed Vanderbilt's role as Accessory Transit's New York agent. Morgan was quick to replace some of the old directors with his own supporters and arrange his election as company president. William Walker, then in Nicaragua, allied himself with Morgan and Garrison and managed to get Vanderbilt's Accessory Transit charter rescinded and a new one issued to the Morgan-Garrison group. While the *North Star* party enjoyed its long tour from England to the Baltic, the Mediterranean, and the Aegean, the absent New York commodore unwittingly lost control of his own company. Perhaps Morgan and Garrison anticipated the different form of fireworks that would issue from Vanderbilt's office on his return.

9

The Holdout,
Samuel Samuels

T HE WRIGHTS, Thompsons, and Marshalls gave the Black Ball Line its fame, which was earned by the line becoming the first transatlantic packet service. The innovative firm was imitated early and often during the sixteen years that the founders controlled the business. They withdrew not for fear of competition or because they anticipated that steamships would obsolete their fleet but because their interests lay primarily with their family textile enterprises. They could not have foreseen that, within six years, Cunard's steamships would be the first threat against the life of sail transport on the Atlantic. Ten more years would pass before the British steamship line would meet a serious challenge. Even after the Marshalls withdrew, two years elapsed before Edward Collins assembled The Dramatic Line of sailing packets out of his Gulf Coast fleet, and ten years before Enoch Train sent his first formally scheduled sailing packet between Boston and Liverpool. Ample space was available for the windjammers.

For all the fame that Black Ball richly deserved, a Nantucket-born sea captain, Charles Marshall (no relation to the textile Marshalls), won honors for Black Ball in extending sail transport well into the age of steam. Jonathan Goodhue & Company took over the line in 1834 and named Marshall as its agent. Shortly afterward, Marshall bought out the Goodhue shares, ended his seafaring, and assumed active management of Black Ball to raise the standard of sailing packets to even greater heights. At that point, the individual who became arguably the century's hardiest and most aggressive master of sail, Samuel Samuels, not yet twelve years of age, set out on his first saltwater adventure.

Emerging from the Pennsylvania coal fields, the Schuylkill River could be deceptive as it curved south of Philadelphia, where its gentle flow attracted lovers, poets, and artists to its shores. The kindly waters left visitors unmindful of the fury that could roll from the depths as the stream found its way into the sea. A river's ripples speak not of the storms, howling winds, tumultuous waves, and icy shores to which they distantly connect; of the evils carried out on the vessels plying the ocean's broad surface; or of the hardships of life too long spent away from land. They whisper only of serenity amid pastoral charm.

It was not the Schuylkill's charm that called to Sam Samuels but his awareness that the river led to adventure on the broad Atlantic. From there, a person could go anywhere, to the rocky coast of Nova Scotia or the sandy shores of Florida, the romantic and sunny Mediterranean, the pirate-infested waters of the Windward Isles, and perhaps even to the savage islands of the great Pacific. This estuary near his home, narrow enough that he could swim across, would be his gateway to the world.

He was tall for his age, gangly and lightly built, with a mass of unruly black hair. His dislike of schooling was not for inability to learn but that he found it to be dull and rebelled against its discipline. On the Schuylkill, Sam had learned to handle a boat, and he thrilled at being in command of the little world of wood and hemp that carried him on the stream. He was quick to understand why the boat swung one way when its tiller was pushed in the opposite direction and why one turned a wheel to the left to aim a vessel to the right. He felt the wind on his face and was quick to sense how it could be harnessed.

When his mother died, Sam Samuels was just old enough that he would remember her for years to come and young enough that he failed to understand why the father-son relationship changed when his father remarried. Although his stepmother had a son the same age as Sam, he was not destined to become the companion for Sam that his surviving parent had hoped for but a rival for the attention that he needed. The lad spent more time with his books of adventure, away from home and school, hanging around the river, getting to know the boatmen, and learning the language of the waterways. Sailing on the river, he could let his imagination roam and face challenges that fulfilled his day, rather than the petty issues of dealing with two strangers in a house full of contention. He saw resolution of his problem in departure from what he felt was no longer his home. Sam and his stepmother had argued too often about matters that little interested him. At age eleven, he struck out on his own and signed on as ship's cook with a pair of Jerseymen. Their families knew Sam's father, and, after Sam suddenly left their employ when the schooner arrived in New York, they reported to his father that the boy had been a better helmsman than a sea cook.

After three years at sea, Sam returned home and recounted his adventures since his short-lived job in the Jerseymen's galley. The skipper of his next ship, the *Rio,* gave him a home between voyages, and the captain's sister taught him a bit about cooking. Samuels had a way with people. He charmed the females; hoodwinked the men; and, by various means, learned to control the truculent of both sexes. It was sailoring that he wanted, and, despite seasickness in the Gulf Stream, he learned to climb the rigging along with another green boy who had joined him. During a Gulf hurricane (in 1836, according to Samuels, but more likely the devastating storm of the following year), the boys were engaged in handling sail when the ship took a heavy roll and both fell toward the waves curling alongside. Sam's partner was lost overboard and never found, but Sam was saved when the helmsman, waist deep in water, managed to grab him. Through the storm and a subsequent grounding in the Gulf of Mexico, Sam proved his mettle enough to earn the arbitrary rating of able-bodied seaman (A-B). He had done the work of cook poorly, ship's boy eagerly, and ordinary seaman well.

No doubt, Sam also reported on his six-month tour at $18 a month as an A-B on the Revenue cutter *Jefferson.* While speaking proudly of the

Jefferson's armament and military discipline, he might have skipped the particulars of how he had deserted the *Rio* on its arrival in Mobile, Alabama. He probably failed to relate that he was chased down and jailed for the desertion, although that might have come out if he explained how he had learned the Liverpool style of boxing. This ungentlemanly skill would prove handy throughout his life at sea.

Mobile was a malignant seaport, its waterfront teeming with crimps clustered like cockroaches around taverns and rooming houses, men who preyed on dry and destitute sailors. The returned mariner also probably did not tell how he and his drugged shipmates had found their way to the *Jefferson* after he was released from jail. It is unlikely that he told his family much about his troubled friend, French Peter, an alcoholic given to vicious rage when influenced by the bottle. Peter had taught Sam a large measure of seamanship, but he had also taught the lad to drink. The two were on liberty when they were caught in a brawl in a boisterous Mobile dance hall. Drunken Peter was rendered unconscious, with Sam striving to save him, when both were shanghaied onto a ship ridden with cholera. Hustling from the ship at the first opportunity, the pair wound up in Liverpool.

Liverpool proved to be as degrading a port as Mobile for Sam. After a few days, he and Peter once again jumped ship to sign on board the British freighter *Emily,* bound for Galveston. Again, Sam tried his hand as cook and again failed. For that, he was nearly beaten by the hungry crew before his jail training came to his aid. Taking no such ill treatment, he turned the seamen's entertainment at punishing a poor cook into a series of fistfights, one after another, with the offended crew members. The captain, admiring the young man's spunk, shifted him to deckhand, an assignment much more to the lad's liking.

In the Caribbean, the *Emily* was chased by a faster, well-armed pirate ship. Twice the renegades came alongside to inquire about the cargo, until they suddenly departed in pursuit of a more appealing quarry. That ship was identified by the relieved sailors as the *Crown Prince William* of Rotterdam, and it was never heard from again.

In Galveston, Texas, Sam signed aboard the Texas frigate *Houston.* When the *Houston* encountered the same pirate ship that had accosted the *Emily,* Sam earned his keep by being the first to identify it. After a brief battle, the *Houston* lost sight of the pirate and was unable to claim its destruction. Then, yellow fever broke out on the frigate. Because of his quick observance of the pirates, Sam was assigned to the prize crew of a schooner recently captured in the Mexican War. The vessel was to be delivered to New Orleans, Louisiana, and its crew thereby escaped the *Houston*'s contagious curse. In New Orleans, Sam found himself in customary fashion broke again. He next shipped on board the *Chester* for Philadelphia. After three years of roaming and growing into his midteens, he had come home to Pennsylvania.

Sam made more half-voyages during the next year and continued the practice, not uncommon among sailors, of jumping and signing on whatever ship seemed appealing. For so little schooling, Samuels displayed much capability and some culture and gave due deference to his superiors. In 1840, he signed onto the *St. Lawrence* under a Captain Drinker. His memoirs reflect his perspective from the forecastle in failing to mention—perhaps he did not know—the surnames of the captains under whom he sailed as a seaman. When he joined them in the cabin, the captains' first names and knicknames appear in his writings, although it is unlikely that he ever addressed them by those names. Later, when he achieved his own command, he would be on a first-name basis with Admiralty lords, a New York governor, and the pastor of Manhattan's Grace Church. The *St. Lawrence* also carried the sons of its three owners as supercargoes on a long voyage that proved broadly educational for Samuels because he spent much of it in company with the gentry.

The ship sailed around the Cape of Good Hope to Australia, where the first of its cargo was offloaded. Then, in the South Pacific, the mariners came upon an uncharted island near the Carolines that was inhabited by savages. The captain sent out a boat that was greeted by dozens of frightening natives who overturned it in an effort to capture the white visitors. The boat crew, including the adventurous Samuels, was outnumbered but the men managed to fend off their attackers and return to the ship. The natives were thought to be cannibals. Later, on another island where crewmen befriended a fully tattooed, admitted associate of cannibals, they learned that they might well have supplied a meal if they had not escaped.

The *St. Lawrence* then sailed to Manila in the Philippines, where the crew broached the remaining cargo made up chiefly of spirits. Sam was among those found drunk, and he was clapped into irons. In their ine-briated state, the seamen felt that their shipmate was unfairly treated. When the captain returned to the ship, a fight ensued between the crew and the captain and his mates. The crew insisted that Samuels be released. Cutlasses were drawn and the captain was throttled during what became a full-fledged mutiny. In a rare burst of responsibility, Sam shouted to the shore for guards. The American consul and a squad of soldiers arrived, and the rebellious crew were sent to prison. After a four-week detainment, the captain and crew reached a compromise and the prisoners returned on board. On his return to the ship, Sam learned that one of the passengers was the American port captain's twelve-year-old son, who was traveling to Baltimore to visit his grandparents.

Crossing the China Sea, the ship was caught in a typhoon, during which a crazed Malayan servant cut his own throat to the windpipe and survived. Barely able to talk, he claimed that he had wanted to marry the young passenger's mother, whom he had served in Manila. He was in a jealous rage and had intended to get revenge by killing the boy before a superstitious urge had him put a knife to his own throat. The man was capable of getting around while wearing headgear that kept his bandaged throat free of further injury, and he insisted on resuming work.

During the same storm one of Sam's close shipmates was mortally in-jured and buried at sea. The death resulted in Sam's advancement. Given the opportunity for an introduction to navigation by Captain Drinker, he enthusiastically accepted.

After the cursed ship made it back to the United States and dropped anchor in Delaware Bay, Drinker and the supercargoes went ashore and left the young boy behind. The crazed Malayan, aflame with jealousy, was again determined to kill the youngster. He found a knife but was dis-armed by the crew and confined to private quarters. There, he discovered a rusted pocketknife and once again tried to cut his throat. This time, he was successful, even disemboweling himself. In his dying agony, he bit off the end of a finger. Needing no further proof that the ship was doomed, Sam and most of his shipmates had reason enough to sign off as soon as they could.

By the time that the *St. Lawrence* had returned to the United States in 1844, passenger-carrying steam vessels had increased in number along with a disproportionate increase in sinkings, explosions, and fires at sea. Ocean travelers found sailing ships to be safer, more comfortable, and often faster. Federal legislation passed in 1838 had called for routine steamship inspections, but they had done little to force improvements. By then, Edward Knight Collins had moved his base of operations from the Gulf of Mexico and established it in New York, the better to urge the administration to consider mail-carrying subsidies for England-bound steamships. Sail and steam both strove to command the Atlantic route.

THESE WERE maturing years for Sam Samuels. Before he was eighteen years old, he had sailed on a dozen ships. He had been shanghaied three times—would he ever learn? He was jailed twice. His wild behavior barely skirted justice on either land or sea. He had been in conflict with pirates twice and with cannibals once, and he had sailed for weeks with a murderous madman. Yellow fever, which more than once had taken his shipmates to their deaths, had not touched him.

The *St. Lawrence*'s arrival in Philadelphia ended Samuels's unruly life as a common seaman and his years of sailing before the mast. He had gained a wealth of experience and a modicum of maturity to the extent that Captain Drinker recommended him for a second mate's berth. Although living and eating in officers' quarters, a second mate was more of a petty officer responsible for dispensing supplies from the boatswain's locker, doing work alongside the foremast hands, and even going aloft with them as needed. His first assignment in 1842 gave the new Mr. Samuels no trouble. Despite his rowdy behavior ashore, he was well disciplined in his work on board ship.

From the *St. Lawrence*, Samuels moved to the Fielding Brothers' 1,200-ton *Caledonia*, where the ship's master, a Captain Pine, took the seventeen-year-old Samuels on as chief mate. Pine, an Englishman who had sailed in American ships, was impressed by the American standard of discipline. That was what the British ship's new chief officer delivered when it sailed for New York with eight hundred emigrants battened under the hatches. Samuels was tall and strong, and he practiced the tactics of hard-driving officers. He had rubbed shoulders with enough Liverpool sailors to know that they respected good seamanship and a firm hand. Before the *Caledonia* was out of the English Channel, the tough, young American had his roughneck crew in hand.

Meanwhile, Captain Pine's wife continued Sam's education in mathematics and navigation, which qualified him for several later berths as chief officer. On the *Rockall*, Samuels met a lady whom he determined to make his wife. Soon afterwards, they were married before Sam departed on a voyage to London. The North Atlantic was becoming the territory that he knew best and winter the season that he most favored.

Samuels never mentions his wife by name in his memoirs and extant records preserve her near anonymity, but he speaks well of the refining influence of marriage and the extent to which her pious serenity softened his turbulent disposition. At some point, she joined him on his voyages and he became a born-again Christian. Mrs. Samuels was very much a part of her husband's life, although he leaves his readers wondering about her name and background and the names of their three daughters. The family head must be forgiven for being all seaman in Victorian times.

Although Samuels might have been tamed, he was no less vigorous on the quarterdeck. A bit of this vigor is seen in the report of his assignment in 1843–44 (as paraphrased below) after he joined the *Manhattan* as chief officer. At age twenty-one, he took over the full-rigged vessel as his first command.

At that time, Cornelius Vanderbilt was building his lavish Hudson River fleet of steamboats. The steam-assisted *Savannah* and the steamship *Robert Stockton* failed to prove that American steam power had an immediate blue-water future, and sailing packets remained dominant. Yet, far-sighted Edward Collins was seeking a way to convert his own shipping line from sail to steam. Only Samuel Cunard, supported by generous British subsidies and the help of Enoch Train's merchant competitors in Boston, had shown the courage and capability to send steam-driven paddle wheelers routinely across the ocean. Donald McKay was about to build a line of sailing packets to enable Train to expand his English trade. The forces reaching for control of the North Atlantic drew closer.

Samuels was already a father in 1845 when he was named captain of the *Manhattan* and also designated as its "nominal owner"—a free agent to determine subsequent trading activity after discharge of the initial cargo. He had a new all-Dutch crew when he sailed for Genoa and undetermined eastern European ports, destinations influenced by the season and prevailing freight rates. American seamen not infrequently deserted in foreign ports when they found the treatment by American officers to be too oppressive. The hard-driving skippers were unperturbed. Forsaken wages and replacement by lower-paid foreign sailors contributed to the profits of the voyage. As he gained experience, Samuels would meet the same situation. The new captain had a limited command of Dutch, but he expected the crew to take commands in English.

With more self-confidence than prudence, Samuels attempted a nighttime entry into the Dardanelles and was taken by the current some 20 miles off course. After losing a day in regaining his route, he anchored among some twenty-two vessels waiting to proceed through the passage that held the outposts of the Turkish guards and the first approach to the treacherous Black Sea. The barometer fell, the wind came up, anchors dragged, and the *Manhattan,* along with other ships, fetched up near the plains of Troy. Veering out full chain, the ship began to leak badly as it thumped on the hard bottom. The U.S. consul, expecting that the vessel would go to pieces beneath them, advised Samuels to put his men ashore. The captain rejected the suggestion. The wind shifted in time to check the adverse current in the straits while the crew heaved 50 tons of ballast over the side, carried out anchors, and worked the leaking hull off the bank. This was extreme work for the sailors, but it would have been impossible for any ship then propelled by steam.

On the day before Christmas, 1844, the *Manhattan* was the only American vessel in a fleet of sixty ships bound for Constantinople. Under full sail, it raced a Turkish corvette to lead the fleet into the Bosporus. The chain of events from near shipwreck to a glorious arrival at the Golden Horn brought Samuels's reputation for ship handling to the attention of the naval pasha. While the *Manhattan* underwent repairs, the American consul reported that the pasha was interested in appointing its captain to the position of admiral in the Turkish navy. Declining the pasha's generous offer, Samuels pleaded fealty to his wife and child in the United States, which was just as well, considering the highjinks that Samuels and some of his fellow captains engaged in while they were delayed in the Turkish port.

Eventually, the *Manhattan* sailed to the Black Sea port of Odessa. Later, when it was homeward bound through the Bosporus, the American consul cautioned Samuels that he should not pause at once friendly Constantinople, suspected as he was of complicity in the escape of a concubine from the pasha's harem. She was not on board the *Manhattan,* but, for reasons never explained to his crew, Samuels hastened his disguised ship through the Dardenelles and willfully bypassed the legally required clearances at the Turkish castles.

That adventure in Samuels's narrative strangely mirrored the plot of an eighteenth-century comic opera, yet its authenticity was later affirmed when Samuels, then a famous mariner, was in New York. Several officials, including a customhouse official and later clerk of the New York Court of Common Pleas, were witnesses to the recounting of the tale on the deck of Samuels's ship by a Swedish sea captain and his wife. She was the escaped concubine, and he was the man whom Samuels had assisted in managing her escape.

His first voyage as captain was successful enough in the vessel owner's view that he gave Samuels permission to take his wife and, by then, two children with him on the next voyage. After the *Manhattan* was loaded with a cargo of sugar, his family, a stewardess, and most of the crew from his previous voyage, Samuels got under way for Leghorn on the Italian west coast and Batavia in the Dutch East Indies. Near Sardinia, a strong southwester came up astern. Approaching the lee shore of the mainland at night with the bottom shoaling rapidly, the ship repeatedly luffed into the wind, pitched heavily, and blew out some of its sails. Under a lightning storm, the wind suddenly reversed direction, a heavy sea struck, two crew members were lost, and the leadsman called "five fathoms." Lightning illuminated the nearby shore, breakers could be heard, and the depth went to $4\frac{1}{2}$ fathoms. Mrs. Samuels, on her knees in the cabin, was praying. The wind calmed as she came on deck to report to her husband that her prayers had been answered, she who sighted a light as the wind began to blow from the shore. Gradually, Samuels eased the vessel away in a light breeze and, guided by the lights, brought it to anchor in four fathoms at 2 A.M., close to Leghorn harbor. Samuels knelt in prayer with his pious wife.

The *Manhattan* arrived at Leghorn in the midst of a rebellion. Despite the presence of a U.S. naval squadron, Samuels and his crew were tracked during their shore activities by a members of a villainous band who sensed that the captain would be taking money on board for the next leg of his journey. Surrounded by sixty allied seamen, Samuels managed to secure $80,000 in Spanish pillars on board. Then, a gang of twenty men, led by a one-eyed bandit, boarded the ship. They returned to their boats after Samuels leveled his pistol at the leader while his crew surrounded the others with cutlasses and pikes to foil the attempted robbery.

Few of Samuels's adventures came to a tidy end. He often experienced a recurrence of whatever evil he had successfully overcome. Swindlers whom he had encountered earlier under the guise of pilots, apparently in league with the bandits fended off in the harbor, chased the *Manhattan* in two boats crowded with men as it sailed into the Mediterranean. This time, Samuels avoided a boarding, and the chase halted after he ordered the crew to fire balls and shot at close range into each vessel.

Seventy-eight days out of Leghorn, the ship arrived at Java Head, sailed into Sunda Strait, and anchored in the Bay of Batavia. There, for more than five weeks, the Samuels family led an elegant life. Mrs. Samuels was the first American lady ever to visit the place. Disregarding orders to await advice from Amsterdam concerning return cargo, Samuels loaded the ship with coffee, arrack, sandalwood, spices, and rattan on the American consul's advice. Portions of his ship were rotten, and he planned an earlier and slower passage home.

Following an easy run to the Cape of Good Hope, the *Manhattan* was caught in a southwest gale. Two of her lifeboats were lashed, bottoms up, above a gallows frame forward of the house near the stern, which afforded a shelter from some of the breaking seas. With the ship sailing under close-reefed topsails, Samuels stood under the boats. Momentarily forsaking the sailor's rule of one hand for the ship and one for himself, he raised both hands to his mouth to shout orders to the men forward. A heavy sea struck the ship on the quarter, stove in bulwarks and part of the house, and washed the two boats and the skipper overboard. Unabashed,

9–1. *Samuel Samuels (1823–1908), daring driver of ships and men.*
The Mariners' Museum

Samuels swam for one of the boats floating upright and clambered over its shattered gunwale while his ship sailed on. The splintered boat was nearly full of water as waves broke around it. Using his sou'wester as a bailer, he worked and waited for six hours for the return of his vessel.

Three times, the chief mate, as acting captain of the ship, had searched but could not locate his drifting superior. On his fourth effort, he found Samuels and hauled him out of the boat with a towline about his torso. The sea that washed the captain overboard had nearly drowned his wife, his children, and the stewardess. Much of the bulwarks and deck gear was damaged, and the ship was leaking badly, with both pumps working full-time to keep the water from gaining. Still, as the wind moderated, the captain ordered canvas added aloft.

"Sailors soon forget past dangers," Samuels wrote, "and only live in the present." In calmer seas, they found most of the leak above the waterline, and, with a more stable trim, they eased the work on the pumps and shaped a course under southeast trades for Saint Helena. There, stopping for little more than a day, they were able to trim the ship enough to seal the sprung strakes and stop the leak. They took on fresh water and vegetables and, later in northern latitudes, encountered an English schooner from which they procured onions, wine, ale, and cheese.

In his memoirs, Samuels goes on for pages about the joys of fresh provisions taken on board as they approached the Azores and adds, almost as an afterthought, "At 4 A.M. one morning, I was made the happy father of a baby girl." The mother, of course, only a month before had nearly drowned and had faced the anguish of worrying for six hours about her husband missing in storm-tossed waters. Samuels resumes his narrative with a discussion of the multiple skills that a shipmaster must have—sailmaker, rigger, carpenter, cook, lawyer, navigator, merchant, and, yes, doctor and clergyman.

Bringing the tired old *Manhattan* into Falmouth, England, two months earlier than the owners expected affirmed Samuels's reputation for swift ship handling. The vessel was repaired, painted, and caulked, putty and paint providing cosmetic aid to a rotted mizzenmast, until as Samuels wrote, "I felt as proud of my ship as I did of my wife." Surely that put things in order.

After making the short haul across the North Sea to Hamburg, Germany, the captain paid off his crew and arranged for their transport back to Holland, where they had signed on board. In 1849, an epidemic of cholera raged across northern Europe. In Hamburg, deaths among the shipping community alone were as high as 160 a day. The Samuels family and stewardess remained on board the *Manhattan,* but it appeared that the captain's extraordinary run of good fortune was about to end as symptoms of the disease appeared. He soaked in steaming hot mustard baths and imbibed a mixture of brandy, cayenne pepper, laudanum, and Angostura bitters. He wrapped himself in turpentine-soaked cloths, choked down the burning broth, and willed himself the fortitude to resist the disease. The treatment, coupled with his wife's prayers, cooked off the hellish affliction before it could do him in.

His health restored and the last of his cargo discharged, Samuels arranged the sale of the rotting old ship for $8,000. Declining an offer to remain on board under the new owners, Samuels and his family took passage to New York on the packet ship *Catharine.* Afterward, he took a single-voyage berth as the *Catharine's* chief officer under John ("Bully") Edwards, from whom he acquired the hard-driving technique of the top captains. Together, they boarded the *Angelique* as master and mate, and Samuels took over command for its next voyage on the familiar route between New York and Amsterdam.

Sam, the foremast hand, had sailed on more than nine ships; Mr. Samuels, mate, on thirteen more; and Captain Samuels on two of his former ships. He had cruised to the far side of the world and knew well the North and South Atlantic; the Mediterranean; the Indian Ocean; and the Aegean, Black, and China seas. He had avoided yellow fever, pirates, shipwreck, and being lost when he was washed overboard at the height of a gale. At the age of twenty-six, with a wife and three children, he was ready to prove himself on the Great Circle of the Atlantic.

III

The Kingdom Captured

What fates impose, that men must needs abide;
It boots not to resist both wind and tide.

WILLIAM SHAKESPEARE

10

Converging on the Great Circle

Like the scent of sea crashing on the shore with a rising tide, in the mid-1800s the fresh air of experimentation was wafting through the United States with the surge of industrial change. Samuel Morse's magnetic telegraph, demonstrated in 1844, promised that, with the stringing of wires information could be exchanged across the land in minutes rather than weeks. Louis-Jacques-Mandé Daguerre's New York portrait gallery captured living images on metal plates without use of sketchpad, palette, and brush. Electric motors held promise for easing the labor of man and beast; people looked forward to the day the machinery would replace the horses drawing New York's new railcars.

In lower Manhattan, the five-story American Museum housed a collection of exotic live animals once thought to be the stuff of folktales—a duck-billed mammal, neither fish nor fowl; a leather-skinned unicorn, later identified as a rhinoceros; giraffes, scientifically billed as camelopards by showman Phineas T. Barnum. Barnum's exhibits thrived on strange creatures brought from across the seas. An astute mix of suspect humbuggery and authentic peculiarities generated the public's readiness to accept as real nearly anything that was extraordinary. More fascinating than the animals was the museum's congress of human oddities—Chang and Eng, twin brothers from Siam, joined at the hip for life; a dog-faced man, allegedly brought from the Russian steppes, covered with hair from crown to waist; South Seas savages; a towering 8-foot giantess; a nearly fleshless "living skeleton" with hardly an ounce of fat; and most famous of all, Barnum's tiny friends, the personable Charles Stratton and his wife, Lavinia, "only inches" (perhaps 30) in height. The nation's first steam locomotive was named for Stratton—Tom Thumb.

Meanwhile, steam engines powered looms, dug canals, and outperformed the wind in crossing the Atlantic. Richard Henry Dana's report in his *Two Years before the Mast* on the continent's little-known west coast, called Spanish America before its accession, fired the drive to build a rail crossing from sea to sea. Short-line railroads were common elements of urban centers. The eastern states were already connected with federally subsidized rail lines, and the prospect of a transcontinental path loomed high. On both sides of the Atlantic, the economic focus moved from wide-open agrarian societies to sooty industrial clusters nestled under plumes of smoke and steam. Newly macadamized roads and multilevel canals connected inland and coastal communities expanding with factories, warehouses, and docks.

Shipping and foreign trade flourished. Wealthy, aggressive speculators stepped in to build the steam plants and risk the installation of heavy machinery in hulls more suited to wind and waves, then to convene and cajole the workers whose wheels and paddles would churn the oceans. A new breed of laborer came to the seaports. Burly men migrated from the freshwater steamboats and inland foundries to work deep in the hulls amid complex machinery, boilers, and fireboxes—coal passers, stokers, steamfitters, oilers, and wipers who were willing to sweat in stifling confinement below decks for marginally higher oceangoing wages.

Enticed by the prospect of exploiting an emerging saltwater domain, dozens of firms intent on capturing a share of expanding intercontinental trade arose in the port cities. They centered on New York and Liverpool, two pulsing arteries that fed the traffic of the Great Circle. The struggle among the would-be titans for rule of this Atlantic kingdom was a contest without rules, one in which contenders set their own measures of success—punctuality of scheduled departures; crossings of shortest duration; fastest day's run; largest vessels; or, for a given busy period, most passengers or greatest tonnage carried and revenues earned. They boasted of the achievments of their own ships in their drive for increased revenues and spent what was necessary to sustain their claims. Rarely was profit a measure; it was a goal to be achieved only after dominance was won.

Not all changes were beneficial. Industrial growth in the cities was accompanied by overcrowding, poverty, and often rampant disease. Despite the threat to life and limb at sea, shipboard life was healthier than that prevailing in waterfront neighborhoods. Provided that individuals with infectious diseases were barred at the gangway, crew and cabin pasengers enjoyed clean, fresh air, an ample supply of victuals, and easy disposal of sewage. The sequestered, cramped quarters of steerage, however, were ripe to foster the outbreak and spread of infections.

The term *packet* originally meant sail transport between designated ports, with regular schedules essential to the exchange of mail. In time, the designation applied to steamers, as well as to the tall sailing craft that appeared by midcentury. Several clipper ships were built specifically for packet duty. Because the term *packet* once referred to the tidy brigs under 500 tons that first held to announced departure dates, the term *packet ship* more commonly identified the smaller, wind-driven passenger liners.

Investors measured steamships by horsepower, tonnage, and passenger-carrying capacity. Passengers measured them informally by comforts and duration of passage, as they sought more of the former and less of the latter. Speed under sail always had been judged by poor standards—crossing times and individual days' runs—with every new record sending all prior achievements to oblivion. Such measures gave little account to differences in sizes or loads of competing ships. Record passages might have had modest hourly runs, even the fastest at relatively low speed, but the triumphs were achieved through a moderate, sustained pace, day and night, over extended periods. Weather, wind, and routes were vitally important factors, but, until most liners standardized one element of the crossing by consistently following great circle tracks, weather and wind were rarely mentioned in noting accomplishments.

After 1842, when Matthew Fontaine Maury was appointed to the U.S. Navy Department of Charts and Instruments, his massive study of ocean currents, the Gulf Stream in particular, and tables of seasonal wind expectations helped to reduce passage time. Hull design came into its own when marine architecture, associated with the development of clipper ships, became formalized as a profession. Donald McKay's elder brother Lauchlan, in analyzing distinct differences of design in his text on naval architecture, ignored the actions of hard-driving skippers and their crews during wild weather. Their actions often made a difference in the results, yet they were taken for granted. There were ample occasions when resolute command and courageous labor aloft outdid the accomplishment of coal and steam. Speed, however achieved, eclipsed thoughtful consideration of safety precautions that were vaguely assumed to be in place.

Among many businessmen who sought a place in the transatlantic trade, the principal contenders, one British and three American, were men of substance well before they sought to rule the Atlantic. By 1841, Samuel Cunard, building on his enterprises in the Maritimes, had the great circle route well in hand and later strengthened his company's grip by announcing plans for connecting lines to Africa and India. Enoch Train supplemented his Baltic, Gulf Coast, and South American trade with an irregular Irish export and emigrant service. Edward Collins gained fame and fortune through his Dramatic Line of flashy sailing packets. Latecomer Cornelius Vanderbilt's fabulous wealth accrued from his steamboat operations in New York and expansions to the Gulf of Mexico and Central America before he engaged in European transport. As family men and moneyed heads of successful businesses, they were respected leaders within their own circles. For the three American ship operators, Train, Collins, and Vanderbilt, the Great Circle glistened like a scimitar to be wrested from the grip of Cunard, the quiet Briton. Other companies joined in the struggle but ever in the wake of these four men. Meanwhile, a seaman with narrower ambitions but as strong a drive in his own sphere, Samuel Samuels, awaited the full development of steam's tall-masted competitors. Throughout his extraordinary career on sailing ships, nothing challenged him so much as the advent of steam power, not to harness it but to better it under canvas. Meanwhile, Donald McKay, among the best of the tall ship designers, was preparing to deliver tools that might do it.

THE RIVER MERSEY was far behind. Cape Clear and the Fastnet had dropped below the horizon as the *Britannia* set out along the Great Circle on its way to Halifax. Conversation about the glorious departure on July 4, 1840, had faded, although the event would linger long in memory (Chapter 5). Those making the maiden voyage took comfort in the presence of Samuel Cunard and his daughter, for the new steamship had a rough westward journey. The engines, untested on a passage of such length, throbbed heavily as the vessel tossed through unusually stormy seas for early summer. The initial deck layout proved cumbersome. Conforming to that of traditional sailing ships, even if the sails were to be little used, the wide, spoked double wheel was positioned aft directly over the steering gear that it controlled. From that location, the high paddle boxes obstructed the views of helmsmen and watch officers. Paddlers did not respond well at low speeds, so that, in close quarters, the watch favored a conning position on a bridgelike structure above the midships engine room. From there, orders could be delivered by voice tube or cord-rung bell directly to the engineer below. Hand waves or a loud hail aimed sternward sufficed for helm orders. In the open sea, the mate took his customary position on the quarterdeck near the wheel, there being little need under the circumstances for engine orders. After a few trips, adjustments would be made to relocate the steering station to the more practical location. On ocean-going vessels, the high central wheelhouse—the traditional ship's bridge—owes its origin to that experience. The *Britannia* was hermaphrodite-rigged, fore and main masts carrying square topsails above gaff-rigged, fore-and-aft courses, and a gaff-spanker at the mizzen, all small in size considering the ship's 207-foot length. The sails were meant more for stabilizing than for driving, in accord with Charles MacIver's desires for steamship operations.

On the ninth day out, in high latitudes, the steamer slowed to pass through a field of icebergs. However distraught the passengers might have been, they put their uneasiness behind them at the end of the twelfth and last full day at sea when the owner shared the news passed to him by Captain Woodruff. During the previous twenty-four hours, they had traversed 273 miles, the fastest day's run that any steamer had ever achieved. The 1,135-ton paddle wheeler steamed into Halifax on July 17 and docked at Cunard Pier at 2 A.M. The crew and longshoremen hustled to give it a quick turnaround while Cunard remained on board. Nine hours later, the flagship departed alone for Boston amid cheering crowds on the Halifax wharves. The consort *Unicorn,* having prepared the North American ports for the flagship, turned off on its feeder run to Quebec. The next day, at nightfall, *Britannia* approached the Boston pilot station, just eighteen months after Samuel Cunard's eyes first brightened at the prospect of transatlantic steam service.

The Boston merchants, expecting that the *Britannia* would depart from Liverpool on July 1, had planned for its arrival three days earlier. It was to have been accompanied en route by Junius Smith's *British Queen* bound for New York, both the ship and its destination considered by the Bostonians to be strong rivals. Celebratory flags remained lowered and cannons stilled as the Port of Boston awaited news of the *Britannia.* Word of its arrival in East Boston did not circulate until the next morning, Sunday, a day of piety in the Puritan-bred seaport. It was a day of quiet joy as the people learned of the *Britannia*'s fourteen-day, six-hour passage, having beaten the *Queen* to America by more than two days.

Two more days elapsed while civic officials prepared the welcoming ceremony and alerted all of New England to the event. From the time of the Tea Party, Bostonians had relished any opportunity to gather in raucous convention—tax rebellion; the Red Coat evacuation; news of the ringing of Philadelphia's Liberty Bell; a Bostonian's discovery of the Columbia River overlooked by English explorer George Vancouver in 1787; the return of the victorious, locally funded *Constitution*—all expressing American antagonism over the English powers across the sea. Now, they did a turnabout to welcome their good British friends in the name of commerce.

At its pier, the visiting steamship was adorned stem to stern with flags and evergreen branches, with the British flag on the mainmast and an

American ensign hoisted to the fore. The USS *Columbus* and the Revenue Cutter *Hamilton* hovered off *Britannia's* stern, both fully dressed in signal flags. On an arch erected across the street leading from Cunard Pavilion, the succint marine history of steam power was emblazoned in three proper names: "Cunard" across the top in gold letters, flanked by canvas with "Fulton" over an American eagle on one side and "Watt" over Great Britain's rampant lions on the other.

The new Maverick House was decked out in flags for the afternoon's inaugural banquet, its balconies aflutter with the parasols and kerchiefs of hundreds of colorfully outfitted ladies. A second arch bore the inscription: "Liverpool-Halifax-Boston," above the names of the Cunard Line's four new vessels that would unite the cities by the power of steam. The firing of a signal gun followed by an artillery salute announced the formation of a triumphal procession. Two thousand people, eight abreast, marched behind the brass band of the Boston Brigade from the new pier to the hotel. Speeches followed, with Harvard College President Josiah Quincy Jr. as keynote speaker. In introducing the Honorable Samuel Cunard, Quincy recalled that Abraham Cunard, born in Philadelphia, had lived in New York until the end of the Revolution, thus making Samuel a "grandson of America." Shy and gracious as always, Cunard responded briefly, so soft-spoken that he could be heard only by those seated next to the podium.

Composer Thomas Arne put James Thomson's poem, "Rule Britannia," to music especially for the occasion. Performed as a march, no one doubted at its conclusion that *Britannia* indeed ruled the waves. Famed orator Daniel Webster was followed by the British consul, editors, bankers, and merchants, all congratulating not themselves but a London-based businessman. The shipowner was presented with a great silver cup, embossed by a Boston silversmith with an emblem of the *Britannia*. After sunset, the day came to a spectacular conclusion when the *Hamilton* sent off a round of rockets to initiate a display of fireworks from the surrounding hills. Boston was again united with its mother country across the water by the establishment of steam-powered postal service.

There were curious nuances to this turning point in international commerce. The Boston merchants were backing a British steamship pioneer instead of conservatively investing in the extended packet service of one of their own. On the face of it, their risks were greater and, in the long run, what had they to gain? A small fraction of well-fixed travelers passing through the city would be hardly enough to bring long rail lines to the New England seaport, certainly not to the extent that overseas freight was bringing business to rival New York Port.

During the first six months of transatlantic operations, Cunard ships ran at eight to nine knots and sustained an average passage time of fourteen days. In January, in the midst of a windy winter, the *Columbia* crossed in an astounding twelve days. That was a noteworthy exception, for safety ranked high in the priorities of Cunard management. As their experience grew, Cunard ships became known more for cautious operation than for speed. In Liverpool, Charles MacIver was responsible for servicing the fleet. So seriously did he take his port captain's role that he practically disenfranchised the masters by limiting their traditional free use of authority. In orders to the captains, he wrote:

> We rely on your keeping every person attached to the ship, both officers and people throughout several departments, up to the highest standards of discipline and efficiency which we expect in the service. . . . You must not stop or delay the ship on the passage for any purpose, without previously consulting the Admiralty agent and having his sanction. Treat the Admiralty agent as a respected passenger. . . . The mails require the captain's best attention. Have them always ready to hand at the respective ports in England and in America as the first duty after the ship is secured. . . . The trust of so many lives under the captain's charge is a great trust. It will require great vigilance day and night. . . . Good steering is of great value. Pick out some of the best helmsmen for this duty. Let them steer the whole voyage out and home—such sailors to be paid five shillings per month extra wages ranking as quartermasters—but not to be so rated in the ship's articles. . . . It is to be borne in mind that every part of the coast board of England and Ireland can be read off the lead and ships from abroad making their landfall should never omit to verify their position by soundings. But masters eager to obtain credit of making a short passage rather than lose a few minutes in heaving the ship to, will run the risk of losing the vessel and all the lives on board.

MacIver's admonitions were buried in precautions concerning fire prevention in the dock and at sea; adherence to strict voyage schedules; training of the crew; limiting the use of canvas to steadying the vessel in a gale; and matters of cleanliness, ventilation, and ship handling in icebound ports. Coal consumption was "not to exceed the specified number of baskets of fuel each hour, each basket to contain not more than fifty pounds weight," a limit more for conservation of fuel than out of consideration for the coal passers. The engineer was to blow off the boiler hourly, thus reducing the risk of excess pressure while clearing soot from within the stack. He was to count the revolutions of the engine every two hours. Such detailed regulations must have rankled the captains, yet most of them earned reputations for their loyalty and dedication to the company.

Based in Halifax, Samuel Cunard and his son Edward took charge of the American end of the business, careful always to report to their London and Liverpool counterparts any hints of developing competition. In April 1841, David MacIver wrote to Samuel, "I have yours of Saturday enclosing the Prospectus of an Iron Steam Coy. [*sic,* Company] to New York—Quackery—not worth noticing—would only do harm to publish it—would excite more attention than it deserves. 'Delano and Rathburn' spoke the other night as if Collins had no chance of getting up Steamers— All he is asking of the American Government is, liberty to tax the settlers he carries." It is likely that Cunard had sent MacIver a brochure prepared in conjunction with the Collins letter to President Van Buren.

CAREFULLY RATED chronometers had been carried for decades on board ocean vessels, along with the almanacs and complex tables needed for longitude computation, an arcane and error-prone procedure. In 1843, the enduring problem, coupled with poor visibility, contributed to the Cunard Line's first loss, the wreck of the fast-steaming *Columbia* off Sable Island, Nova Scotia. Through the foresight of Charles MacIver and to the credit of a well-trained crew, there was no loss of life. The catastrophe gained little adverse publicity, for people routinely looked upon oceangoing as a risky business and weather an ever-threatening curse.

During the following January, Boston found itself in the throes of one

10–1. *RMS* Britannia *departs from icebound Boston.*
The Mariners' Museum

of its most bitter winters. The *Britannia,* coming down from Halifax late in the month, slogged its way through a thickening layer of sea slush. The temperature dropped far below freezing, where it remained for a week. While docked in East Boston, the steamship became locked in ice 6–8 inches thick. Troubled by the growing popularity of the packets sailing out of New York, the Boston merchants were as anxious as Cunard management to see the Liverpool schedule maintained. A coalition of businessmen collected several thousand dollars and put out gangs with sleds, plows, axes, and saws to cut a 60-foot-wide channel through several miles of ice.

In addition to hundreds of workers at the channel's edge, thousands of Bostonians thronged the frozen harbor as they celebrated the unique affair, walked and skated across the ice, and even bundled up in horse-drawn sleighs to glide over it. One of Nathaniel Currier's ubiquitous observers was on hand to capture the scene for the printmaker when the

Britannia thrashed through the freshly cut pathway on February 3, only two days behind schedule.

Meanwhile, Enoch Train's White Diamond Line took shape in the recently introduced Boston–Liverpool packet service. Ignoring the British steamers and the plentiful New York packets, Train was convinced that he could successfully compete with them (Chapter 7). In the second week of December, a ruinous gale roared over the Atlantic during the voyage of Train's *Dorchester.* A month later, on January 11, 1845, the first news of its loss arrived when the New Line's packet *Rochester* arrived in New York with passengers rescued from White Diamond's foundering flagship.

Train's misfortune turned to his benefit, an uncanny situation in his reach for the Great Circle. The two men, builder and operator, could not have foreseen the startling expansion of the immigrant trade following the onset of the Irish famine. When it arose, White Diamond Line was poised to capitalize on it with the larger and faster *Joshua Bates.* Initially, McKay's small East Boston yard financially backed by Train was producing but one vessel a year.

The first vessel from the yard was the packet *Washington Irving,* co-owned by Train and its captain, Eben Caldwell. It joined the *Joshua Bates* on the Boston–Liverpool route in September 1845, about the time that the youthful George Francis Train joined his cousin's firm. McKay and Train remained uninterested in steam-powered vessels. The brigs ran at significantly lower cost of operation; they found that they could afford to sail with less than full bottoms. The wind was free, and crowded dormitories in steerage were earning more revenue per cubic foot than did most dry cargo.

Packed steerage earned Train his profit even though it gained him no reverence among his Yankee business associates. Unlike the Cunarders, Train passengers streaming down the gangways onto the Charlestown immigration piers brought no money into Boston. The Irish poor brought only strong backs and a willingness to work at less than going wages. One miserable Atlantic crossing turned most of them forever against seagoing; the hardiest went no farther than the docksides as longshoremen. They brought a gentle charm and a ready wit that found them jobs in the lowest levels of local government, such as walking police beats and running errands for ward politicians. They also brought children and a strong Catholic faith that soon demanded churches, schools, and hospitals in that traditionally Protestant city.

Years of living on the edge of poverty made the Irish less than adequate tradesmen. Instead, they cleared the land for the Public Gardens, transported the rocks that filled in the swampy Back Bay, and hauled granite blocks and carried the mortar for churches rising on the hills of a dozen neighborhoods. The Irish women cooked, cleaned houses, taught in the schools, and tended the libraries. The ditches for the nation's first subway were dug by the first native-born Boston Irishmen. Enoch Train received no credit for the way that his migrant ocean shuttle changed the makeup of the city over little more than a generation. Although he was one of Boston's wealthiest citizens, he was little recognized by the Boston Brahmins with whom he associated, whereas his Nova Scotia–born shipbuilder rose to prominence.

Train's hold on good fortune was tenuous, even as demand grew for his company's low-cost transport. To meet the increase, he ordered the packet *Anglo-Saxon* for his own account. The 894-ton ship was less than a year old when, during the winter of 1846, it was lost off Cape Sable. Train's line was not the only company to suffer losses. Through two dozen years of packet ship ascendancy, 1824–48, one in six vessels was lost to storms, fog, fires, or shoals. Yet, on average, packet transport sustained a lower casualty rate than did transient shipping. Among the New York ocean packets, whose reporting foreshadowed the style of reports to be issued by common carriers a century and a half later, only six per hundred thousand passengers lost their lives through calamities.

Resolute in facing setback, Train added three fast packets to the White Diamond fleet before the end of 1846. They supplemented Train's other ships in making significant inroads on the English trade. The packets booked three classes of passengers, and full holds carried Staffordshire potteries, Manchester dry goods, and general cargo for as many as 150 consignees per voyage. That performance enticed Train to put what would become his proudest vessel, the *Ocean Monarch,* into packet service in 1847 to increase the flow of Boston-bound Irish immigrants. White Diamond's ships lacked the prestige of first-class ticketing, but the returns from steerage consistently formed the most profitable part of its business.

Telegraph connections between seaports did not exist in 1848, and wireless transmission would not occur until the twentieth century. Communications across the water traveled unhindered at their own pace. By midcentury, news generally arrived from Europe within three or four weeks of its dispatch. Sea captains meeting with other ships passed along departure-day newspapers and gossip and sometimes put aside commercial rivalries to exchange information. At the minimum, they logged observations of vessels sighted en route. Ships approaching pilot stations during daylight were frequently identified from shore, and semaphore towers transmitted word of their arrivals to the cities of destination. On boarding an arriving vessel, pilots exchanged local news for information from across the waters. In an innovation introduced by James Gordon Bennett's *New York Herald,* fast-sailing news boats cruised beyond the approaches to seek information that might influence the financial markets. When a ship entered a harbor, the more important events were shouted from deck to passing craft or to piers where an audience was always available and eager to carry the tidings to the broader populace. An early hint about European commodity prices could send the recipients of the news scurrying to the exchanges hours before the ship carrying the details eased into its slip.

Delays in scheduled arrivals caused no immediate concern because people were accustomed to crossing times that varied with the weather. As the days stretched out, however, shipowners and waiting relatives began to relate reported sea conditions and the extent of detainment. After a long unexplained delay, those waiting at the waterfront for news grew in number and anxiety peaked for word about a tardy vessel. Months sometimes elapsed before all hope for an unreported vessel expired.

When the *Ocean Monarch,* James Murdoch commanding, was overdue in September 1848, an arriving steamship approached its Boston pier to encounter over three thousand people collected along the waterfront and crowding the wharves. The steamer's captain stood on the bridge with his brass speaking trumpet in hand. Before the first lines were hauled to their bollards, he shouted down the news. "The *Ocean Monarch* was burned off Orm's Head. Four hundred passengers burned or drowned. Captain Murdoch taken off a spar by Tom Littledale's yacht. A steamer going to Ireland passed by, and refused to offer assistance. Complete wreck, and complete loss."

The grim message was followed by a moment of stunned silence. Then, wild excitement burst out as people rushed for newspaper and shipping offices. George Francis Train was among those on the wharf. He raced on horseback past the ferry pier and up State Street to bring the news to the Merchants' Exchange. Two weeks elapsed before ships arrived with papers bringing detailed reports from the captain and other survivors. The tragedy took place in the Irish Sea, four miles off the coast of Wales, on the morning of August 24. Littledale's yacht, *Queen of the Ocean,* returning to Liverpool from a cruise to North Wales, was first on the scene. It was joined in the rescue operation by the *Affonso,* a Brazilian steam frigate making a courtesy visit to England and carrying several notable passengers, including an admiral of the Royal Navy and his daughters. The Ireland-bound steamer first reported was not identified.

The fire aboard the *Ocean Monarch* was already out of control and a distress flag flying when the rescuers approached. Two lifeboats had been quickly launched, the remaining ones lost to the fire. Several passengers and crew were found clinging to wreckage in the choppy seas when the yacht put out a small boat, joined by five others from the Brazilian warship. The *Ocean Monarch*'s blazing mizzenmast crashed over the stern and was soon followed by the main. Several passengers rushed forward to distance themselves from the flames and clung in panic to the *Monarch*'s jibboom and bowsprit. The crew of the *Affonso* placed a stern cable on the bow of the burning ship and persuaded a few of the hovering emigrants to climb along it, hand-over-hand monkey style, or to jump clear. Several passengers were stretched out on top of each other in clusters on the long jibboom when the *Monarch*'s foremast crashed, and the jibboom fell into the water with its load of screaming passengers.

Captain Murdoch threw over the topgallant yard for flotation and then went into the sea himself to cling to a plank until he was rescued by Littledale's crew. Other vessels joined in the rescue. A seaman from the

American *New World* swam with a line to the flaming wreck. He clambered on board to assist in clearing off the last of the stranded victims and helped them into boats before he jumped into the sea just ahead of the flames. The abandoned *Ocean Monarch* burned to the waterline and sank in ten fathoms of water. Sources differed in reporting the number of people on board, to be expected considering the diffused hand-kept records during that era. Of some 390 people on board, 216 were saved, including all but 2 of the 25 first- and second-class passengers. In the days that followed, 170 bodies washed onto the shores of Wales.

10–2. *Burning of the* Ocean Monarch, *from the eyewitness sketch.*
The Mariners' Museum

The fire could have been started by a steerage passenger attempting to use a ventilator as a stove. It raged out of hand almost at once and swept through the lower decks. Amid wild confusion, flames took control of the ship too fast for the captain to ground his vessel in a flood tide. Fortunately, Captain Lisboa, the *Affonso*'s commander, and Admiral Grenfell took command of boats to gather the unfortunates. The young Prince de Joinville, third son of a former French king—he would go to America in 1861 to fight for the Union in the Civil War—was among the *Affonso*'s guests. While he assisted in bringing on board the *Ocean Monarch*'s desperate survivors, he managed to capture the scene in a sketchbook. The *Illustrated London News* published his grim drawing of the disaster soon afterward.

ASSESSING HIS grip on the North Atlantic, Samuel Cunard was unconcerned about the sailing packets but, in 1847, expressed anxiety over the new New York and Liverpool United States Mail Steamship Company. "The American ships will be different," he told his managers. "They will introduce all our improvements together with their own. We shall also have national prejudices to contend with, so that every attention will be required to meet them." Encouraging a watchful eye, he concluded with some confidence, "I do not despair of getting our fair share and the intercourse between the two countries will yearly increase."

10–3. *Port of New York, 1851, largest seaport in the United States.*
The Mariners' Museum

By 1848, Cunard had doubled his fleet to eight vessels and was working toward doubling it again. During the following year, his company replaced the old *Britannia* and *Acadia* and arranged a new contract with the Admiralty that provided a subsidy of £145,000 per year. In return, Cunard promised to bring service to the growing New York Port, where he arranged terminal facilities at Jersey City, directly across the Hudson River from the Manhattan piers. From there, the line scheduled weekly American departures for direct transport to Coburg Dock at Liverpool, alternating the New York Port departures with the customary Boston-Halifax-Liverpool route. Edward Cunard moved from Halifax to become the line's New York agent. On December 29, 1848, the *Hibernia* arrived from Boston. On New Year's Day 1849, in a quick turnaround, it departed on the first direct New York–Liverpool run, and the *Cambria* followed two weeks later. Within a year, Cunard's New York business exceeded that of the eight-year-old Halifax and Boston service, with New York cargoes half again more than those shipped at Boston.

In 1850, Cunard's New York shipments nearly doubled those of Boston. By then, the Cunard family had acquired a sweeping piece of property on the highest land in Staten Island and had made New York their home. Invoking the further expansion of his ocean schedules, Samuel Cunard convinced the Admiralty to increase the mail subsidy; annual contributions reached £173,340. Mirroring the Hudson River rate wars, the Atlantic steamship rivalry took on the aspect of a high-stakes spending struggle. With American maritime ventures at a peak, Uncle Sam and John Bull faced each other with the strategies, tactics, and diversions of a nautical jousting match. David MacIver's earlier jest about the Americans asking their government to tax the settlers echoed hollowly, for the Britons were behaving the same way but on a grander scale.

CUNARD'S MOVE signaled a long-term trend in the striking growth of New York Port, but the shift in business from other East Coast facilities to New York was obscured by an overall period of expansion in foreign trade. Boston's foreign trade more than doubled from 1840 to 1848, the immigrant arrivals nearly all accomplished without benefit of steam. That port's heyday had passed, however, and it slipped into a rarely reversed decline. Economically myopic Enoch Train remained undisturbed, deluded as he was by the growth of his own business. Most transatlantic traders had similar feelings, and their respective shares of the total market went unexamined during the heady period.

Donald McKay expanded his yard from the foot of Border Street along the shores of East Boston and put down ways that delivered three vessels in 1848, four in 1849, and six in 1850. Productivity grew quickly following the installation of a steam-powered sawmill. It was his own invention, suspended in such a way that heavy timbers could be cut to shape and beveled by three men faster than formerly accomplished by a dozen men with handsaws. The great beams were hauled and dropped into place from a derrick swung into position by oxen; steam winches were not yet considered vital to the apparatus.

Abruptly, the props were knocked from under the American presence in the North Atlantic when the startling pull of California gold diverted the interest of several East Coast shippers and whalers. Demand for fast passage to the West Coast soared. In 1849, Boston cleared 151 ships for California, many of which failed to return because their captains and crews abandoned them in San Francisco. The Irish famine tugged from the other direction, as it brought on a new wave of European immigration. Enoch Train was quick to offer accommodations as he arranged new passage offices in Liverpool and Cork, and he put his new partner, George Francis Train, in charge of the Liverpool agency. Lingering in Boston, the impetuous young man took advantage of his position to urge McKay to build clippers for the interocean route to California as an extension to White Diamond's business. At first, the suggestion failed to interest the conservative Enoch or his shipbuilder. McKay saw the Great Circle to be a rainbow rising from his own dockyard, the pot of gold glistening at his feet. Train was prime among owners of sailing ships who were determined to exploit the Atlantic and increase the size of their fleets while replacing their older vessels. Their demand sustained the East Boston yard until McKay worked up the design of a vessel suited for the long, two-ocean voyage to the gold fields.

In October 1850, McKay launched the Atlantic sailing packet *Daniel Webster* for Train and fitted out his first clipper for Boston's George B.

Upton. Relishing the potential of the costly tall ship, Upton joined forces with the Sampson & Tappan shipping firm to send out the 1,534-ton *Stag Hound* under Captain Josiah Richardson, the first McKay vessel to sail for the Golden Gate. Enoch Train was not yet ready to concede to his cousin's urging, whatever the attractions, even as Donald McKay started to lay out lines for even larger California clippers.

One might wonder whether Enoch Train saw the Liverpool assignment as an opportunity to get the fluent but ever eccentric George Francis out of the way. Following the launching of the *Stag Hound* on December 7, 1850, George made plans to move to Liverpool but with little sense of urgency.

Widowed in 1848, McKay remarried during the following year. His secretary, the romantic Mary Cressy Litchfield, while unable to provide the shipwright's advice of her predecessor, took a strong interest in her new husband's work. Artistic in nature, she assumed as her special task the naming of the McKay vessels. A series of fanciful names given to his clipper ships, some borrowed from the British, bears witness to Mary's influence.

McKay sensed that tall ships built to his designs could outdo steamers in the rush to the equator and outmaneuver them by circuiting South America. Sturdy sailing vessels were the only ships that could handle the lengthy voyage to California. Paddle wheelers were considered too risky for the stormy waters off South America's southern tip, and the 3,000 mile passage lacked adequate coaling ports in the Southern Hemisphere. Between Rio de Janeiro, Brazil, and Valparaiso, Chile, engine-repair facilities were nonexistent. On both the Atlantic and the Pacific coasts, steam vessel operators weighed the potential of a connection across Central America to meet the demand for transport to the gold fields. Such a route would require breaking through the isthmian jungles and paving swampland for the interocean connection.

Cornelius Vanderbilt was first to prove the shorter overall travel time achieved by combining a double steamship route with a cumbersome land crossing at Nicaragua, although he did little to compare the operating costs of the two routes. Sail's economic advantage over steam came not just from the wind but from smaller crews of skilled labor that kept the ships in condition while under way. Even with the longer passage time, rapid turnaround still gave windjammers a competitive edge. Sailing vessels carrying their own craftsmen—carpenter, sailmaker, and boatswain—had no need for machine shop mechanics and ironworkers at both ends of the route. Coal weighed heavily on the balance sheets of steamship companies. The net effect was that the longer the passage, the more suitable was sail transport. Despite the elaborate furnishings of some steamships, travel on them proved no more pleasant than on the large ocean sailers. In fact, during a rough passage, a stable sailing ship was the

10–4. *Grand saloon of the SS* Atlantic, *elegance at sea.*
Peabody-Essex Museum

more comfortable—deep-keeled, quieter, cleaner, heeled to a steady angle, and never rolling to the extent of its steam-powered counterpart.

While steamship proponents studied the issues, master of sail Samuel Samuels held out for wind-driven transport. In 1850, he joined the sailing packet *Angelique* as chief mate, New York to Amsterdam, and took command of it within a year (Chapter 9). Having cruised the world, the North Atlantic became his territory, and the mastery of tall ships his calling. Under Samuels, within three years the *Angelique* gained notoriety in periodic listings of packet performance, and shipowners were quick to take note of the skilled captain.

LATE ON THE scene, Edward Knight Collins started his steam packet operation in 1850 (Chapter 6). On April 27, the extravagantly outfitted *Atlantic* sailed from New York, to be joined before year's end by the *Pacific, Arctic,* and *Baltic.* Each would be identified as a "United States Mail Steam Ship," or USM, to counter the British RMS. The public, taking mail for granted but fascinated by steam, settled for the simpler designation of SS, an acronym that would last for more than 150 years. The vessels were matched in size, each about 2,800 tons, some 1,000 tons larger than the average Cunarder, and crossing, on average, in one less day.

The *Atlantic* boasted two great saloons, 67 feet long and 20 wide, paneled in rosewood and satinwood, and separated by a steward's pantry. Furnished as dining and drawing rooms, the latter was so embellished with mirrors that a passenger spoke of having encountered six repetitions of himself. Marble-topped tables, lavishly upholstered sofas, and tufted, gilt-edged chairs on thick carpets were surrounded by stained glass ornamentation bearing politically suitable geographic themes. Each Collins ship had an insulated room that stored 40 tons of ice.

The narrow passenger staterooms were steam heated and equipped with individual signaling gear to call the stewards. Tin commodes stood near the washstands. Several bathrooms were shared among multiple staterooms, a significant improvement over the Cunard Line's sparse bathing facilities. Centered amid the staterooms was a striking tonsorial parlor, its adjustable chair equipped with an inclined back and stuffed leather headrest, seat, and foot trestle. An "experienced surgeon" was advertised as part of the staff on each Collins ship. A Collins innovation that would endure for more than a century—a smoking room, an odiferous deck-house graced with hand-painted spittoons—offered gentlemen a retreat from the vaporous conversations of mixed company. In theory, the *Atlantic*'s staterooms accommodated about two hundred passengers berthed in pairs, scanty for comfort but at a lower fare per person than that charged for roomier single berthing.

The start was not auspicious for the hundred people making the *Atlantic*'s maiden voyage. Paddle blades were damaged in a grounding on Sandy Hook. Because the water was too rough for repairs, the ship was obliged to thump its way uneasily across the Atlantic. After six days, a water condenser failed, and the ship hove to for forty hours while it was restored to operation. Thirteen days elapsed before its arrival at the Mersey River, and a three-week layover was needed to complete repairs. Fortunately, the difficulties occurred on the eastbound voyage, and the adverse publicity was slow in echoing back to the home port. The line saved face on the flagship's return to New York, with the run accomplished in a record-breaking ten days and sixteen hours. It justified the enthusiasm that Collins publicity had generated during the long outfitting period and that continued through the year. The American public was delighted to read of the *Atlantic*'s overall high performance and quick to forgive its incommodious departure.

In May 1851, the *Pacific* sailed with two hundred and forty-three passengers, the largest number ever embarked on a steamship, and brought in $36,450 in passage money. To add to its fame, the *Pacific* also crossed in record time and briefly took the honor from Cunard's *Acadia*. In approving the design of the four ships supporting his promise to operate the fastest steamers on the North Atlantic, Edward Collins put himself in a nearly untenable position. Side-wheelers driven by single-expansion engines normally gave limited propulsion. The paired engines of the Collins ships required additional coal to feed them, which amounted to an extraordinary waste of fuel. The *Arctic* burned 68 to 79 tons of fuel per day. Speed was achieved by constantly pushing the machinery close to capacity and putting the sturdy wooden hulls under intense stress from engine vibration. Additional pressure on shaft bearings, even with vigorous injection of lubricants, wore down surfaces to the extent that the engines had to be shut down for hand scraping at the conclusion of nearly every voyage. A hot bearing while under way, even in the best of circumstances, hardly could be tolerated for the loss of time and the reaction of passengers to the disturbance.

Adding to operating costs was the exorbitant standard of food and drink that Collins had established to draw clientele from both the Cunard Line ships and the familiar sailing packets. Each vessel was equipped with a soda fountain, and passengers were stupefied when they were offered four full meals a day. The Collins Line was expensive to run, and, in its effort to pluck a greater portion of the trade, it lost money at a startling pace. Any form of rate war with the British would prove disastrous.

11

Portents

After Collins's *Pacific* took the Blue Riband from Cunard, *Hunt's Merchants' Magazine,* the bible of maritime affairs, began logging voyage lengths in days, hours, and minutes. Facing a diminishing share of transatlantic trade and unable to match the technical superiority of the new Collins ships, Samuel Cunard found his position threatened. He exhorted Charles MacIver (port agent David had died in 1845, and the extent of his control in the company had passed to his brother) to come up with any measures that might protect or improve their situation, something that MacIver had been dwelling on since the *Atlantic*'s first visit to Liverpool. There, he met with Brown, Shipley, Ltd., the Collins Line agents, to offer a proposal that was certain to appeal to the Americans because it eliminated the threat of a price war. During negotiations, both Samuel Cunard and Edward Collins kept their distance and left the details to their subordinates. The two groups ironed out an agreement, not to be made public, fixing the minimum rates for both passengers and cargo. Either company could charge higher fees and keep the difference; only rates lower than those agreed on were prohibited. Adult first-class passage from Liverpool was set at £35 and second class at £20 (about $171 and $98, respectively). The return voyage rates from

America were set at $120 and $70, accordingly. Freight was fixed at £7/7 per ton, with various adjustments for small shipments. The schedule recognized that individual reputations in their own countries gave the British ships an earnings edge on the westbound trips and the Americans a similar advantage on eastbound passages.

The curious part about the contract, in spite of the public appearance of intense competition, was an agreement to pool the earnings for subsequent allocations adjusted to the earning capacity of individual steamships, the Collins ships having greater passenger and cargo space than the Cunarders. The arrangement was finely tuned to be equitable by basing pooling on a triple voyage plan—earnings on one American westward transport of cargo and passengers were balanced against two British voyages; eastbound pooling arrangements encompassed only the carriage of passengers. Should either company's gross transatlantic earnings be less than one third the sum of all voyages of both, the other would pay the necessary amount to bring them up to one third of the aggregate. Further details anticipated the issues of transshipment of goods for Cunard's European routes, the carrying of high-freight specie, and allowances for passenger provisions and the expenses of loading.

The initial agreement, to cover a period of nineteen months, went into effect on May 25, 1850, and was renewable into 1853 when it would be reviewed and revised as needed, with settlements to be made at the end of each period. Both parties resolutely agreed to the secrecy clause, as they well knew that they should. Although such a rate-stabilizing arrangement might be suspect under the traditional and often flaunted free-trade policy of the United States, the international cartel was not illegal. Antitrust laws governing restraint of trade did not exist on the books of either nation. The agreement avoided the destructive chaos that had been introduced by Cornelius Vanderbilt on inland waters. History has long proved that such accords can be beneficial to all parties in the trade.

Samuel Cunard now felt comfortable, and he firmly intended to maintain his usual level of prudence as he vigorously competed. Edward Collins was exuberant and looked on the one-third floor as near assurance that his subsidized venture would be profitable. His showmanship came forth as he strove to make his shipping line famous in both hemispheres. In

September 1850, diva Jenny Lind, the Swedish Nightingale, departed from Liverpool as the *Atlantic*'s star passenger, standing on the casement of the paddle wheel and waving farewell to her English fans as the ship got under way. Her impresario, Collins's friend Phineas T. Barnum, planned a formal welcome on her arrival in New York, where he had already generated a staggering amount of public anticipation.

Barnum arranged to stay at the Staten Island home of New York Port Health Officer Sidney Doane, so that he could be the first to greet the singer when the ship arrived at the quarantine station. He boarded at the first opportunity, with newsmen in close pursuit, and rushed to the diminutive soprano's stateroom. There, he found her nearly hidden by a great bouquet of roses being presented to her by the shipowner. Edward Collins, aided by the *Atlantic*'s captain, had arranged an earlier boarding to welcome his famous passenger. Momentarily outdone, Barnum recovered fast. The next day at the Canal Street dock, thousands of fans crowded the waterfront and cheered for a singer from whom few had ever heard a note. A phalanx of young ladies in flowing white gowns led the star to Barnum's carriage drawn by a pair of prancing white horses, the grinning impresario himself at the reins. Posters nearby, advertising her forthcoming concerts, carried Barnum's name in large type joined with Jenny Lind's. Edward Collins and his steamship were left to memory.

Barnum's collection of investments in real estate, museums, and several show business ventures put him among New York's gentry. Although he had escorted his performers to Europe many times, he knew nothing about shipping. His embarrassing encounter with Collins had made it evident that power accrued to steamship owners and enticed him to take a fling at the shipping business. For advice on how to approach it, Barnum sought out fellow New Yorker Cornelius Vanderbilt.

"Is it possible you are the showman who has made so much noise in the world?" Vanderbilt breezily addressed Barnum when they first met. "I expected to see a monster—part lion, part elephant, and mixture of rhinoceros and tiger."

Barnum proved to be a gentlemanly, optimistic, self-confident, and shrewd opportunist; the last trait was held in common by the two millionaires. They drew up a partnership with Cornelius Vanderbilt guiding the showman and his colleagues in the formation of the Barnum Line, with the Commodore retaining half ownership of the line's 1,500-ton *North America*. The first sailing to Ireland was planned for June 17, 1851, but it was delayed a week and finally canceled outright. The ship had a paltry crew, the hull floated high with less than full load, and the passenger list was sparse. The Barnum staff learned that the shipping business was not for them.

At the time, Vanderbilt was seeking broader support in the Pacific for his planned interocean service. He sent the *North America* through the Strait of Magellan to San Francisco where it joined the Vanderbilt Line's *Pacific*. Barnum recouped most of his ill-chosen investment by selling his share to the rascally Daniel Drew, thereby making Drew one of Vanderbilt's distant business associates. Vanderbilt seemed undisturbed by the transaction. For some years, he and Barnum continued a casual friendship that ended when the shipping magnate went into railroads and the entertainer into politics.

The *North America,* a responsibility of the Vanderbilt Line's San Francisco agent, soon developed a bad reputation. Only two meals of poor quality were served per day. The crew's seamanship was so bad that the ship grounded on the Mexican coast on a bright moonlit night. No lives were lost, but the ship was, following wild drunkenness and looting. According to his usual practice, Vanderbilt did not cover his ships with insurance. He tended to distance himself from his West Coast investments and never admitted to responsibility for their shoddy operation.

IN MID-FEBRUARY 1851, the renowned *Atlantic* was long overdue. Delays were no surprise during the winter, but the days passed without word of the ship and concerns for its whereabouts increased. It had departed Liverpool on December 12 and was known to have been spoken four days later by a sailing vessel also destined for America. That information had been recorded during the first week of February when grim rumors of its fate, all without foundation, had circulated throughout the city. Ocean traffic was at its annual low; shipping messages decreased as fewer vessels hazarded the storm-swept seas.

A year earlier, Cunard's *Niagara* had worried everyone for days until it

11–1. *SS* Atlantic, *first and most famous Collins steamship.*
The Mariners' Museum

arrived safely under sail, its machinery broken during a troubled crossing. The shaft of a rolling paddle wheeler is subject to excessive strain as one wheel pushes through deep water while its counterpart flails the air. Two engines driving separate shafts must be synchronized by connecting machinery, which is equally at risk in beam seas. What boiler explosions were to the steamboats of inland waters, collapsed paddle wheels and cracked shafts became to the hard-driven ocean transports.

Lookout stations at Coney Island and Sandy Hook sent their sightings into New York City from signal towers, but, with fewer hours of daylight during winter, their messages fell short of reporting all of the traffic arriving in the Narrows. After nightfall on February 15, a vessel approached and, as it crossed the Upper Bay, fired its guns, a signal that it carried urgent news. Slowly entering the port in darkness, the ship continued to fire for more than an hour as hundreds of people rushed to the Battery and strained to sight the blue and red lights that marked ships of the Collins Line. The vessel headed toward the transatlantic steamships' North River berthing area, as shouts echoing across the water identified it as the Cunard Line's *Africa*. Did it bring any word on the *Atlantic*?

A hush fell over thousands of people on the Manhattan piers while the *Africa* continued on the route to its Jersey City pier. Finally, it eased into its berth, and a mate climbed to the top of a paddle box to announce, "The *Atlantic* is safe; she has put into Cork with a broken shaft."

Within the hour, shouts of jubilation were heard throughout Manhattan as men stopped each other on the streets to share the good tidings. Theatrical performances were suspended to announce the news. Newsboys in knickerbockers rushed to street corners, hawking special editions carrying the news in its barest particulars, "The *Atlantic* is safe." The next day's papers furnished more details at readily paid prices much above the customary two cents. The *Africa* was carrying passengers who had survived the *Atlantic*'s troublesome voyage and had later boarded the Cunard freighter for its regular crossing.

Before it was out of the Mersey River, the *Atlantic* had encountered terrifying gales. The pilot could not be debarked, but the captain insisted on continuing the voyage rather than returning to port. For more than three weeks, winds of hurricane force plagued the ship. On January 6, while the ship rolled in mountainous seas, a giant wave broke against its port paddle wheel. It fractured the main shaft and put both engines out of commission. Without steam power, the vessel was nearly helpless and in danger of capsizing. The captain was forced to spread all sail, "little handkerchiefs in comparison with our immense craft," according to one of the passengers. Already halfway across the ocean, the skipper attempted to continue westward until adverse winds compelled him to change course for Bermuda and caused further damage. The ship lost its bowsprit and a jibboom in head seas, paddle boxes broke, and wheels bent. The captain now had no choice but to turn and run back to Ireland before nearly overpowering winds. The beleaguered vessel arrived in Cork on January 22, six horrifying weeks after leaving Liverpool. The crew was exhausted, and the passengers, all unharmed, were ravenous, having been cut back to two meals per day under reduced rations. Several dauntless travelers resumed their crossing on the *Africa.*

LATER THAT year, Collins's *Baltic* took the Blue Riband, the *Atlantic* scare notwithstanding. The recognition came at a heavy price. During their first year, the Collins vessels were losing an average of nearly $17,000 per voyage. Speed became critical to the line's operation—speed to register record crossings; speed to outdo all the sailing packets and the newly arrived clippers; and, most important, speed to impress the postal service. Since its foundation, the U.S. Post Office Department prided itself on efficient delivery of mail, which was not readily accomplished across the ocean. Letters must be kept moving, if for no other reason than hastening commercial transactions, more so in overseas banking than in domestic finances. Prompt departures after mail closings and rapid delivery at the other end helped to ensure a contract renewal for the carrier. British mail ships faced similar pressures from the Admiralty. Timeliness was the standard of operation, a costly but better alternative in the eyes of the shipowners than debilitating rate wars. What they ignored, eclipsed by the generous subsidies, was the cost of speed in daily operations, damages, and losses.

Of the six principals in the ongoing struggle to grasp the Great Circle, three were advocates of the tall, sturdily built clippers and three were staunch steamship supporters. With the exception of the Train-McKay association, until the rivalries became intense, no face-to-face meetings among the six men were recorded, and but a single instance of correspondence through intermediaries was noted. One can imagine the scene if, just once, they had all convened, say for the transfer of the fastest-passage award from British hands to Edward Knight Collins, proud owner of the steamship *Baltic,* in 1851. Samuel Cunard might be the focal point of this imaginary meeting, curled white hair ringing his head, his high brow and slight features, and his small mouth perhaps fixed in a wry smile. Shorter than average, Cunard is standing in the midst of the group. Handsome Donald McKay, tall and clean-shaven, his dark hair flowing to his shoulders, leans forward to engage in conversation with Cunard. Accompanying McKay is his major client, the thinly built Enoch Train dressed in a dark frock coat and, at his throat, a high collar and black, string tie. His forehead is furrowed above a craggy, ascetic face. Train's distant cousin, George Francis, is not present; he had been tactfully sent away by his employer. Two other men stand on the trio's periphery. Pouting like a bulldog as he awaits recognition, stumpy Edward Collins seems unwilling to approach the reserved Cunard or distinguished Train. Young Samuel Samuels, newest captain of the fast ocean packet *Angelique,* the only dedicated seaman among this group of shipping moguls, fidgets nervously, being far more comfortable on the quarterdeck of his own ship than in a business conference. Samuels is a thickset man, nearly as tall as McKay, sideburned in gentlemanly style, confident that he can hold his own on matters concerning the design and handling of fast sailers. He has not yet had the chance to prove it to the other men, and, for him, action precedes words.

Collins, displeased that he is not the center of attention—he is a splendid conversationalist and natural showman—senses that he can shift the focus to friendly banter with the courageous mariner and, intent on discourse, approaches Samuels. His timing is poor, for into the room barges the assertive Cornelius Vanderbilt, well-tanned, graying side-whiskers spreading across his shoulders like a pair of stunsails, the portliest man among them, and certain to be his customary unrefined self in this group.

The glint in Vanderbilt's eye does not hint at recognition of opportunities across the North Atlantic. That aspiration and its fulfillment are years away. The Commodore's reputation as predator is well known. If, overcoming his succinct manner, he should express interest in the other men's achievements on the Great Circle, what heated discussions might ensue? Or, might they be tempered by the arrival of the ladies—Train's courtly Almira, matronly and richly outfitted Sophia Vanderbilt, youthful Mary Ann Collins, the self-assured Mary McKay? The pious Mrs. Samuels, quiet and unassuming, stands demurely beside her husband. Cunard, long widowed, has not remarried. Tonight he serves alone as host. He raises a glass of Madeira and invites the guests to join him in a toast to the new holder of the Blue Riband before they sit down to a meal of steak and kidney pie.

Of course, no such meeting of the titans and their consorts ever took place. It would have made for a grand evening of gracious Victorian conversation, delicately threaded with hints of ruthless rivalries. A ten-year history of ocean conquest might have been encapsulated in the passing of a few hours, and the outlook for the next ten years perhaps made clearer.

During Donald McKay's most productive year to date, 1850, he sent six ships down the ways, half for North Atlantic service, and two others were under construction. His drafting boards carried the nearly fulfilled plans for what again was to be his largest ship. Ordered by Enoch Train, at 1,783 tons, it was the first of three clippers launched by McKay that year. The

11−2. Flying Cloud, *Train's short-term investment.*
The Mariners' Museum

year before, he had built a packet of 1,100 tons for the New York firm of Grinnell, Minturn & Company. When a company manager made a follow-up visit to the yard and saw what was on the ways, he went directly to Train with an offer amounting to twice the cost of Train's contract. A doubling of investment in a matter of months hardly could be declined. Anticipating the delivery of McKay's next clipper in June, Train accepted the offer and sold the ship for $90,000 shortly after the April launching.

George Francis Train later claimed that he had given the clipper its name, *Flying Cloud.* The assertion was worthy of the same credence to be given to his boast of having sent forty clippers to California—a thread of truth in the fabric of a whimsical memory. George was first to recognize what Donald McKay's designs could accomplish in meeting the demand for travel to the gold fields. Ultimately, McKay produced fourteen ships that sailed to the West Coast at least once from either Boston or New York. Many other ships followed from nearly every eastern seaport, their owners surely unaware that they were contributing to George Francis Train's self-serving accounting. His later claim to naming the *Flying Cloud* reflects a tiff concerning the name of McKay's next clipper that followed the launching, a small matter that jarred everyone into their proper places.

The sale of the *Flying Cloud* brought quick profit and a lifetime of regret to Enoch Train as it went on to become the most famous clipper of all. The ship, 235 feet overall with a 40-foot beam and 20-foot fully loaded draft, contained nearly 1 million board feet of oak and 50 tons of copper fastenings, even before copper sheathing was applied below the waterline. The hull's interior was paneled in satinwood with mahogany and rosewood frames. When the masts were in place, the truck towered 166 to 200 feet (authorities differ) above the main deck. Three masts carried up to twenty-two sails, plus four stunsails in light airs. Only under conditions seldom achieved could all sails be set together, but it was equally uncommon, among hardy seamen, that upper masts were lowered or more than a few sails furled.

The *Flying Cloud*'s passage time on its maiden voyage, New York to San Francisco, was a stunning eighty-nine days and twenty-one hours, which reduced by a quarter the times set two years earlier. Of more significance was the vessel's earnings record. A freight rate of thirty-five cents per cubic foot might have been profitable. The shipowners were able to charge three to four times that rate for transport to California. On the *Flying Cloud*'s return to New York eleven months after it had first put to sea, the ship had earned $200,000. McKay had deftly balanced speed and capacity so that, during the course of a year, it could carry the maximum volume of cargo. Here was the ideal sailing vessel, flawless in design, perfectly executed, stately in its slip, and magnificent in motion.

Train's appetite had been whetted. He took his gains from the *Flying Cloud*, sold his packet *Anglo-American* to a British firm, and invested the proceeds with his partner in the extreme clipper *Staffordshire*, Captain Albert E. Brown. Built in 1851 for the Liverpool service, on the first transatlantic voyage the vessel carried Train's newly married daughter on the start of her European bridal tour. Departing Boston under Captain Brown's command on December 10, the richly outfitted vessel sailed side by side with the Cunard steamer *Asia* for several hours until the latter turned off for Halifax. The promising start was justified by a record twelve-day passage to Tuskar Light, and the *Staffordshire* arriving at the entrance to the River Mersey in light airs on Christmas Eve. On the ship's return to Boston, in a gamble intended to demonstrate the advantage of sail over steam, Train and Brown booked it for a voyage around the world. The first leg from Boston to San Francisco took a commendable 101 days, and the last leg from Calcutta to Boston eighty-two days, a remarkable journey overall. Thereafter, Josiah Richardson, Train's longtime associate, signed off George Upton's *Stag Hound*, relieved Brown on the *Staffordshire*, and took it into regular service on the North Atlantic. No vessel was more the favorite of Enoch Train than the *Staffordshire*.

By now, McKay was turning out four ships a year, all close to or over 1,500 tons. Undaunted that their construction and operating costs were climbing out of proportion to their size, McKay again produced his largest ship, this one for his own account, and put brother Lauchlan in command. While the ship was in the stocks, meddler George Francis Train, not yet relocated to Liverpool, had the idea that this extreme clipper, not intended for the White Diamond fleet, would suitably honor the head of Train & Company if it were named for him. He reported his idea to the

Boston Post's maritime reporter and recounted Colonel Train's remarkable career but failed to consult the proposed honoree. The *Post* published a description of the new ship along with its name, *Enoch Train.* "Premature," huffed Colonel Train when George showed him the article. Aware of Mary McKay's prerogative, the elder Train would have no part in the proposition. George might declare, as he did in his memoirs, that it was he who undertook the change of name, but what it became seems suggestive of Mary McKay's poetic bent—*Sovereign of the Seas.*

11–3. Sovereign of the Seas, *a forest of clipper rigging.*
   The Mariners' Museum

THE WHITE DIAMOND fleet had some twenty-four vessels sailing between Boston and Liverpool, and Lewis Wharf was no longer adequate to service them. In 1852, Enoch Train purchased Constitution Wharf, moved his headquarters to State Street, and also arranged for an office in Liverpool's famous India Building. It was time to get George Francis packed and out of Boston and send him to England. The *Daniel Webster* was to sail in October, and Train made sure that his cousin would be on board. Striving to book the packet to capacity, George lingered until the last minute. Within minutes of departure, he was still at the booking desk, with one more berth to be sold, when Ralph Waldo Emerson appeared in the office, a wad of bills amounting to the fare of $75 in hand. Together, the pair made a pierhead jump, and George and Waldo were off to England.

Enoch heard news of the pesky young man earlier than he had expected. Long since sold by Cunard, the old *Unicorn* was found sinking, not far from Halifax, with some 150 passengers and an unruly and incompetent crew on board. The *Daniel Webster* hove to alongside the *Unicorn* to save the passengers, whom George thought at first were Cunard passengers. On arrival in England, he was quick to report to the *Liverpool Courier* the shocking conditions that led to the *Daniel Webster*'s rescue of 174 desperate souls from the British liner.

An operational difference prevailed among the long-established Western Ocean packets and the tall clippers to which Train had turned. Sailing vessels routinely carried their own craftsmen in the crew. While they were at sea, the crew did nearly all the work of maintenance between wind and water. Initially, Lauchlan McKay had signed on four mates and ninety-six men to the *Sovereign*. Arranging berthing space and provisions for such numbers was a challenge, especially for the three-month passage to the West Coast. The operators gradually learned to economize and reduced the size of clipper ship crews by one half to two thirds with more work for all and little reduction in the established practice of shipboard maintenance.

The older packet ships often sailed with only two mates and fewer than twenty men. Maintenance was continued in port during discharging and loading of cargo. The packets took longer to turn around and then sailed intensely, their captains more willing to risk a sail being blown to shreds than to haul it in. Samuel Samuels on the packet *Angelique* was of that persuasion. He signed on men to sail, sending them aloft to set more canvas rather than assigning them on deck or in the lower rigging with paint pot or tar bucket.

The Black Ball Line, first of the packet operators, stayed the course and collected regular, if modest, profits under its new owners. In 1834, one of its most seasoned captains, part owner Charles Marshall—he had crossed the Atlantic ninety-four times before retiring from the sea at age forty-two—took over management of Black Ball until it discontinued operations thirty years later. In 1848, Marshall experimented with a wooden steam-paddler, the *United States,* built by famous New York designer William Webb. The ship did not serve Black Ball's interest and was sold to a German company within a year. Marshall's ships were no less hard driven than their spirited competitors, but, under his control, they somehow reflected more care. For years, the Black Ball's *Independence* held the westbound sailing record of fourteen days, six hours. The tidy ship cruised the Western Ocean for twenty-nine years; made 116 round-trips without loss of a seaman, sail, or spar; and brought thirty thousand immigrants to America. Two hundred marriages and fifteen hundred births took place on board. If there was a lesson to be drawn from Black Ball's performance, it went unheeded by shipping's other leaders.

The year 1852 was one of marked change. Donald McKay's fascination with immensity and speed—the two seemed to go together, while their expenses were ignored—turned his interests away from the frugal White Diamond business. The 2,421-ton *Sovereign of the Seas* was the acme of McKay's famous works. In July 1853, Lauchlan McKay took it along the Great Circle in fourteen days and two hours; with time differences considered, two hours were shaved from the current record. Also, that year, the owners of the New York–based Red Cross Line selected Sam Samuels to supervise construction and take command of the *Dreadnought* for the Liverpool service. David Ogden, formerly an associate of McKay's one-time partner, John Currier, joined with New York merchants Francis Cutting and Edwin Morgan, later governor of New York, to put a fast packet on the Atlantic route. General agent Ogden had experienced more than his share of shipping losses—six vessels, four of them on the North Atlantic. The planned *Dreadnought* would be the only ship remaining in the desperate Red Cross Line. In February 1853, it was launched from the Newburyport yard (where Donald McKay had his start), readied for sea, and sent to New York to begin packet service. Under Captain Samuels, its first round-trip voyage took fifty-eight days, unimpressive except that it cleared a $40,000 profit for the skipper and owners. A packet captain's customary share in the earnings came to 5 percent of freight charges and steerage and a quarter of cabin-class fares. Samuels waxed enthusiastic as his line's single ship contended in the reach for a firm grip on the North Atlantic route.

During 1852, the first vessel of any kind crossed the Atlantic in less than ten days to arrive at Sandy Hook, nine days, twenty hours, and fifteen minutes out of Liverpool. The steamship *Pacific* took the honors, and Edward Knight Collins took the glory for the westward passage. Nevertheless, after the first financial reconciliation of their agreement at the end of 1852, Collins and Cunard independently became aware that neither company had benefitted by the rivalry. The busy sailing packets, their owners largely uninterested in garnering the top tier of the transatlantic business, were of little concern. The cream of the business was turning sour. By year's end, Charles MacIver estimated that Cunard had lost £30,000 to the new Collins line. Well backed financially, with operations in the Maritimes and Europe and a planned route to India, Cunard management became impatient with the single-minded Collins. His call, six years earlier, to drive the Cunarders out of business continued to resound through the corridors of Liverpool and London.

In New York, a worried Edward Collins leaned over company ledgers, his bent shoulders propped on arms pinned to the desk with tightly curled fists. The finely cursive entries on the bookkeeper's sheets gave unnerving evidence that the line could not turn a profit without additional funding. Divested of all but the steamship fleet, Collins, in characteristic fashion, prepared to capitalize on the *Baltic*'s fame by sending it on a lobbying journey to the nation's capital.

From its delayed start, the voyage was beset with troubles. When the ship's regular captain became ill, Collins turned command over to naval observer and first officer, Lt. Gustavus Fox, the man later to be named President Abraham Lincoln's assistant secretary of the navy. Halfway up the Potomac River, while carrying several dignitaries, the *Baltic* fouled an anchor and ran aground. Overcoming both difficulties, Fox anchored the ship off Alexandria, Virginia, as close to the capital as its draft permitted. There, Collins put aside his financial problems and reigned over an affair planned to top his best publicist performance. President Millard Fillmore, accompanied by his cabinet, selected members of Congress, several foreign ministers, and assorted military officers with their ladies, arrived to a twenty-one gun salute. Champagne, wines, and liquors flowed so generously that speeches and even spontaneous toasts were curtailed to keep some semblance of decorum. The crowd of visitors, invited and uninvited, who climbed on board to tour the vessel and feast on the plentiful spread became so oppressive that the president and several others, perturbed and poorly fed, departed early.

Later, the press, its reporters no doubt elbowed away from bar and board, frowned on the affair. Despite adverse commentary in the New York papers on the costly entertainment, the Collins subsidy was raised to a total of $858,000, or $33,000 for each of twenty-six round-trips. At the same time, a nervous election-year Congress stipulated its right to end the increased subsidy on six months' notice. Subsidy aside, the Collins share of the two lines' combined revenues within the covert price-fixing agreement had crept up from a shaky 35 percent of the total in 1850 to 41 percent in 1852. Because the line had carried 50 percent more passengers than Cunard, its lesser share of earnings pointed to extravagance, which was clear on the ledger books but somehow ignored by Collins management. Simply cutting costs might have gained a profit; instead, the improved American figures relieved Collins's worries. He concluded that the Cunarders were concerned for their own future.

Following the February 1853 renewal of the agreement, Cunard introduced a screw-propelled vessel that bypassed Manhattan and docked directly at the company's Jersey City piers in obvious competition with the *Atlantic*. The agreed cargo rate to New York was then £5 per ton, but Charles MacIver had no compunction about charging only £3 for delivery to Jersey City. In December, when it appeared that a second screw-propelled ship would enter into competition with the *Pacific,* Collins Line president James Brown wrote directly to Cunard to complain: ". . . If Mr. MacIver pursues this course we see no remedy but dropping our rate for freight, as it will not do to come away with half cargo. We desire to act in good faith and each expects the same from Mr. MacIver." After additional admonishments, the screw-propelled ships were diverted from the route. There were other disputes, generally of a minor nature, because both parties felt, as Cunard put it to one of the managers who had signed the original agreement, "No bargain can be expected to exist which is not to conduce to mutual agreement." Adjustments had to be made by both sides as schedules changed; special rates were introduced by one line or the other to induce travel and when unanticipated circumstances arose. By and large, the renewal negotiations and conformance activities were amicable. The cutthroat practices of the Hudson River were not to be replicated in the North Atlantic cartel.

Meanwhile, Donald McKay rode the tide of clipper ship fame. Within a single year, 1853, he produced *Empress of the Seas, Star of Empire, Chariot of Fame,* and *Romance of the Seas,* all names specified by Mary McKay. Finally, in the fall of that year, before thousands of spectators, he launched what was to be his largest ship, the 4,555-ton *Great Republic.* Fitting out was incomplete when a steam tug towed the ship from East Boston to its South Street berth in Manhattan prior to a worldwide voyage emulating the *Staffordshire*'s successful venture with Lauchlan McKay as skipper. On Christmas Day, shortly before departure, a warehouse fire burning out of control across the street leapt into the *Great Republic*'s rigging. Before the ship could be scuttled, all the rigging, masts, deck, and upper portions of the hull were consumed in flames. The loss of the underinsured clipper brought a turnaround in clipper ship design and maritime fortunes, while it reflected the Americans' exceptional resiliency. The *Great Republic* was razeed under the supervision of Nat Palmer, once a confidant of Edward Collins and a Dramatic Line captain. McKay rebuilt the vessel as a bark with reduced rig and returned it to sea to capture new records on the Cape Horn route to San Francisco.

During that same difficult year, Cornelius Vanderbilt returned from his long vacation on the steam yacht *North Star* to find that he had lost control of Accessory Transit (Chapter 8). Whatever plans that he might have made during his visit to England for extending his operations across the Atlantic were deferred. Venting his anger in a string of expletives, he penned a note to the devious managers Morgan and Garrison:

> Gentlemen:
> You have undertaken to cheat me. I won't sue you, for the law is too slow. I'll ruin you.
> > Yours truly,
> > > Cornelius Vanderbilt

11–4. Dreadnought, *the "Wild Boat" that put steamers on edge.*
The Mariners' Museum

Threats of suits and countersuits followed. The press thoroughly covered all charges and countercharges as Vanderbilt took his revenge. William Walker, the ambitious central American adventurer whose supply lines Vanderbilt had once controlled, was also implicated in the takeover and faced the Commodore's wrath.

WHEN THE *Great Republic* burned, Samuel Samuels was striving for another fast *Dreadnought* voyage. Winter blew into the North Atlantic, but Samuels defied it as he struggled eastward in twenty-four days. Sailors had commenced calling the *Dreadnought* the "Wild Boat of the Atlantic." Shortening sail only in extreme conditions, Samuels was so demanding of his crews that all but five of the American crew jumped ship when it docked in Liverpool. Writer Nathaniel Hawthorne, who had been appointed American consul by President Franklin Pierce, had ample work in tracking the deserters. For Samuels, the loss of a few men was routine; he wrote off the missing crew and arranged their replacement from among the hardy Liverpool "packet rats" whom he had known off and on through the years. He liked their courage but trusted them not at all. By his own admission, aside from his wife, who was not on board during this voyage, the most loyal member of the crew was Wallace, his dog. Commenting on the Liverpool seamen, Samuels stated that "they had not the slightest idea of morality or honesty," yet he admired their willingness to face the worst weather and to put up with less sleep and harder knocks than any other sailors.

Ignoring a warning that the last thirty men available to join him were a set of pirates plotting to kill him and take over the *Dreadnought,* Samuels signed on a full crew. He was determined to deal with them in their own fashion. After reading the rules of the ship to the men, he ordered them to have the carpenter break off the ends of their knives. That brought the would-be renegades to the brink of rebellion, but Samuels held to his word and most of the men sullenly obeyed. Some of them had sailed earlier with the captain. As a youth, he had spent time in the Mobile jail with at least one. He told them that he knew of their plans but was glad to have them where he could teach them a lesson or two about life. The *Dreadnought* was not to become theirs, he said, nor was he about to go for his last swim. The scowling sailors were not curbed. The helmsman drew his unbroken sheath knife on the skipper. With Wallace's help, Samuels knocked the man down and put him in irons. The sailor's defiant shipmates then refused to work unless he was released.

Refusal constituted mutiny, and Samuels put the rebels—two thirds of his crew—on reduced rations and tighter watches. Steerage passengers hovering on deck from the mainmast aft were panicky witnesses to all that happened. Samuels, fully armed, strengthened his position. He cut off all food and water for the rebellious sailors until the full crew returned to duty. Tensions tightened like a cable on a windlass as undermanned watches continued throughout the night. The hungry mutineers were confined forward, the captain in his place on the quarterdeck, a mate at the wheel, and fearful passengers watching events unfold while the *Dreadnought* pressed on and the wind increased. At dawn, the mutineers refused the skipper's call to furl the royals. "Work before you eat," insisted Samuels. The passengers, many of them Germans who knew nothing of "blood-boat" ways, took the side of the rebels and begged the captain to end the standoff. "If you don't join me in quelling the mutiny," he responded, "consider what you face with these men in charge."

Several passengers turned to support him; the others went below to pray for a rapid and satisfactory outcome. Armed with iron bars taken from the cargo, the braver passengers stood behind the skipper and his pistols as he advanced on the renegades confined to the forecastle. Seeing a clear passage, the captain walked forward with Wallace in advance. Abreast of the galley housing, he gave the order, "Go ahead, Wallace." The dog reached the forward corner of the house and let out a deep, slathering growl. As the skipper and dog passed, two men lurking in the shadows jumped them from behind. Warned by his canine companion, Samuels aimed a pistol at one while the dog went for the other's throat. More growling, shouting, and tussling followed before the rebellious pair was locked in irons. Another watch passed without food; now three men were secured on bread and water.

Finally, the leader of the mutineers pleaded, "Captain, I have had enough." His knife went over the side. The three mutinous leaders were put on their knees to holystone the deck, and the attempted takeover came to its end. Not only was it ended, but the captain, influenced by his Christian wife's earlier coaching, gave them a lecture and forgave them their trespasses. The fortunes of the Liverpool packet rats were generously turned in their favor by the man whom they had planned to send to the ocean's floor.

FORTUNE SHIFTED against Samuel Cunard when his original agreement with the Admiralty came back to haunt him. Great Britain had become embroiled with Russia in the Crimea, and the issues burst into hostilities in 1853. America's foreign trade benefitted and generated a burgeoning financial period for U.S. farmers. In England, the war remained unresolved long enough to threaten Cunard with the Admiralty's requirement to withdraw ships from the Atlantic for conversion to wartime objectives. The year 1854 stood to become decisive for the combined efforts of American shipowners, both clippers and steamers, to end forever the Cunarders' dominance of the North Atlantic.

Collins was not prepared to grab the territory. His constituency in Congress had weakened under opposition to the increased subsidy. New Postmaster General James Campbell noted the wide discrepancy between the subsidy given to Collins and the subsidies granted to other American mail-carrying lines. When Collins countered with a list of his line's rapid crossings, the objections subsided, but he had no financial base from which to expand his operations.

Enoch Train and his seafaring partners took a closer look at the costly tall ships and evaluated whether conversion to steam or a return to more economical smaller packets would be the appropriate move. McKay had formerly equated size to sustained speed in strong winds, which was thought to be ideal for the North Atlantic. At one time, construction costs could be recovered by a single voyage to San Francisco, but such was not the case for the Liverpool run. Even Donald McKay now realized that clipper costs had become excessive, and he turned to reducing the size of the ships on his drawing board. The *Chariot of Fame* was the last vessel that Train ordered from his longtime associate. McKay, driven to reach perfection in the design of the perfect long-haul sailing ship, looked instead to supply England's Liverpool-Melbourne service. He well could have received encouragement for the venture from his admirer and former advocate, George Francis Train, by then operating his own shipping business in Australia. McKay had reason enough to turn away from the Great Circle. After completing a fast Atlantic crossing in January 1854, his clipper *Star of Empire,* less than a year old, disappeared during its next voyage without explanation and was never heard from again.

Samuel Samuels was undeterred by the *Dreadnought's* nearly successful mutiny. He knew the ship whose construction he had overseen from keel to royals, and he reveled in commanding the hardiest sailors whom he had ever known to run it. In 1854, he drove the ship in six one-way fast passages between New York and Liverpool. In December, following a troubling twenty-nine-day crossing in the fall, he broke all sailing records, New York to Liverpool, in thirteen days and eleven hours. That was close enough to steamship averages that it worried the paddle wheel operators, who could not deny that sail and steam were weaving over each other's wakes in the North Atlantic.

For both interests, the contest remained open, but lessons were both learned and ignored in the rush for control. Safety of passengers and crew at sea was to be gained more through routine prudence than under government regulation, even at the expense of speed. Profits would be elusive for sail and steam alike if vessels continued to grow ever larger; somewhere there was a point at which size, comfort, and cost came into balance. The most subtle challenge, one that would be ignored for a century more, lurked under unstable labor costs and government subsidies, two forces not seen to be associated. Maritime labor was severely undervalued. Desertions and mutinies were minor sparks whose flashes warned of future conflagrations. Unless given better treatment and improved wages, the common seaman would eventually seek redress not by individual or concerted desertion but by an organized refusal to work.

The immediate reaction to such an event would be an increase in operating subsidies, supported by the government's desire to keep the mail moving and to maintain an active reserve fleet for naval enhancement. In effect, should the government join the paymaster in every voyage settlement, the result could lead only to perpetual escalation. The prospect, far beyond the imagination of visionaries during the mid–nineteenth century, would become a reality during the twentieth century. Shipping leadership looked no further for its goals than winning commercial control of the trade route spinning out to the Atlantic's horizon and ruling that kingdom at whatever cost to investors and government.

12

Fall of the Titans

THE STRUGGLE for possession of the Atlantic sea lanes grew intense after 1853, while the pathways to profit grew murkier. Enoch Train, worried about the principal business of the Boston windjammers, began to move White Diamond's organization closer to the corporate structure of steamship operators by sharing control with his financiers. The Irish famine eased, but poverty and political strife kept the stream of Irish and German immigrants at high levels. Providing their passage to America attracted even the New York steamship lines. Fugitives from European factional skirmishes and disease-ridden seaports found easy transportation, their destination port often determined by the lowest fare available.

For Samuel Cunard, his short-lived support of the Admiralty's wartime needs provided the occasion to modernize his fleet. Impressed by technical developments in the Clyde shipyards, he contracted for the construction of an iron-hulled ship before the Admiralty was fully won over to the design. Collins, continuing his boasts of the superior service to be found on his massive vessels, was reluctant to curb the lavish expenses that drew the top clientele and bought him fame. Shrewd Vanderbilt set out to win back his Central American facilities and cast a covetous eye on

12–1. *Listing of mail steamers, Vanderbilt's target for inclusion.*
Library of Congress

the commercial routes to Europe. In the turmoil that emerged from these diverse interests, no one envisioned that the downfall of the titans would be brought about not through their scheming but by the nature of the Great Circle itself.

Edward Collins maintained a close relationship with his wife's large family; his father-in-law, Thomas Woodruff, had even named him executor of his estate. The Woodruffs perhaps furnished Collins a surrogate for the siblings whom he never had. In the summer of 1854, the two families planned a joint European tour. Mary Ann would join her brother Samuel and his wife with the youngest of the three Collins sons, Henry Coit, and their only daughter, named for her mother. Edward's activity in rallying congressional support for the steamship subsidies prevented his accompanying them, although twenty-eight years of marriage had not diminished the devotion between him and Mary Ann. During the period of separation, the two were determined to test the depth of their affection by an experiment in thought transference. They agreed to set aside specific times when they would quietly concentrate on each other and record what they thought the partner was saying. On Mary Ann's return, they would compare notes to see if clairvoyance had any validity in their lives.

Following a period that was remarkably free of artifice, the couple's efforts would not have been deemed outlandish. Conditioned by the flood of new technology, people were open-minded toward the sensational—Barnum's amazing collection of living oddities, new substances that eliminated the pain of dentistry and surgery, magnetic telegraphy, photography, and portable electric power. Six years earlier, the mysterious Fox sisters, Margaret, Katherine, and Leah, had reported establishing communications with the spirit world and, soon thereafter, routinely gave séances. *New York Tribune* editor Horace Greeley, in bringing them to Manhattan for demonstrations, attested to their honesty in invoking other-world apparitions. Spiritualist churches arose across the nation as spiritism and clairvoyance captured the interest of hundreds of thousands of credulous Americans and eventually spread in a countercultural flow across the sea to Europe. Edward and Mary Ann Collins were among the tentative believers, and the *Arctic* in midocean gave them a venue for experimentation.

Their contemplation would have to hurdle the late summer fog brought on by cold northern water swirling into the warm currents of the Gulf Stream. Saturated air hovering over the sea can reduce the radius of visibility within minutes to less than a ship's length. Charles Judkins, the Cunard Line's top skipper, commanded substantial respect among the fleet's administrators. In disputing one of Charles MacIver's admonitions, he proposed that the best way to handle an encounter with a patch of fog is to tear through it at full speed, thus reducing the time spent within it. Suppose two men must cross a street in a downpour. Who arrives drier, the one who strides at his regular pace around the puddles or the one who hastily splashes across the street through the same volume of rainwater?

The question of risk of collision arose, but Judkins suggested that fishermen alone in their dories would hear a steam paddler in ample time to clear the path. Sound your horn periodically, he counseled. The steam whistle, a new innovation, could be heard for a mile or more. Put a lookout forward where he is not distracted by the sounds of the engines, and he will pick up other horns if they are blowing. The idea is to get out of the fog bank as fast as possible.

Packet skippers generally agreed with Judkins. They felt that there was small chance of traffic converging in the vastness of the sea and speed was advantageous in returning to normal. The captains of Collins Line steamers, heedless of dangers presented by ice fields and poor visibility, particularly risked trouble in pursuit of speed records. Around midday on September 27, 1854, while hurtling through a wind-whipped blanket of mist, the *Arctic's* Captain James C. Luce heard a shout from the bow lookout, felt a shudder forward, rushed to the foredeck, and saw a steamship under his massive ship's starboard bow. The little iron vessel, with its forepeak apparently cut off, continued to scrape roughly against the *Arctic's* hull. Swinging wildly, the strange ship plunged its stern against the *Arctic's* wooden side. As the *Arctic* rode the crest of a swell in the heavy seas, Luce and his crew looked down on the small vessel in the trough and assumed that it was sinking fast. It was quickly identified as the French steamship *Vesta*. Valiantly, Luce called for one of the *Arctic's* boats to be lowered to aid in a rescue.

At the close of the 1854 European travel season, the Collins flagship had a prestigious passenger list. On board were the Duc de Gramont, newly appointed attaché to the French legation; many wealthy New York businessmen; and several prominent members of the academic and scientific communities. Also occupying first-class berths were seven family members of Collins's banker, James Brown; Captain Luce's wife, daughter, and eight-year-old crippled son; and Mary Ann Collins, her brother and his wife, and two of Mary's children.

The ship departed Liverpool on September 20 and was expected in New York at the end of the month. During the first days of October, anxiety grew among those awaiting its arrival in the Narrows. A *New York Herald* newsman contacted Collins and on Saturday, October 8, reported, "Mr. Collins attributes the detention of the *Arctic* to the breaking down of her machinery. He is of the opinion that, instead of putting back, she is coming on under sail, and may be expected to arrive at this port today or Sunday." The suggestion was plausible, Collins knowing well the extent of wear on engines routinely driven to capacity. The instance of the *Atlantic*'s frightening bout with the seas before its successful return to Liverpool was still fresh in mind. Carrying such a distinguished roster of passengers, the *Arctic*'s captain could be expected to exercise every precaution. There was, in Collins's opinion, no deep cause for concern.

In fact, the *Vesta*'s iron hull remained intact, and it limped into St. John's, Newfoundland, around the first of October, while the *Arctic* was severely damaged below the waterline. At about the time that the *Vesta* reached safety, two of the *Arctic*'s lifeboats, partially occupied, washed up on the shores of Newfoundland's Broad Cove. The development of Morse's telegraph had followed the newly forming railroads; it had not yet snaked its way along the coast between the British colonies and New York. Reliable news still took days to be compiled and sent south by turnpike and waterway.

The day after the tragedy, the crew of the ship *Huron,* on its way from Saint Andrews, New Brunswick, to Quebec, spotted a raft with a lone occupant, *Arctic* crew member Peter McCabe. The lad would be immortalized in graphic portrayals of the disaster as reported by survivors. On

12–2. *Loss of the SS* Arctic, *America's shocking sea tragedy.*
The Mariners' Museum

October 10, the bark *Lebanon* arrived off Sandy Hook with eighteen *Arctic* survivors. During the early morning of the next day, the pilot boat *Christian Berg* brought them into harbor.

Summarizing the event and the subsequent investigation, William S. Lindsay wrote in his *History of Merchant Shipping and Ancient Commerce:*

> ... [T]he *Vesta* appeared at first to be so seriously injured that in their terror and confusion, her passengers amounting to 147, and a crew of fifty men, conceived she was about to sink, and that their only chance of safety lay in getting aboard the *Arctic*. Impressed with this idea, many of them rushed into the boats, of which, as too frequently happens, one sank

immediately, and the other, containing thirteen persons, was swamped under the quarter of the ship, all on board of her perishing. When, however, the captain of the *Vesta* more carefully examined his injuries, he found that, though the bows of his vessel were partially stove in, the foremost bulkhead had not started. He therefore at once lightened his ship by the head, strengthened the partition by every means in his power, and by great exertions, courage, forethought and seamanship, brought his shattered vessel without further loss into the harbour at St. John's.

In the meantime a frightful catastrophe befell the *Arctic,* and one so little anticipated that the persons on board of her, supposing she had sustained only trifling injury by the collision, had launched a boat for the rescue of the passengers and crew of the *Vesta.* It was soon, however, discovered that their own ship had sustained fatal injuries, and that the sea was rushing in so fast through three holes which had been pierced in the hull below the waterline, that the engine fires would soon be extinguished. The *Arctic's* head was therefore immediately laid for Cape Race, the nearest point of land, but in four hours time from the collision water reached the furnaces and soon afterwards she foundered.

As it was blowing a strong gale at the time, some of the boats into which her passengers and crew rushed were destroyed in launching, others which got clear of the sinking ship were never heard again of, and only two, with thirty-one of the crew and fourteen passengers, reached Newfoundland.

Collins was returning from Washington to his New York office when the first details of the calamity reached the city. He took the ferry from the Jersey City train depot across the Hudson to debark in Manhattan at four in the morning. There, he read the first cursory news of the tragedy. Lacking the critical information that he was anxious to obtain, he went directly to Larchmont and eventually received a long, detailed letter written by Captain Luce following his nearly two-week stay in the hospital: ". . . It becomes my painful duty to inform you of the total loss of the *Arctic,* under my command, with many lives, and I fear among them must be included your own wife, daughter and son, of whom I took a last leave when the ship was going down." Luce lost three members of his own family, who went down with the son, two daughters, and two grandchildren of the Collins Line president and financier, James Brown.

Lindsay's history continues:

... Among those who perished were the wife of Mr. Collins and their son and daughter, but the captain, who remained on board to the last, and the first as well as the second and fourth officers were saved. Seventy-two men and four females sought refuge on a raft which the seamen, when they found the ship sinking, had hastily constructed, but one by one they were swept away—every wave as it washed over the raft claiming one or more victims in its prey; and at eight o'clock on the following morning one human being alone was left out of the seventy-six persons who, only twelve or fifteen hours before had hoped to save their lives on this temporary structure.

The solitary occupant of this fragile raft must have had a brave heart and a strong nerve to have retained his place upon it for a day and a half, after all his companions had perished, for it was not until that time had elapsed that he was saved by a passing vessel: his tale of how he and they were parted was of the most heart-rending description. . . .

As a large portion of the first-class passengers of the *Arctic* consisted of persons of wealth and extensive commercial relations in the United States, as well as in England and her colonies, besides more than one member of her aristocracy, the loss of the *Arctic* and the terrible incidents in connection with her fate caused an unusual amount of grief and consternation on both sides of the Atlantic.

In his book published twenty-two years after the tragedy and during the steep decline of America's merchant marine, Lindsay did not dwell on the failure of *Arctic* crew members to save the vessel or the panic and lack of discipline that led to the abandonment of floundering women and children. It was impossible to determine if any action, however extreme, might have kept the *Arctic* afloat under the horrifying circumstances. Although the loss was not the direct cause of the nation's crumbling maritime fortunes, the circumstances that brought it about were symptomatic of the precarious state into which American shipowners had evolved. Heavy reliance on government funding, a blind eye for the balance sheet, disregard of safety precautions in an environment considered dangerous under the most benign conditions, performance over prudence in the reach for power—all were prophetic of ultimate failure on a grand scale; anything that the cruel sea could deliver might topple the structure that technology had built.

Talk circulated throughout Manhattan that Edward Knight Collins was either deranged or dead. The grief-stricken man was neither. Rather, he was determined to recover from the disaster, and, after a period of mourning, he and Brown resumed their efforts to take possession of the Great Circle, deadly as it had proved to be.

Contrary to Vanderbilt's risky practice, Collins had taken care that the *Arctic* and its cargo were fully insured against loss. Neither ship was held liable for the accident, there being no international rules of conduct at sea. Had the two vessels sighted each other in ample time, with the *Vesta* approaching the *Arctic* on the latter's starboard bow, common practice would have had each ship turn sharply to the right (helm a-port) to avoid close approach. The sea was indeed vast for maneuvering. It would have been a time to flaunt the advantages of sail were New York Port not in such deep mourning. Captain Samuels brought the *Dreadnought* into port after one of its longest crossings—he was in Liverpool when the *Arctic* departed—to find flags at half-mast and the New York waterfront greatly subdued.

IN FEBRUARY 1854, the screw steamer *Alps,* Cunard's first ship lacking a final "a" in the name, arrived in Boston with British mail. It was followed unexpectedly by a sister ship, *Andes,* when Cunard announced that the regularly scheduled *Niagara* had been taken over by the Admiralty to serve as a military transport. The *Alps* and *Andes* had been hastily assigned to replace it.

By midyear, Cunard was running nine ships on tightly stretched schedules between England and North America. In response to the British government's need for support in the Crimea, the line was further obliged to withdraw from the New York–Liverpool route and send its ships to the Black Sea with troops and mail. American shipowners were heartened by their adversary's weakened position on their jointly coveted route. Biweekly sailings to Boston continued, but Cunard's ongoing affection for the port certainly brought no pleasure to Enoch Train.

The acknowledged American shipping leader who was in trouble, however, was Edward Collins. Vanderbilt wasted no time in taking advantage of the situation as he moved to organize the Vanderbilt European Line.

Within two months of the loss of the *Arctic,* Collins was astonished to learn that the Commodore intended to apply for a subsidy of $15,000 per full voyage for biweekly transatlantic round-trips. He headed directly to Vanderbilt's office. The New York papers closely followed the doings of the two shipping magnates. Their conversation was reconstructed shortly after the confrontation during this single instance of their meeting.

Collins tried to persuade Vanderbilt to ask Congress for $33,000 per voyage to match his own receipts. Promising to support the request, he explained that the service could not possibly be done for less. "Why, I'm not making any money on my steamers, as all the world knows," he said.

"No," responded Vanderbilt, "I'm patriotic in this matter. If an Englishman can do it for $16,000, I'm sure I can, and I won't admit that a Britisher can beat me in anything."

Collins shook his head, "That's not business, Vanderbilt. I can't make it pay as it is." In five years, the Collins Line had never paid a dividend.

"Then you have got into a business that you don't understand. Let me have the opportunity and I'll make it pay." On that chilly rejoinder, the meeting ended.

They were both headstrong individuals. It occurred to neither one that, by joining forces, their combined presence would have been difficult to counter. Collins had the fleet, the fame, and the approval of Congress. Vanderbilt's additional funding could have put a joint venture in the position that he so much enjoyed, one in which he could dictate prices and terms. Neither one had the temperament to be or to accept a silent partner.

Before the end of 1854, Vanderbilt had ordered two new steamships, the 2,000 ton wooden side-wheelers *North Star* and *Ariel.* Soon after, his advantage was increased by another disastrous event, the loss of White Diamond's worldwide voyager and major carrier of European emigrants and transatlantic cargo. It was a devastating year for Enoch Train. His twenty-one-year-old son, Enoch Jr., died. Then, he lost one of his most admired associates, top-rated sea captain Josiah Richardson, and the ship that he had commanded, Train's favorite *Staffordshire.*

The ship's chief mate, Joseph Alden, orally related the story:

We had a measure of trouble earlier in the week when we lost most of the foremast, the bowsprit and rudder head. Then the day before the accident Captain Richardson—a close friend of Colonel Train's, he was—had gone aloft, whether to extend his view of the ocean—'twas still violent—or to examine a piece of ill-fitting gear I do not know. He lost his footing and fell to the deck, some thirty-five feet. He struck his back severely, injured an ankle, may have cracked some ribs. Anyway, he was in desperate pain, and could hardly move. We stretched him out, wrapped in thick blankets, and carried him below to his bunk. Through it all he remained conscious, groaning with every shift of his torso, but still in command.

We took two hundred and fourteen emigrants aboard in Liverpool. The passage across was not fast in the stormy waters, twenty days as we neared landfall on the Seal Islands. Then the snow thickened and visibility fell to nought.

The mate paused in somber recollection. His tale continued:

You can imagine the horror brought by the sound of timber on rock, motion suddenly arrested, the hull lifted to a crazy angle, yards and masts askew. Shouts along the deck rose above the sound of surf breaking around us. We had come up on Blonde Rock. I put men to sound the bilges at once, backed the sails to turn the vessel, and attempted to beach her. For nearly a glass we struggled, twenty minutes at least, then the steering gear broke and she came into the wind. There was no hope. Men at the pumps could not stem the water surging through the spaces below. From his berth the captain gave the order to abandon ship, and we turned to launching the boats. It was slow work in the stormy conditions while the ship was foundering, out of control. I took a hand below with me to save Captain Richardson, to carry him to a boat. He refused. The ship is so close to shore, he claimed, she'll strike hard before she would go down.

"It is impossible," I told him, "for she will sink in a few minutes."

"Then if I am to be lost, God's will be done." Those, I'm saddened to report, were the man's last words.

On December 30, 1854, Josiah Richardson went down with his ship. One hundred and sixty-nine people, mostly steerage passengers, went with him. The loss of the *Staffordshire* marked the fifth major disaster for Enoch Train. The *Dorchester,* the *Ocean Monarch,* the *Anglo-Saxon,* the *Star of Empire,* and now the *Staffordshire* presented a grim record within the space of ten years. The vessels were soundly insured, and White Diamond survived financially, but the loss of several hundred lives was haunting. From every direction, screams echo across the gray water; darkness sets in as the calls weaken, diminishing in number, wails, whimpers, a desperate gasp. Finally, only silence competes with the slap of the waves. That thought tormented the shipowner. Enoch Train's spirit was broken.

AT SEA WHEN the *Staffordshire* went down, Samuels was driving the *Dreadnought* on its fastest crossing, New York to Liverpool, in thirteen and one-half days. Learning of the loss, he remained unfazed. With ample reason, he considered his own life to be charmed as he overcame one challenge after another. There would be no pause in his drive toward new records. He had become known as the skipper of the Wild Boat of the Atlantic, a reputation that he savored and intended to maintain.

THE LAST HALF of 1854 marked the climax of the struggles of sail and steam. The terrible loss of the *Arctic* overshadowed all transatlantic travel. Cunard's steamship lead was shrinking. While Samuel Samuels established new sail-crossing records, Donald McKay continued to launch elegant California clippers that would achieve enviable records in the Pacific. Inventions were introduced that helped his tall ships get taller. Two New England sea captains simplified sail-furling tasks aloft. Frederic Howes patented the addition of an extra topsail yard, an improvement on the double topsail invented by Robert Bennett Forbes thirteen years earlier. McKay included both devices in his ships and raised his topgallants even higher above the water.

Could anyone confidently predict when or how the parallel progress of sail and steam power would be resolved? Few transportation experts doubted that the age of windjammers was nearing its end. The technical advances of midcentury assured it. The American merchant marine had peaked in most measurements—number of ships, tonnage, revenues—sparked by industrial developments on both sides of the Atlantic. Dozens of short-line railroads fed American seaports while increasing the availability of steam engines and the people to operate them. The real unknown was what would happen to increase the pace of change.

Vanderbilt, the steamship advocate with the broadest experience, became an unpredictable element in the fray. In February 1855, he formally submitted his low bid to Postmaster General Campbell:

> Sir: The Cunard Line between New York and Liverpool having been withdrawn, and a frequent and rapid communication with Europe being so essential to the interest of our commerce, I submit the following proposition to the Postmaster General:

> I will run a semi-monthly line, which, by alternating with the Collins line, would form a weekly communication. And I will perform this proposed mail service for the sum of $15,000, the voyage out and home—the contract to exist for five years. . . . Good and sufficient steamers shall be put on the line within thirty days after the contract is signed.

Vanderbilt's proposal brought the mail subsidies into debate before Congress. The old battle cry, "Drive the Cunarders off the sea," initiated by Collins when first seeking government aid, was revived.

At this point, Campbell sharpened his earlier arguments before Congress. He pointed out that the Collins Line had been relieved of the necessity of carrying the passed midshipmen and that the Post Office had never sent out the planned mail agents. Collins delivered only twenty-six voyages for his $858,000, whereas Cunard, soon to resume full service, performed fifty-two voyages in return for the Admiralty's equivalent payment of $866,700. Among the postmaster general's recommendations, he suggested that the six-month notice specified by the 1852 act be issued, after which the increased subsidy be withdrawn. Derogatory phrases concerning the situation—harmful to broader commercial interests, destructive of competition, and gratuitous creation of a monopoly—certain to raise the ire of businessmen were bandied about. Aware of New York's importance, the ports of Boston and Philadelphia, joined by southern interests, picked up the cry and vied for aid in establishing steamship lines on the Great Circle. Mississippi Congressman William Barry, referencing the *Arctic*'s loss, spoke out, "If they had spent in lifeboats for that vessel what they spent in gingerbread ornaments and decorations, there might have been hundreds of valuable lives saved." Edward Collins put hope in the fact that his contract was not with the Post Office but with the Navy

Department and not scheduled to expire until 1860. The postal contract with the Bremen and Havre shipping lines would run out in 1857. Collins suggested that the money be diverted to his own increasing needs.

Collins had strong political support in the face of the postmaster's opposition. Representative Edson Olds, chairman of the Committee on the Post Office and Post Roads and once opposed to Collins, proposed that if Collins would build a fifth vessel as replacement for the *Arctic,* his payments should be continued and the six-month notice to end the subsidies should be rescinded. Collins advocates suggested that Cornelius Vanderbilt was trying with his bid to corner Collins into buying the *Ariel* at a high price, a tactic that would not have been beyond the scheming shipping magnate. Vanderbilt found a supporter in Representative William Smith of Virginia and joined him in Washington. In the Commodore's defense, Smith commended him for his yachting expedition, "a matter of pride and glory to our country," while he criticized Collins for his floating palaces and extravagance of habit "wholly at war with that simplicity which ought to belong to republican institutions." Overcoming such craven posturing, the Collins appropriation bill passed, only to be vetoed by President Pierce as a monopoly-fostering "gratuity." Talk of bribery circulated, all of which Vanderbilt roundly denied. Finally, the supporters of Edward Collins were able to work around the veto by adding an amendment to a Navy appropriation bill that insured the continuance of payments to his line.

Despite the setback, Vanderbilt went ahead with his plans just as the Crimean War ended and Cunard resumed full transatlantic operations. The Commodore found himself fighting battles on multiple fronts from his South Street headquarters. Through clever purchases of stock, he regained control of Accessory Transit Company. William Walker, allied with Cornelius K. Garrison and Charles Morgan and encouraged by a Nicaraguan revolutionary, managed with a makeshift army to capture Grenada and to set himself up as head of a new government. He then agreed with the ousted Accessory Transit leaders to annul its charter. In reaction, Vanderbilt withdrew his vessels from the route. "It is a duty I owe the public," he said. The ships were tied up at piers in San Francisco and New York when he approached the owners of the two Panamanian lines, William H. Aspinwall and George Law, and demanded a combined payment of $40,000 per month to keep his line shut down. Oral agreements were reached and several payments made in what Law and Aspinwall supporters saw as outright blackmail. That term haunted the Commodore from his earliest days on the Hudson River, but he remained undeterred.

When Morgan and Garrison continued to operate their own vessels at a fare of $175, Aspinwall stopped Pacific Mail's payments. Vanderbilt threatened again to revive his defunct company and promised, this time, to destroy the Nicaraguan line that Morgan and Garrison had started. Through that intimidation over a two-year period, Vanderbilt drew $1.2 million in payments from Pacific Mail and United States Mail while, at the same time, he took revenge on the unholy trio in Nicaragua. The devious Walker was not trying to annex the Central American nations for the United States, as had first been thought, but was hoping to establish a military dictatorship that would exclude the United States. Patriotically, Cornelius Vanderbilt made certain that his government was aware of this information.

INSPIRED BY THE collision of the *Vesta* and *Arctic,* Matthew Fontaine Maury included a section in his 1855 sailing directions, "Steam Lanes across the Atlantic," in which he recommended multiple great circle eastbound and westbound routes, separated by 100 miles, to avoid risks in fog. Improving on his recommendation, shipowners devised a composite pathway following eastbound and westbound rhumb lines in the western ocean south of latitude 42 degrees to the end of truncated great circle routes clear of fog and ice hazards. In announcing the planned addition of the new *Adriatic* to his fleet as replacement for the *Arctic,* Collins advertised that his ships would follow this safer path.

At that time, Enoch Train and Donald McKay concluded that sailing vessels would not be able to compete much longer for passenger trade. Both of their businesses were doing well in spite of setbacks. The Train Line maintained twenty-four packets on the Boston-Liverpool run. McKay's yard was enjoying a peak period of production. During 1854–55, McKay built six clippers, including the magnificent 2,515-ton *James*

Yours truly
M. F. Maury
Lt. U. S. N.

12–3. *Matthew Fontaine Maury (1806–1873), Pathfinder of the Seas.*
The Mariners' Museum

Baines and the 2,084-ton *Lightning,* both of which set new speed records. By 1856, he had built thirteen clippers for the California trade.

Steamships had made inroads on the bookings of the New York packet lines while the Cunard Line recovered from its wartime reduction, and Collins drew up plans to put the *Adriatic* into service. At 3,760 tons, it would be the world's largest wooden paddle steamer, 70 feet longer than Collins's other vessels. In reaction, Train and McKay assembled a group of fellow investors to form the Boston and Europe Steamship Company. Distracted by their ongoing successes, slow to convert their ambitions to reality, and ultimately stopped by worldwide financial restraints, the proposed business never came to be.

There was ample competition in the Atlantic when the announcement of "Vanderbilt's European Line of Steamships" appeared in April 1856. Cunard found himself squeezed by one of his own countrymen after the Inman Line, which had offered steerage service from Southampton to Philadelphia since 1850, moved its North American terminus to New York. Both Collins and Cunard ignored steerage carriers. In their view, they were classified among the sailing packets that attracted little interest from the carriage trade arriving at the steamship docks. With the acquisition of an iron screw-propelled vessel built by a Clyde shipbuilder, Inman gave it a new terminus in Liverpool. The line then sought to combine the prosperous steerage business with first-class trade and mail transport. In March 1857, the Inman Line formally changed its name to Liverpool, New York and Philadelphia Steam Ship Company, which brought to eleven the total number of transatlantic steamship lines operating out of New York. Only Collins, Cunard, and Inman offered direct steamer connections to Liverpool.

During this period, David Ogden and Francis Cutting's revived Red Cross Line boldly guaranteed to deliver goods on a sailing packet between the New York and Liverpool ports within a specified time regardless of weather during the voyage or forfeit the charges. The ship, of course, was the *Dreadnought,* and the skipper was Samuel Samuels. He carried no official mail, but he twice slipped between the steamers to bring the latest news to Europe ahead of them. For nipping thus at the steamers' sterns, the *Dreadnought* commanded rates midway between those of the sailing packets and the steamship rates secretly agreed to by Cunard and Collins. Edward Mills's Ocean Line, the first American company to be granted a federal subsidy, continued to operate the *Washington* and the *Hermann,* both more than ten years old, between New York and Bremen. The presence of iron hulls, screw propulsion, and liners carrying multiple classes of passengers on several transatlantic routes marked important shifts in maritime commerce. The sketchy grasp that each of the major competitors, with Cunard and Collins leading the pack, maintained on the North Atlantic routes could sustain little in the way of setbacks. The forces in such events were too many and too great to prevent the competition from taking over.

12–4. *Cunard Line's RMS* Persia; *iron finally arrives.*
The Mariners' Museum

AFTER HIS STINT on the Vanderbilt family cruise, Asa Eldridge, the *North Star*'s captain, returned to Collins's employ to take command of the *Pacific*. Having gained the Admiralty's approval of iron in his mail carriers, the *Andes* and the *Asia,* Cunard introduced the iron-hulled *Persia* to his regular transatlantic fleet. He expected to set a crossing record with the *Persia*'s new 3,800-horsepower Napier-designed engine with little effort. In January 1856, someone suggested an unofficial race from Liverpool to New York between the *Persia* on its maiden voyage and the *Pacific* on its homebound trip. Who proposed the idea never became clear; it might have originated with the press. Adopting it was more in the style of showman Edward Collins than the conservative Samuel Cunard or his Liverpool port captain, Charles MacIver. The *Pacific* departed Liverpool on January 22 with 141 crew and a scant 45 passengers.

In command of the *Persia,* Charles Judkins, despite his outspoken view in dealing with fog, cautiously waited some days at Huskisson Dock for severe weather to clear. After setting out, the *Persia* faced three days of strong wintry seas. Judkins was compelled to set sails to stabilize his ship before hurricane-force winds rose to blow out a trysail. At 2 A.M. on the sixth day at sea, the *Persia,* running at eleven knots, entered head-on into an ice field. The captain called to stop the engines, but momentum drove the ship against an iceberg that blunted the bow and sliced 16 feet of rivets from the starboard side. After resuming power, Judkins maneuvered the vessel to free itself from the ice, but protective iron bars and floats were torn off and the rims of its paddle wheels were twisted. Chastened by the incident, the captain clawed his way to New York.

On pulling the weather-scarred steamer into its slip, Judkins learned that the *Pacific* had not been reported. Other ships that had passed through the same area described the field as made up of chains of bergs heavily blanketed in fog. The *Pacific* was never heard from again. Some days later, during its passage to Glasgow, the *Edinburgh* reported sighting ornamental floating doors "with white or glass handles," but they were not firmly identified with the lost ship. The Great Circle had taken another toll.

Ample evidence seemed to indicate that Edward Collins was a man with a curse. Shortly before the *Pacific* had departed from Liverpool on its final voyage, the New York pilot schooner *E. K. Collins* was lost with four crewmen off stormy Sandy Hook. The shipwreck might not have been connected with its namesake and his tragedies were it not the final chapter of an eery coincidence. Fifteen months earlier, when newspapers had reported loss of the *Arctic,* they had printed news about the burning of a Great Lakes steamer, also named *E. K. Collins* in the shipowner's honor. Two vessels named for the shipowner met destruction as his liners encountered terrible fates—could Mary Ann Collins somehow have influenced the losses to issue a warning from the bottom of the sea?

Collins chartered ships to maintain the mail sailings even with limited passenger bookings, and that expense added to the line's already staggering cost of operation. Deeply in debt, Collins found himself unable to adhere to the terms of the secret pact with Cunard. Gamely, Charles MacIver agreed to a suspension until the *Adriatic* became part of the plan.

The once vibrant transatlantic passenger business groaned from disaster and overexpansion. Cornelius Vanderbilt intended to drive a wedge into its middle. He had the *North Star,* his 2,300-ton yacht, refitted to start service to Havre on April 21. That was followed by the *Ariel* in May with a scheduled stop at Cowes, England, for passengers and freight. The line set the first-class fare at $130 and second class at $75 but soon cut them to $110 and $60. Competitors ignored the predictable Vanderbilt ploy and held to the original fares as "standard." The number of passengers carried by the new line, about one hundred per voyage, was inadequate to be profitable, but the steamers earned a reputation for speed. Refined to days, hours, and minutes, crossing times were carefully clocked and recorded. The eastbound passage averaged twelve days and seventeen hours, westbound nearly a day longer. The Collins Line still held the records. Vanderbilt's single-expansion engines could not sustain the pace; his ships added an extra day to the schedule set by Collins.

Cunard, intent on safety and ever conservative with fuel, matched Vanderbilt's passages. Edward Mills's Havre Line took a day longer, which put the Collins Line in even better light. Because patrons were enamored of speed, Collins attained the top of the business. Nevertheless, talk persisted that, on arrival of his ships in New York, their engines routinely underwent extensive repairs to offset the strain of routinely running them at capacity. The thoughts of the firemen and coal passers were not documented.

The unsubsidized Vanderbilt European Line was no better off. Contemptuous of his adversary's extravagance and reliance on federal subsidies, Vanderbilt found that his earlier bravado with Collins was unfounded, for he was barely making his own service pay. With the planned addition of the *Vanderbilt,* the Commodore sought to carry the mail to Havre at small charge to the government. The wooden-hulled vessel, costing over a half-million dollars, began service between New York and Havre in July 1856. With sixteen watertight compartments, 335 feet in length, and a 16-foot beam, at 4,500 tons it was bigger than Collins's forthcoming *Adriatic* and promptly claimed honors as the "largest Atlantic steamship." Two walking beam engines, each 2,500 horsepower, made it a reliably fast ship. Profits were achievable, but they were meager.

Meanwhile, burdened with the ornate old *North Star,* Vanderbilt decided to exercise some of his enmity toward William Walker in Central America. Up to his old tricks, Vanderbilt turned again to the two inter-ocean carriers, Pacific Mail Steamship Company and United States Mail Steamship Company, then paying him $40,000 per month indemnity, and offered to abandon his Nicaragua Line if they would buy his *North Star* for $400,000. The offer was not accepted; the two lines were content in the transport of forty-niners (California gold seekers). Ocean trade is a notoriously fickle friend. Within a year, one of United States Mail Steamship's vessels, the newly named *Central America* (formerly the *George Law*) would encounter a fate that would drastically alter the picture.

The U.S. Congress, concerned that money was being poured wastefully into the improvident and troubled Collins Line, sent notification to the shipowner in August 1856 that his subsidy would be withdrawn in six months. Two months later, Vanderbilt took advantage of the situation. Struggling to maximize his thin profits, he sent the *North Star* to Southampton and Bremen and put the *Ariel* temporarily on the Panama route, where it would be more profitable in competing with George Law's United States Mail Steamship Company. The Commodore kept a clean desk. Carrying most of his affairs in his head, he conducted his business orally. Over the years, his spelling and grammar had made little improvement. Aided by his longtime clerk, Lambert Wadell, he produced a summary of his findings:

> The experience of six months has satisfied me that it is utterly impossible for a private individual to stand in competition with a line drawing nearly one million dollars from the National Treasury, without serious sacrifice. The extravagance which a compensation so munificent naturally engenders is utterly inconsistent with the exercise of that economy and prudence essential to the successful management of any private enterprise, and I have become satisfied that no private individual can be expected to enter into competition with a line drawing such material aid from the general government.

The words may not have been the salty Commodore's, yet they were more than hand-wringing over the misdirection of money going to unworthy shipping lines. His ample experience as an operator had taught him that the aggregate cost of modern ocean transport—iron hulls, compact but powerful steam plants, first-class amenities, ever-faster crossings—was far greater than passengers and shippers were willing to pay. Like all shipowners, he gave no attention to what seamen were truly worth for their labor and the risks that they took. A half century would elapse before labor costs, low as they might be, were factored in. The British experience in the Crimea taught that the necessity of maintaining a ready supply of potentially useful warships justified government support as much as did mail transport. At the time, even that was a radical suggestion.

Vanderbilt applied for subsidies for himself while competing successfully against Aspinwall's and Law's heavily subsidized lines servicing Central America. Then, with his usual abrupt tactics, he shifted the *Ariel* to a regular schedule on the Bremen route and set first-class fares at $80—cut and thrust. That action captured enough bookings from the ten-year-old Hamburg and Bremen Line that it was soon forced out of business.

The *Vanderbilt* remained alone on the New York–Southampton–Havre route. The vessel was fast. In 1857, it captured the Blue Riband from Cunard's *Persia* when it steamed from Sandy Hook to the Isle of Wight in nine days and eight hours. Handicappers equated that to a Liverpool passage of nine days and one hour, which made it two hours better than *Persia's* best time. Sweat in the stokehold and fine-tuning of the timepieces won the day.

The Vanderbilt Line could claim several accomplishments, as it did in a self-published broadsheet. Cornelius Vanderbilt achieved them without partners or subsidies. He demonstrated the reliability of more economical beam engines, which had been customarily thought unsuited to ocean waters. His ships achieved the quickest steamship passage while they offered the lowest fares. He boasted that he had come from the owner of a small schooner on Long Island Sound to the owner of the world's largest steamship. His statement, "No passenger ever lost life or limb by any kind of disaster," on the Vanderbilt Line stretched the truth and ignored the

12–5. *SS* Adriatic, *costliest and last Collins liner.*
The Mariners' Museum

catastrophes of his West Coast operations. Despite the claims, the European line had a poor reputation for service and living conditions. One of his ships even faced a mutiny until the rebellious seamen were sent ashore and replaced by a polyglot crew.

WHILE THE great hope for the Collins Line, the *Adriatic,* lay in its slip with fitting out incomplete, a number of Boston's prominent citizens sent an invitation to Collins to visit their city in his new vessel before it went into regular service. It is unlikely that Enoch Train was among them, but the courtesy extended to Collins was indicative that the New England merchants wanted to draw attention from New York. "Permit us to say," the invitation ended, "that besides our personal gratification in your acceptance of this invitation, we believe that such a visit as proposed would be an event of great interest and pleasure to all who feel pride in the success of the American commerce, and in our fellow citizens generally." Were the Bostonians tiring of the Britons' steady success?

Collins accepted the invitation and attended a dinner in his honor on October 11, 1856. Nothing more than a pleasant evening—no offer of pier facilities, no welcoming brass band—seems to have come of the visit. Nor did the ship itself grace Boston harbor. A month earlier, George Steers, the *Adriatic*'s designer and a close friend of Edward Collins, had been trampled to death by a runaway horse. The ship was beset with engine problems, and its sea trials were deferred for months.

In February 1857, Congress withdrew Edward Collins's subsidy and entered into a contract with Cornelius Vanderbilt for the transport of transatlantic mail. As a result, Vanderbilt became the major American steamship operator in the Atlantic. The Commodore had made his point, and the marginally profitable Vanderbilt Line paid its director well.

That same year, incited by Vanderbilt's wrath, the hostile Central American states closed in on the self-appointed president of Nicaragua and forced William Walker to surrender to the U.S. Navy. Walker was again tried for violating his country's neutrality and again acquitted. Out of power but free to resume his knavery while Vanderbilt dusted his hands in vindication, Walker blamed his defeat on the overreaching Navy.

With his eldest son now a member of the firm and financier James Brown continuing as president, Edward Collins was finally ready to put the *Adriatic* into service. The maiden voyage was scheduled to start on November 21, 1857, but adversity set in again. On that day, John Collins, Edward's uncle and lifelong mentor, then the line's marine superintendent, died. The sailing of the Collins Line's last hope for survival was deferred for two more days until it was finally under way with thirty-eight paying passengers.

The end of the Crimean War in 1857 had its effect on business interests halfway around the globe. Credit withered overseas, and the bottom dropped out of foreign demand for American agricultural goods. In October, excessive European speculation in American railroad development added to the economic crisis. It was inevitable that the short-line railroads that had been springing up for twenty years would be eventually connected by federally funded rail lines stretching across the vast continent. It had not happened in the thriving manner once expected, and, looking at Europe's depression, the American people lost confidence in their own nation's economy. Facing a downturn in financial markets, investors began converting their assets to gold or cash. Confidence crumbled when the *Central America* sank in the deep waters off Cape Hatteras, the tempestuous Atlantic taking its tribute even from the forty-niners. The paddle-wheeled steamship was carrying miners and their families from Panama to New York, along with more than 20 tons of California gold, some the property of the federal government. The year's series of depressing events combined to bring on the third and most destructive panic in the nation's history.

Still, 1857 was a good year for Cornelius Vanderbilt. He had taken to curbing expenses by laying up ships during the winter months when traffic was expected to decline. Although travelers were not pleased with the European line's irregular service, his three vessels running across the Atlantic had carried 2,194 passengers eastward and 2,669 westward. The impressive total of 4,863 passengers was behind Cunard's 5,534 but exceeded the Havre Line's 3,252 passengers. Collins's dying line carried only 1,516 passengers. The British Inman Line held the top position with its steel hulls and screw propellers transporting a grand total of 11,924 passengers, mostly immigrants, between Liverpool and New York. All steamship lines on the Atlantic carried a grand total of 54,746 passengers. Sailing packets, unable to match the service or speed of the steamers, took a much smaller portion of the trade. The halting transition from sail to steam now had validity. Vanderbilt was not content with less than 9 percent of the steamship business, and the aging opportunist already had his eye on the bargain-priced railroads.

By 1857, the British government was paying out the equivalent of $5.5 million per year in mail transport subsidies, with Cunard drawing the lion's share, which was far more generous than U.S. payments made to the Collins Line. For Collins, the nation's financial crisis was the coup de grâce. The line owed crew members $3,000 in back pay. The City of New York had claims of $39,000 in unpaid taxes for the years 1856–57. The federal government held a $115,000 lien on the steamers. Unpaid charges secured by a $500,000 mortgage bordering on default faced the firm. The Collins line ran out of cash needed to operate on schedule. The great wooden paddle steamer *Adriatic* made its last voyage for Collins during the dreary winter of 1857–58. Costing more than $1 million, it had come on the scene too late to save the line from bankruptcy. On the round-trip to Liverpool, the *Adriatic* carried only 10 percent of its passenger capacity, while the *Atlantic* and *Baltic* struggled to hold together a schedule of monthly sailings. On February 10, 1858, the shipping pages carried a brief notice, "The Collins steamship *Atlantic* will not sail on Saturday next for Liverpool, as has been announced." To no one's surprise, the Collins Line expired.

On April 1, the Collins ships were put up for auction. With Edward Knight Collins in absentia, all three ships were sold through an agent as a package to James Brown. He paid $50,000 in cash for the three ships, with 20 percent down and the balance due the next day. Thus was sealed the fate of the bankrupt line.

THE PANIC OF 1857 caused Donald McKay to close down his yard. Enoch Train chartered another builder's clipper, the *Cathedral,* and sent it on a run to the Pacific. The route, although potentially lucrative, was a peculiar one for Train to have specified, but the fate of the *Cathedral* was not, considering its operator's grim touch. In a storm off Cape Horn, the ship rolled onto its beam ends and was wrecked with the loss of several lives. The defeated shipowner withdrew his White Diamond Line from service. He was not alone among packet operators, as the panic engulfed even the steamship companies. Philadelphia's Cope Line went out of business, as did the two-ship Ocean Line when Congress withdrew all subsidies. Cunard continued to lead passenger companies in refitting the Great Circle to Maury's designated routes. The company began experimenting with iron construction on its steamy Suez–East Indian routes.

Iron hulls and screw propulsion introduced new discomforts in return for safety and speed. With the withdrawal of side-wheel propulsion, steamship lines eliminated one of the likeliest threats to safety, but regular transatlantic passengers lamented the ultimate passing of the ponderous paddle wheelers. The iron ships were noisy, cold in wintry waters, ovens in the tropics, and, at times, they took on a disturbing corkscrew motion.

In January 1858, Vanderbilt's *Ariel* was missing. When it was shortly out of Southampton, the ship's starboard shaft broke in a winter gale. Had the wheel dropped off, the vessel would have capsized. As it was, it crept into Queenstown under shortened sails, the crippled wheel strapped to its side. It was shipping water and without steam power. Its passengers completed their voyage on a Cunard Line vessel at Vanderbilt's expense. Again, in December, gale-whipped seas swept over the weary *Ariel,* killed its captain, and severely damaged the ship. The hard-pressed Commodore must have looked with even more favor on the railroads in which he was dabbling.

Vanderbilt threatened to reopen Accessory Transit in 1858. On June 9, the two interocean shippers raised his "stipend" to $56,000. Then, after years of political maneuvering, trickery, and stock manipulation, the Vanderbilt scheme to link the oceans came to an end. His victims discontinued their payments, and he put his Central American vessels up for sale. By then, 20,000 passengers had crossed on the Nicaraguan route.

Unwilling to continue skirmishing with the increasingly assertive Germans, Vanderbilt discontinued his Bremen service in 1859. Meanwhile, Samuel Samuels kept the heavily rigged *Dreadnought* sailing under the severest conditions. In March, he established a new packet ship speed records, New York to Liverpool in thirteen days, nine hours; just nine days, seventeen hours from Sandy Hook to Queenstown. There he was slowed in light winds in completing the passage to Liverpool. The minutiae of that voyage have been disputed—might it have been a few hours longer and thus no record, the skeptics asked. Their challenge was based on contemporary reports in the Liverpool newspapers, taken from the *Dreadnought*'s log, quibbling over the delay that occurred between Queenstown and arrival at the Mersey. The severest opposition to the accuracy of Samuels's accomplishment came from those who noted, after his death, that he had failed to mention the voyage in his memoirs. A plausible reason for the absences exists in Samuels's final voyage on the *Dreadnought* as the American Civil War spread to midocean. The voyage capped all that the last great holdout for sail power had ever accomplished. Influenced by compelling, war-fostered circumstances, that adventure turned the skipper of the Wild Boat of the Atlantic to steamships.

13

Aftermath

URING THE half-dozen years between the loss of the *Arctic* and the outbreak of the Civil War, the United States merchant fleet was considered to be among the world's largest. That achievement was scuttled, along with an alarming number of vessels, through a wartime threat to the commercial shipping of both belligerent forces—government-sponsored raiders sent out in place of the renegade privateers outlawed in 1856 by international agreements. The bulk of American shipping belonged to the North. The Union was quick to set up its maritime defenses and commandeer vessels for blockading the southern coastal cities. The South, for lack of ships in the ports that it seized, was slower to react accordingly in northern waters. Eventually, a hastily formed Confederate navy put out fast, moderately armed raiders to cruise nearby trade routes and capture or destroy the Union's extensive fleet of merchantmen and those of neutral nations that carried contraband to or from Union ports.

England attempted with difficulty to retain its neutrality during the conflict. Heavily dependent on the Confederate states to supply its looms with cotton and on Union purchases of industrial goods, it tried to service both without confrontation. American overseas trade continued,

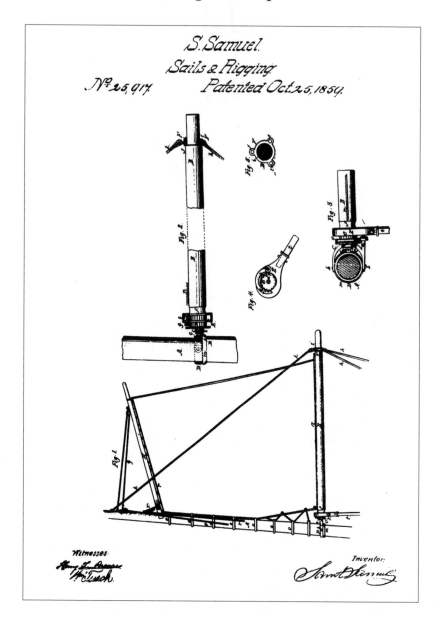

13–1. *Samuels's timely patent, bearing misspelled name.*
    U.S. Patent and Trademark Office

neutral vessels being free to pass through the blockades by presenting cargo manifests that listed no materials of war. Initially, the hostilities between the states had small effect on transatlantic passenger transport because it was critical for both sides of the unresolved dispute to keep their routes open to Europe. Cabin space on the *Dreadnought*, booked as much as a year in advance, remained filled. The Confederate blockade fleet ranged the Caribbean in search of northern commerce until late in 1862 when its raiders began cruising like hungry sharks along the Great Circle. To avoid attack by an enemy raider, an unarmed merchantman needed the speed and agility of a clipper to outrace it. A heavily armed steamship's smoke was apt to give it away. Before their topgallants were sighted, tall ships often could detect a raider's proximity and then show their heels to escape confrontation.

SAM SAMUELS never commanded a McKay-built vessel. The *Dreadnought* was designed and built in the rival Currier and Townsend yard expressly for Samuels's command, with modifications that he imposed while supervising its construction. Although the vessel gained fame for the builders, a series of cost overruns during production financially crippled the partnership and contributed to its demise.

At 1,400 registered tons, the *Dreadnought* was what the builders termed a *semiclipper.* It carried sturdier, reduced upper rigging, the better to keep heavy canvas aloft in strong winds. In the opinion of many packet skippers, the extreme clippers' royals and skysails with their flimsy spars and removable upper masts could do little to achieve constancy of speed if they were lost when gales blew up. The *Dreadnought* was probably equipped with the roller reefing gear patented by Samuels in 1859, not that he was inclined to give it much use. Square-riggers customarily maintained headway while reducing sail; a spread of canvas full of wind was easier for men to reef while leaning across a yard. Such was not the case with sails mounted on jibbooms and mizzenmasts. Fore-and-aft sails were shortened by heading the vessel directly into the wind, pitching it heavily in the seas, and losing headway. During the interim, men stretched out on the yards were prevented from handling the square sails, an extreme measure for hard drivers such as Samuels. His solution was to roll up the fore-and-aft sail like an inverted window shade and furl it along the top of its boom while it still held wind. The invention would have been nearly indispensable during the *Dreadnought*'s final voyage under the hardy skipper.

On a February afternoon in 1862, while headed home from England with a full load of passengers, including several women and children, the ship was struck by a violent gale midway between the Azores and Halifax. The area was known to be raider territory—several whalers had already been torched—but Samuels scoffed at the suggestion that any steamship could get close enough to trouble him and certainly not in heavy weather. The storm's intensity forced him to reduce the ship to as small an amount of canvas as he customarily carried while under way. Through the night, the gale's severity increased. At daybreak, the skipper called for the crew to heave to. After the foresail was furled, they carried bare poles and little more than a set of stormsails with which to wear ship while waiting out the storm's fury. The vessel suddenly careened to port and was heeling close to its beam ends when an immense sea swept over the starboard quarter. Samuels was nearly drowned in the torrent as he hung onto a rack of belaying pins to avoid being washed over the side. He was knocked unconscious by a flying piece of gear and, on coming to, found himself pinned under a heavy spar. The upper half of his body hung in the water outboard of the lee rail, his legs awash on deck and crushed by free-floating spars. His right leg was broken, and his left wrist was useless. He grasped the rail with his right hand until the crew could clear the deck and pull him fully on board.

During a short lull in the storm, his men carried Samuels below to his cabin, where they found the skylight stove in and his papers afloat in a foot of water. Stretching him out on a sofa, they split his right boot and stripped off his trousers to discover a compound fracture below the knee and bright scarlet blood spouting from a punctured femoral artery. After a tourniquet was applied, the purser and a pair of seamen tried without success to set the leg. Then, dosed with a stimulant to spur his recovery, threatened by severe loss of blood, and ignorant of medical procedures, the captain decided on amputation. No one would undertake it, so he prepared to do it himself after giving an amateur's detailed instructions to his attendants on how to tie up the arteries should he pass out. A scalpel and saw were poised for swift action when the second mate, who had gained ample hospital experience when each of his own legs was broken, came below and suggested that they might encounter one of the friendly steam packets, most of which had surgeons on board. The officer successfully pleaded with the captain not to amputate. Together, they bandaged up the limb and bound it into a trough-shaped splint.

After a few restless hours during which he composed himself and his cabin was pumped out and cleaned, the captain learned that the ship had lost its rudder and the carpenter had been killed. The *Dreadnought* was 360 miles from the Azores port of Fayal. While the vessel drifted aimlessly, the crew spent a full day in assembling a makeshift rudder only to lose it when the hoisting straps parted and it fell into the sea. Samuels was frantic. Four days passed. He went sleepless as he subsisted on narcotics, tea, and toast. His leg became inflamed. Nursed by the stewardess and purser, he kept it cool with cold compresses while his officers brought him daily position reports. On the fifth day they encountered a French ship with no doctor and a captain unwilling to take them in tow. For a long, frustrating day, men on both ships worked with hawsers to turn the *Dreadnought* around but to no avail. Finally, the Frenchman said that he could waste no more time. He volunteered to take the floundering ship's mail to Bordeaux for dispatch to Liverpool and New York, and the two ships parted company.

The wind, freshening from the west, was favorable for getting to Fayal if they could but steer. Work on another jury-rudder had started when Samuels decided to make an attempt at sailing the ship stern first on its course. Issuing commands from his cabin, he found that by trimming and furling the headsails and backing the yards, the ship could make sternway at more than three knots. For fifty-two hours, the *Dreadnought* sailed backward and covered 183 miles before the wind died. At that point, the men were able to ship a new rudder in calm seas and resume normal operation. On the fourteenth day following the accident, they sailed into Portuguese-held Fayal.

Samuels was exhausted, completely without strength, his leg in a shocking state, and his body shrunken and covered with sores. Both the

Dreadnought and its skipper needed time in the dock. Two weeks after being taken ashore in the care of a local doctor, Samuels was put under a dose of chloroform and another attempt was made to set his leg. A section of his heel, rotten with gangrene, was removed, but the principal effort was unsuccessful and left a bone spur as large as a tooth protruding from his flesh. Days later, he consulted an American naval doctor, one of a crew assembling to staff the *Kearsarge,* the Union warship assigned to confront the Confederacy's about-to-be commissioned raider *Alabama.* The doctor recommended amputation. Nothing doing, Samuels told him. "Put me on my ship and send me home."

The rest of his tale is anticlimax. He returned to Brooklyn without difficulty, where he had another operation to repair his wrecked limb. After almost a year's convalescence, he walked with a barely perceptible limp, but his commercial career under sail was over.

The Civil War raged on and ended the *Dreadnought*'s regular service. Samuels reported for military duty in 1863 and took his first official command of a steamship, the *John Rice,* as general superintendent of the Quartermaster's Department in New York. In 1865, he commanded the 1,000-ton, wooden steam-paddler *G. B. McClellan,* a transport assigned to the Union's combined military assault on Wilmington, North Carolina. There, Union naval forces captured Fort Fisher during the final major battle of the Civil War. After the war, Samuels captained the steamship *Fulton,* last of the American liners with terminal facilities in Havre, but the fervor of transatlantic competition was gone. Surviving fleets, thinned by wartime raiding and reflagging and lacking the flamboyance of earlier years, settled into more stable steamship operation. The old mariner knew that steam was not in his blood, and he turned to yachting as a hired professional in the territory that he knew well, the North Atlantic. *New York Herald* publisher James Gordon Bennett's *Henrietta* was under Samuels's command when it won the first transatlantic yacht race. He spent his twilight years in a variety of shoreside business enterprises, none very successful, while he worked on his memoirs, which Samuels published in 1887 when he was sixty-four years old. His daughter, Edith M. Samuels, helped him as secretary-typist. Some of his correspondence indicates her name, as well as the captain's explanation of why he failed to include in his memoirs details of the *Dreadnought*'s fastest transatlantic crossing in 1859. Nearly all of his papers, he revealed, were destroyed when his cabin was flooded in the gale of 1862. Several other notes, many dictated by Samuels years prior to his death in 1908, although self-supporting, subtly tend to confirm his accomplishment.

AFTER THE 1857 Panic, when he shut down his shipyard, Donald McKay spent the antebellum years in Europe, where he sold ship timber and studied ironclad construction. The producer of the world's most famous wooden sailing ships, now entertained by the maritime power that delayed Samuel Cunard's conversion to iron hulls, was impressed by the striking shift in technology. He became convinced that Commodore Perry's navy of wooden paddle wheel ships had become chillingly obsolete and returned to the United States to advocate the production of ironclad screw-propelled steamships. In the spring of 1861, he drew up a proposal for a 2,000-ton corvette armed with twelve casemate guns, 9-inch cannons that would put the ship among the most powerful on the high seas. Coming from the acknowledged expert on wooden sailing vessels, the offer made a profound impression on his prospective clients, but the beleaguered federal government, about to be torn asunder, turned it down for lack of funds. McKay returned to England, where he spent most of the war years doing routine business with the Admiralty.

Before the war ended, McKay came home to reopen his shipyard and convert it to the production of iron-hulled ships and locomotive engines. An 1864 venture to produce four naval vessels was a financial loss. Yet, the indominatable spirit of the perfectionist shone forth when he was interviewed in that fall by a reporter for the *Boston Daily Advertiser*. "I never yet built a vessel that came up to my own ideal," he said. "I saw something in each ship which I desired to improve." He continued to build both steamers and sailing ships. The 2,100-ton *Glory of the Seas* was the last ship to come from the McKay yard before he sold it in 1869. Displaying his unfailing confidence in wind power, he built the ship for his own account, accompanied it on its maiden voyage to San Francisco, and lost money on it. Later, he watched it become a swift and profitable vessel for the subsequent owners. The *Glory* lived for fifty-four years.

McKay produced a few more wooden vessels in government shipyards before his enthusiasm waned. He developed tuberculosis in 1877 and retired to his country estate in Hamilton, Massachusetts. There, a disastrous fire later destroyed most of his plans and half-models. The plans for the *Flying Cloud,* believed to be the original outlines, and some for a few lesser vessels were rescued and are preserved at the Massachusetts Institute of Technology's Hart Museum. Severely reduced in both health and wealth, Donald McKay died at his home on September 20, 1880. He was survived by his beloved Mary and most of his fifteen children.

Throughout his years, McKay retained his industrious outlook, artistic perceptions, and patrician joy of life. Nova Scotian by birth, McKay, more than Enoch Train, bore the traits of a Boston Brahmin. One of the city's prominent citizens, a colleague of statesmen Daniel Webster and Edward Everett, McKay was revered by his employees and imitated and respected by his shipbuilding competitors. He enjoyed music, played the violin at home, and reveled in the pleasures of his children. All the while, he welcomed the career support of each of his spouses. Theirs was no token participation of retiring Victorian wives; both his art and his business profited by their interests.

DURING Enoch Train's years as merchant-shipowner, he affiliated himself in traditional Yankee fashion, with the banks that served him—director of the Suffolk Savings Bank for Seamen; major stockholder of the Faneuil Hall National Bank; and, for twenty-seven years, director of the Tremont National Bank. He served for a year in Boston as a justice of the peace and, as a public-spirited citizen, urged the development of Fenway Court. Beaten by the Panic of 1857, he sold his shipping line to the Boston firm of Thayer & Warren, later reorganized as George Warren & Company. The Warren Line fleet was put under the British flag for protection during the Civil War, a practice widely adopted because Confederate raiders would not touch vessels registered to their close allies. Neutral England claimed that alliance and built wooden raiders for the Confederate navy. As a consequence of reflagging and the destruction wrought by raiders, the U.S. merchant marine nearly came to its end. The use of foreign flags of convenience became a curse that still plagues the withering American fleet of the present day. The thinned fleet lost its color and changed its personality as great numbers of windjammers sailed no more in commercially profitable ventures, and steam power converted from paddle to screw propulsion.

Enoch Train's personal financial situation never fully recovered after he disposed of his line. All but facing ruin after the war, he sold his grandiose Dorchester estate and moved to Saugus, a community once famous for producing forged iron for the ships of the Boston dockyards. He died on September 18, 1868, and was buried near his friends Longfellow and Emerson in Mount Auburn Cemetery, Cambridge, the nation's first garden burial ground. He was survived by a daughter, Adeline Train Whitney, who became a widely recognized writer of fiction and verse.

GEORGE FRANCIS TRAIN retained his interest in the tall ships. While managing the English branch of his cousin's shipping firm in Liverpool, he became attracted to the opportunities offered by long-haul sailers out of Australia, and left the Train Line to establish a shipping firm in Melbourne. He claimed to have earned $95,000 during its first year of operation. Unquestionably wealthy, after three years he left Australia in 1855 to tour the world; to establish connections in England, France, and Spain; and to amass funds he would later use in the building of Ohio's Atlantic and Great Western Railroad. He returned to America in July 1856, settled in New York, and devoted his time to writing a series of columns for the *New York Herald.* Digressing from predictable topics, he recounted increasingly sensational observations on life in America. During the next eighteen years, he was to produce speeches, pamphlets, leaflets, and books, a Tocqueville as unrestrained citizen.

In the antebellum period, he went again to England, seeking investors in American railroads, and promoting the construction of street railways in his former haunts of Liverpool, London, and Staffordshire. In 1862, he returned to Boston, where he was jailed briefly for interrupting a public meeting, the first of several such encounters he would have. That same year, he built a showplace in Newport, Rhode Island, from which he undertook speech-making tours on behalf of the Union. Undeniably a gifted talker, in 1866 Train made a fruitless run at the Senate and in 1869

13–2. *George Francis Train (1829–1904), fluent renegade.*
Library of Congress

announced his presidential candidacy, unsuccessfully campaigning from Europe "among the effete monarchies of the Old World."

He was expelled as a Communist from France in 1870, and his caustic commentary on the victorious American Union's behalf made him persona non grata in neutral England. There he spent a short period in jail, where he stated that he was being used as "ransom" for American war claims against England for its part in having built Confederate raiders. When British officials urged him to leave England, his final words to Prime Minister Benjamin Disraeli were, "You go to India by your Suez Canal. I'll go home, build a railway across the continent, and beat you to your goal."

In 1870, cooling off from his various confrontations, Train steamed through Disraeli's Suez Canal and continued around the world in eighty days. In his autobiography, published after the turn of the century, he claimed he had inspired Jules Verne to write a novel of such a voyage.

Once more back in his homeland, Train became captivated by the organization of the Union Pacific Railroad. In 1871, he bought shares of the railroad stock; became a competent lobbyist in Washington on its behalf; and purchased, at low prices, 500 hundred acres of Omaha real estate lying in the future path of Union Pacific tracks. His dark curly hair and newly sprouted chin whiskers contrasted with his white, Mark Twain–style suit, when he gave the keynote speech at the formal opening of the Union Pacific's right-of-way.

Train's increasingly unconventional behavior, far from the mainstream, found him in the company of socialists and advocates of causes that bordered on obscenity. For such he was ostracized and nearly committed as insane. If anything brought him close to Cornelius Vanderbilt, it would have been railroads and his unusual interests, not shipping. He and the Commodore's own strange associates were hounded by the equally odd antismut campaigner Anthony Comstock.

In his own life story, written at the age of seventy-three, George Francis Train, a glib and genuine eccentric, took credit for much of the successes of Donald McKay and Enoch Train. In 1904, two years after the publication of his memoirs, the transportation promoter, commentator, and author died.

CHARLES MARSHALL, the stern-visaged old sea dog who took over the Black Ball Line and ensured its longevity through his management of the firm for thirty-one years, became prominent in New York through a variety of maritime interests. At one time a commissioner of pilots, he was later named head of the Marine Society and director of the Sailors' Snug Harbor retirement home in Staten Island. Marshall was initially opposed to the idea of war between the states, but, once the conflict started, he urged the Union navy to use privateers to tighten the blockade and to undertake a lively pursuit of the troublesome CSS *Alabama*. He died as the Civil War came to an end, but he was outlived by the line of sailing ships to which he had contributed such durability.

SAILING PACKETS built the base for regular transatlantic trade and steam power gave it the energy for spectacular growth. Not until the dual crossing of the *Sirius* and *Great Western* in 1838 did the drama of the Great Circle unfold. Junius Smith, the impresario of transatlantic steam transport, gave up his trading operation after the loss of the *President* and returned to the United States, where he successfully experimented as a tea planter in South Carolina. He was an outspoken abolitionist in the slave-owning South. Tragically, that brought him to the attention of a gang of ruffians, intolerant of what they deemed to be northern interference. The thugs brutally beat him and fractured his skull. He fled to a New York hospital and died from his injuries a few weeks later in January 1853. What John Fitch did for steamboats on the inland waters, Smith did for steamships on the Atlantic. Both men died in misfortune and without due honor for their contributions.

AFTER THE Collins Line failure, Edward Knight Collins turned to the development of mineral properties in Wellsville, Ohio. In 1860, he contracted with Frederick Law Olmsted, the designer of New York City's Central Park, to lay out his Larchmont, New York, estate, in building lots. Five years later, all but fifty acres of the 388-acre Westchester County property was sold at auction to Thomas Flint, who developed the land into what became the waterside village of Larchmont.

Dispirited after his final shipping efforts, Collins spent several years in his marginal Ohio mining business before giving it up to return to New York. He had remarried. Sarah Browne was a widow with two sons who gave him another son, Edward Knight Collins Jr. In 1876, he sold his imposing Larchmont home and moved to a new brownstone on Madison Avenue in the Murray Hill section of New York. By then, he was in sharply straitened circumstances. A few months before his death, his champions appealed to the public for money for his support, unfitting though it would seem for the courageous shipping speculator and showman. Collins, more than any of his competitors, had demonstrated the elegance of ocean liner transport a century before it became routinely expected. He died of heart disease in 1878 and was survived by his wife and three sons. Regrettably, his heirs quarreled over the estate to the extent that no one was willing to pay for a gravestone. Edward Knight Collins lies in an unmarked grave in Woodlawn Cemetery.

CORNELIUS VANDERBILT's onetime partner and antagonist Daniel Drew relinquished control of his inland and coastal shipping businesses prior to the Panic of 1857. By 1844, Drew was pouring money into investment banking and, in 1853, became involved with the Erie Railroad. The panic helped him to force his election as an Erie director, and, in that position, he shamelessly started manipulating its stock. Drew was among the first of a line of rogue financial exploiters. He was destined again to duel with his old enemy, but the railroads had not yet drawn Vanderbilt's wholehearted interest. He had other scores to settle and a troublesome shipping line to put in order.

In the spring of 1856, William Walker, Vanderbilt's Central American nemesis, gained U.S. recognition of Nicaragua's new government and declared himself its president in July. His rule did not last. The following year, he was ousted in a coup and fled to Honduras, where he established a base on the Bay Islands from which he could meddle further in isthmian affairs. Vanderbilt watched patiently from afar while Walker called attention to his own nefarious activities with the publication of his book, *War in Nicaragua,* before launching an attack on Central America in 1860. In that failed effort, he was forced to surrender to the British navy. Closely allied with Honduras, the British returned Walker to Honduran authorities. He was court-martialed and found guilty of fomenting rebellion and violating neutrality. On September 12, 1860, William Walker was shot by a firing squad, and cunning old Commodore Vanderbilt had one less enemy.

Vanderbilt was well tuned to the political stress within his own nation. Seeing the coming of civil war, he moved to divest himself of his Atlantic Line. The line was profitable, probably more so than his central American ventures, but it required more vigilance than he cared to put forth when he considered the tensions between North and South. Retaining his favorite luxury vessel *Vanderbilt*, he sold the rest of the line for $3 million and capitulated to those remaining forces contending for the kingdom of the Atlantic. The U.S. Navy's hasty commandeering of several merchant vessels at the opening of hostilities was not lost on the Commodore. At his own expense, he readied the *Vanderbilt* for conversion to a warship and, in the presence of President Abraham Lincoln and Secretary of War Edwin Stanton, formally presented it to the federal government. Lincoln sent a message to Congress and requested that it make a suitable acknowledgment.

After the unavailing battle of the USS *Monitor* and the CSS *Virginia* (ex-*Merrimac*), Vanderbilt volunteered to take his ship south to ram and destroy the besieged Confederate ironclad. The offer was unaccepted while the *Monitor* hovered in the vicinity to keep the *Virginia* bottled up. Instead the navy sent the armed *Vanderbilt* in a futile search for the elusive raider *Alabama,* and the Commodore joined Union officer Nathaniel Banks in an unsuccessful raiding expedition against New Orleans. Under a government commission, Vanderbilt had chartered ships that proved to be unseaworthy for the venture. Fed up with Vanderbilt's reckless and irresponsible behavior, the Senate investigated the commission's failure and voted for a resolution of censure. The war ended before the resolution could be formally adopted. Ironically, in 1864, Congress had resurrected Lincoln's request and issued a belated resolution of thanks for Vanderbilt's gift of his steamship and his "fervid and large-souled patriotism."

On delivery of the resolve, the Commodore howled as only he could, "Congress be damned! I never gave that ship to Congress. When the Government was in great straits for a suitable vessel of war, I offered to give the ship if they did not care to buy it; however, Mr. Lincoln and Mr. Welles [Secretary of the Navy Gideon Welles] think it was a gift, and I suppose I shall have to let her go." The Commodore's way of thanking Congress for having his name expunged from the Senate resolution was to let the issue of the *Vanderbilt* transfer gracefully expire. Later, he complained to friends, expressing his bitterness over the loss of his ship. The expert in nautical blackmail settled for the gift of a gold medal embossed with his likeness and less criticism of his highly suspect activities. The Navy sent the wooden-hulled *Vanderbilt* on a tour of duty in the North Pacific, far from its familiar waters. There it was sold, converted to a sailing vessel, and renamed the *Three Brothers*. As an ironic and unfitting token of Cornelius Vanderbilt's long maritime career, it ended its days as a coal hulk in Gibraltar and was scrapped after seventy-three years afloat.

Vanderbilt had already started to buy stock in the New York & Harlem Railroad as he turned his back on the deepwater paths to look on the iron roadways stretching westward from Manhattan. In 1863, free of his shipping interests, he prevailed on the City Council of New York to give him permission to extend the Harlem rail line to the Battery. Four years later, he took over the New York Central Railroad and again faced the rascally Daniel Drew. When Vanderbilt started buying Erie Railroad stock because he was eager to get control of the road, he was unaware that Drew was creating and issuing more and more stock and bidding up the price. When Drew sold short, the price of the watery stock caved in, Vanderbilt lost millions, and the illiterate Drew reached the peak of his already extensive fortunes. The nation was aghast at the rampant display of dishonesty by both parties as Erie and Harlem stock soared and fell. Vanderbilt, biding his time, bought shares at low prices because he sensed that Drew and his "short" traders were selling more shares than actually existed.

When the price of Erie and Harlem stock turned up, Vanderbilt forced the issue. In settlement for stock that could not be delivered, he took control of the associated Hudson River Railroad, his revenge on Drew now complete. By 1873, he had connected New York and Chicago by rail, and his Wall Street and overland adventures eclipsed all that he had accomplished on the Hudson River, in Central America, and on the Atlantic Ocean.

On January 4, 1877, Cornelius Vanderbilt, America's richest citizen, died. The precocious Staten Island ferryman, one of the first steamboat captains to poke his ship's bow into the briny waters of the Atlantic, built the foundation of his wealth on maritime ventures from New York to Nicaragua and across the Atlantic to the European continent and the British Isles. Many times a millionaire, his estate was valued at nearly $100 million at his death. He was the father of thirteen children; two sons and all nine daughters survived him. One son died as a youth and another was lost during the Civil War. The Commodore's favorite son and heir, William, was left with the care of the shady ladies of Woodhull, Claflin and Company. The aged Commodore did not live to see Daniel Drew, who boasted of his own millions only a year or two after Vanderbilt's death, die as a broken and despised old man.

13–3. *RMS* Scotia, *Cunard's last paddle wheeler.*
The Mariners' Museum

IN 1862, the Cunard Line launched the *Scotia,* a sister ship to the four-year-old *Persia,* the steamer that, on its first voyage, had paralleled the Collins Line's *Pacific* on the last leg of the *Pacific's* final voyage. The larger *Scotia* was both the last paddler and the company's last Napier-built ship. Its two side-lever engines burned an enormous amount of coal, up to 150 tons per day in forty furnaces, to drive the ship at an average 14.5 knots. Horrified at the expense, Cunard financial managers justified it chiefly by the government's continuance of the mail contracts. The ship took to the North Atlantic under Charles Judkins, Cunard's resolute senior captain. Benefitting from the American Civil War, the *Persia* and *Scotia* were among the most successful vessels operated by the Cunard Line during its twenty-five year history. While English shipyards were producing raiders for the Confederacy, Cunard ships, flying a neutral flag and unhampered by the deadly Confederate marauders, provided safe transport of people and goods between the United States and England. By then, the line's reputation for cautious service was widely recognized, its splendid record of safety due largely to MacIver's early coaching and careful, although frugal, attention to passenger needs. Stewards stood for daily inspection both of the quarters for which they were responsible and of themselves. Scoured fingernails, clean uniforms, and polished shoes were carefully examined as they stood in ranks on the open decks. Crisp service was highly valued and cost less to be delivered than the munificent menus of the few remaining American liners.

A half-dozen years after establishing his transatlantic shipping line, Samuel Cunard was named a Fellow of the Royal Geographical Society. On March 9, 1859, upon Lord Palmerston's recommendation, Queen Victoria conferred a baronetcy on Cunard in recognition of services to his country by the founding of the Cunard Line of steamers. In 1865, Sir Samuel died in London at age seventy-seven. He left estates in England, Nova Scotia, and New York to his extensive family and control of his company to his sons and several of the original investors. After his death, the firm's name was officially changed to The Cunard Steam Ship Company, more easily expressed and broader in potential scope than the name specified on the formation papers. The Great Circle was firmly in its control.

LIKE MYTHICAL gods battling for dominion over an ocean kingdom, the titans of the Atlantic left behind them a tragic wreckage of human lives, lost ships, and squandered fortunes. The Cunard Line, the undiminished survivor, continued to steam prudently over the waves. The humbled Americans had little to build on after the Civil War. A decline in the affairs of America's merchant marine that began with the loss of the *Arctic* continued for ninety years. It was buoyed only by wartime's temporary needs.

Iron-hulled steamships, more easily adapted to the screw propellor, sent the old paddle wheelers into graceful retirement. When bulk production of steel resulted from a British development, the Bessemer process, during the latter half of the nineteenth century, lighter and stronger steel construction replaced heavy iron hulls. In 1869, the opening of the Suez Canal shortened the steamer route to the East Indies and spelled the end of clipper ships as passenger carriers. Suez extended the territory of the British liners and ensured their dominance over half the world from New York to Rangoon. Stiffer shipboard standards of hygiene and health care overcame some of the miseries of steerage. As hotel comforts improved the quality of life above the waterline, vacationers made up a growing proportion of transatlantic trade.

Out of the residue of conflict new order rises. The Civil War converted twenty-seven fractious states into a nation of free people identified by a singular proper noun. Before that war ended, the Industrial Revolution extended the limits of technology at a pace exceeding the Sumerian creativity of five thousand years earlier. Within a century it changed the nature of global trade, aided in massive population shifts, and sharply altered the roles of democratic governments. The North Atlantic provided the venue for radical changes in maritime policies that were to influence the U.S. government's industrial relations for a hundred and fifty years. The notion of a national government subsidizing private commercial operations, introduced by the British Admiralty and adopted within a decade by the United States, persists in the face of intense opposition. In 1890, American Adm. Alfred T. Mahan demonstrated the importance of routine government funding of merchant ship construction and operation and based his arguments on Great Britain's half century of experience. To this day, his theories, studied and adopted by every principal maritime power, remain the strongest argument for continuation of maritime subsidies. Simply put, Mahan stated that naval and merchant fleets depend on each other for mutual survival.

By the twentieth century, the maritime interests of the United States and Great Britain had settled into peaceful coexistence. Briefly, in the years following World War II, the United States achieved leadership in the Atlantic, marked in classic American style with the fastest and costliest liner ever built, the SS *United States*. Although heavily subsidized, it was soon unable to compete with the new advances in technology flying 20,000 feet above it.

The practice of competing companies adopting international agreements on fares and freight, covertly introduced by Cunard and Collins, was affirmed officially in 1908 at the first Atlantic Conference on shipping rates. Ever suspect in its potential for monopolistic collusion, the conference system to balance trade and avoid mutually destructive price wars no longer has validity.

At the end of the millennium, both practices—maritime subsidies and rate conferences—reached the end of their usefulness. The federal government periodically tries to reduce, if not eliminate, subsidies by a variety of disguised proposals. Meanwhile, competing companies enter into confidential shipping pacts with government approval to circumvent their own established conference agreements and to keep costs globally competitive.

Technical advancements had subtle but immense impact on the maritime world. The American innovation of scheduled liners, the packet ships originated by the Thompsons, Marshalls, and Wrights, continued to keep ocean passenger trade in operation long after airlines began offering intercontinental service. The use of Matthew Fontaine Maury's pilot charts reduced the length of the long sailing voyage from New York to San Francisco by seven weeks and saved shipowners millions of dollars. The International Code of Signals, the colorful set of flags routinely used to dress ships, was specified in 1857 for improved visual communications between vessels. Not long after, the international telegraph system facilitated message transfers within minutes; altered the conduct of international trade; and, by the twentieth century, enhanced the safety of life at sea. The introduction of fire and steam on board ships resulted in passage of the first laws requiring supervision of private enterprise for the welfare of the general public. In 1852, Congress established the U.S. Steamboat Inspection Service, which led to formal licensing of pilots and engineers. In turn, licensing gave rise to the first maritime unions, which became major factions in the labor movement of the early twentieth century.

DURING ITS long career, the Cunard Line never lost a passenger through neglect or by accident. The German torpedoing of the RMS *Lusitania* during World War I, Cunard's only major disaster, has occasionally come under scrutiny regarding the possibility that secret military cargoes might have contributed to the sinking. Fifty years elapsed before the *Lusitania's* manifests were made public. Nothing in them revealed acceptable evidence for what happened after the first torpedo struck to send the ship so rapidly to the bottom. Nor has modern deep-sea diving equipment brought up anything to explain the mystery of the vessel's final moments, why the vessel went down so fast.

Following the two world wars, the staid and stately Cunarders resumed regular pursuit of their transatlantic routes and achieved their best years by the middle of the twentieth century with grandeur and speed. When air transport replaced "half the fun" of getting to Europe with ten times the speed, the Cunard Line offered cruises to quaint and colorful destinations around the globe. In time, rising labor costs; the high standards of British registry, first formulated by Charles MacIver; and the expensive maintenance of older vessels coupled with jaded world travelers' diminishing interests in tropical destinations proved prohibitive for the venerable organization. Soon thereafter, the Cunard Line, most of its shares privately held, went up for sale. For some twenty years, controlling interest was in the hands of Trafalgar House, which sold out to Kvaerner ASA, an Anglo-Norwegian engineering and construction group with a fresh outlook on the modernization of passenger transport.

Elegance and immensity—echoes of Edward Knight Collins—loomed as keys to success in the cruise business. Also important was an imaginative approach to transporting passengers wherever they wanted to go anywhere in the world. Kvaerner had the right idea but found that shipbuilding and cruise operations fitted poorly together. The company lost more than $27 million (£16.4 million) during 1995–96. In 1998, it sold the line, then reduced to five vessels with only the exalted thirty-year-old *Queen Elizabeth 2 (QE2)* under English registry, to the Carnival Corporation of Miami, Florida. The conglomerate ship operator is the world's largest in the cruise line business. An American company now owns 68 percent of Cunard, the most experienced shipping line in history.

No case could be made for this transaction being a Vanderbilt-style takeover; if the Commodore could not beat a competitor, he was inclined to buy it out. Rather, for Cunard it was a case of a well-funded deliverer being there at the right time. Collins had fallen victim to the ocean's adversity and his own prodigality; the Cunard Line, prudently riding on fame for superior transport, had failed to keep pace with changing times. Carnival saw how the century-old allure of ocean travel could be conditioned to modern tastes. Vacationers now turn to enormous floating resorts that attract passengers with casinos, celebrity entertainers, exercise, and midocean events—whale migration, eclipses, the circuit of glaciers, and the viewing of volcanic eruptions. More than half the fun comes from staying on board in the company of literally a thousand people.

Fifty years after its peak period, the Cunard name lives on with one ship still flying the red British ensign. No more does Britannia, a metaphor for England's maritime commerce, rule the waves. Who now reigns over the Atlantic Kingdom? In the modern global economy, no one does. Yet, Britannia can take pride that, for a century and a half, it ruled the Atlantic Kingdom with dignity. Keeping to its heritage, the Cunard organization, a subsidiary of Carnival, is working to design the next evolution of passenger liners. They are destined to be floating cities equipped to take on board thousands of travelers, bent as always on getting somewhere with dispatch but undistracted by the once-feared rigors of the sea. Cunard's first new ship in more than thirty years, the *Queen Mary 2,* being built in France and commissioned in 2003–04, will fly the British flag. At 150,000 gross tons, it should be the largest and most spacious passenger ship in the world. A crew of 1,200 will serve 2,600 passengers on transatlantic voyages. Meanwhile, the *QE2* preserves the Cunard reputation by offering the first Cunard Line's original routes among Halifax, Boston, and Bermuda in her schedule of cruises.

Sir Samuel would be pleased.

Appendices

Glossary of Nautical Terms

articles. Performance contract between master and seamen.

bark. Three-masted vessel, square-rigged on fore and main masts, fore-and-aft sails on the mizzen.

belaying pin. Wooden or metal bar, stored in a pin-rack for bending (fastening) of lines.

boatswain. Petty officer responsible for the rigging and for calling the crew to duty.

bowsprit. Heavy spar extending from vessel's bow.

brig. Two-masted vessel, square-rigged.

bulwark. Boards above and around the upper deck, fastened to stanchions.

cabin. Officers' quarters in the after part of a vessel.

clearance. Official permission to leave port after satisfying all local regulations.

condenser. Encased piping for the cooling of steam to water.

coppered. Plating fastened below the waterline to decrease marine growth and wood-eating parasites.

course (of sail). Sail suspended from mast's lower yard; fore course or foresail, main course or mainsail.

crimp. Procurer of crews, usually by dishonest means.

dead reckoning. Determination of position at sea based on direction and distance traveled.

deadrise. Vertical distance from keel to the angular portion of a hull where it turns upward from the bottom.

departure. Last fixed position within sight of land, as opposed to landfall.

double topsail. Second sail above the deck, horizontally split into two portions for ease of handling.

entrance. Convergence of the waterline at the bow and both sides of the stem.

fathom. Measure of 6 feet.

forecastle. Part of the upper deck forward of the foremast; that compartment under the deck where the sailors reside.

frigate. Fast, medium-sized sailing warship.

gaff. Spar, to which the top of a fore-and-aft sail is fastened, fitted flexibly to the mast.

gallows-frame. Amidships framework for the support of spare spars and small boats.

glass. Half-hour sandglass for timing the striking of the ship's bell.

gunwale. Upper rail of boat or vessel.

hawsehole. Hole in the bow through which the anchor cable passes.

heave to. Put a vessel in the position of lying to the wind.

hermaphrodite rigged. Squared-rigged at the foremast, fore-and-aft sails on the main.

hogging. Placing a strain on each end of the hull to bring up its center portion.

holystone. Large stone, often bible-shaped, for scouring the deck.

jibboom. Spar rigged beyond the bowsprit to which jib (foremost sail) is lashed.

lead. Cone-shaped piece of lead to which a length of line is fastened for sounding depth of the water.

leeward. Direction opposite to that from which the wind blows.

loxodrome. Curve intersecting all meridians at the same angle.

mizzenmast. Aftermost mast of a ship.

piragua. Two-masted, round-bottomed open boat; see Figure 3–2, foreground.

quarterdeck. That part of the upper deck abaft the mainmast.

razee. Scraped and cut-down hull by one deck; also, the process of cutting down a hull.

rhumb line. Segment of a loxodrome; on Mercator projections, a straight line.

royal. Light sail, next above the topgallant.

run. After part of a vessel's bottom, rising and narrowing as it approaches the stern post.

schooner. Two-masted, fore-and-aft–rigged vessel.

sheer. Longitudinal distance below the gunwale from stem to stern.

ship, sailing. Three-masted vessel with square-rigged topsail on the mizzen.

shipwright. Carpenter engaged in the building and maintenance of ships.

skysail. Light sail, next above the royal.

sloop. Single-masted, fore-and-aft–rigged vessel.

spanker. Aftermost sail, fore-and-aft rigged.

spars. Booms, gaffs, masts, yards, etc.

steerage. Portion of the 'tween decks forward of the cabin.

stem. Foremost part of the hull that reaches from the bowsprit to the keel.

stunsail. Light sail set outboard of a square sail on boom rigged for that purpose; used only in moderate weather and fair winds.

supercargo. Staff officer on board ship who is responsible for the cargo and its sale and purchase.

top. Platform over the head of the lower mast to spread the rigging and provide convenience for the men aloft.

topgallant. The third sail above the deck, next above the topsail.

topmast. Second mast above the deck.

topsail. Second sail above the deck.

truck. Fastening at the head of the highest mast for the support of signal halyards.

trysail. Fore-and-aft sail with gaff and boom, hoisted on a small mast abaft the lower mast.

'tween decks. Decks within the hold, immediately below the upper or main deck; if two, referred to as upper and lower, dividing hold into three stowage spaces.

yard. Long spar, hung by its center to a mast, on which square sails are spread.

yardarms. Extremities of a yard.

Chronology

Note: When events spanned a number of years, the most significant year is given.

1698   Savery develops an atmospheric steam engine.

1711   Newcomen produces an improved steam engine.

1769   Watt and Boulton develop a practical steam engine.

1782   Watt improves engine with rotary motion.

1783   French steam-propelled *Pyroscaphe* is demonstrated.

1784   Rumsey receives steam navigation rights in Virginia.

1787   Virginia grants steamboat monopoly to Fitch, and he demonstrates oar-propelled steamboats in August. Rumsey demonstrates a jet-propelled steamboat in December. Samuel Cunard is born in Halifax, Nova Scotia.

1788   Rumsey publishes pamphlets on his steamboat work. Fitch demonstrates a steam-powered paddle wheeler.

1790   Fitch puts his latest steamboat into scheduled service.

1791   Fitch patents a steamboat.

1792   Rumsey dies in England before completion of his last steamboat.

1793   Morey demonstrates a steam-powered small craft.

1794   Cornelius Vanderbilt is born in Staten Island, New York.

1796   Livingston acquires Fitch's Hudson River navigation rights.

1797   Fulton works on submarine warfare in England. Morey patents a rotary steam engine.

1798   Livingston briefly holds grant of a New York monopoly. Fitch dies. Roosevelt demonstrates the steamboat *Polacca*.

1800   Fulton demonstrates a diving boat. Cunard is in Boston as an apprentice shipbroker.

1801   Enoch Train is born, probably in Weston, Massachusetts.

1802   Edward Knight Collins is born in Truro, Massachusetts. Fulton and Livingston agree on a Hudson River plan.

1803   New York steamboat monopoly is renewed in names of Livingston and Fulton. Stevens launches screw-propelled *Little Juliana*. Fulton demonstrates his first steamboat in France.

1806   Morey fails in proposing collaboration to Fulton.

1807   Fulton's *North River Steamboat* makes first voyage on the Hudson with a Brown-built hull and a Boulton & Watt engine. Cope Line forms in Philadelphia.

1808   Livingston-Fulton monopoly is renewed.

1810   Donald McKay is born in Shelburne County, Nova Scotia. Vanderbilt starts ferry service between Staten Island and Manhattan.

1811   Ogden loses in opposition to the Hudson River monopoly. Fulton launches *New Orleans* on Mississippi River.

1813   Cunard and father purchase *White Oak,* a British war prize. Livingston dies; monopoly continues as North River Steamboat Company puts *Fulton* to work in Long Island Sound.

1814   Vanderbilt, with government contract to provision forts of New York harbor, gains several boats under his command; he builds schooner to service Long Island Sound.

1815   Fulton dies; Fulton-Livingston steamboat business continues. Ogden purchases rights from next-generation Livingston to run *Atalanta* between New Jersey and New York. Morey gets further patents for steam engine and "vapor engine."

1817   Thomas Gibbons starts ferry operation in New Jersey. Collins moves to New York; with his father, Captain Israel Gross Collins, he conducts a general commission business.

1818   Vanderbilt sails as captain for Gibbons, encourages break with Ogden, challenges Livingston steamboat monopoly, and builds steamship *Bellona,* which makes Gibbons profitable. Black Ball Line of scheduled sailing packets starts operation.

1819   Rolled iron water-tube boilers and double expansion engines are introduced. *Savannah* makes the first steam-assisted transatlantic crossing.

1823   Samuel Samuels is born in Philadelphia.

1824   Collins becomes partner in father's firm. Supreme Court ends Hudson River monopoly and defines control of interstate commerce. William Walker is born in Nashville, Tennessee.

1825   S. Cunard and Company, shipping firm, is formed in Halifax. Collins captures the cotton market.

1827   Collins forms Vera Cruz Line. McKay is apprenticed as a ship carpenter.

1828   First American steam-powered locomotive is introduced three years behind England.

1829   Vanderbilt enters shipping business in coastal waters with *Bellona* and soon starts Hudson River rate war.

1831   Collins takes over packet line to Vera Cruz and control of New Orleans
        Line. Cunard brothers buy interest in steamship *Royal William* running
        between Halifax and Quebec.

1833   Collins corners the New York–New Orleans trade.

1834   Daniel Drew enters steamboat business, competes with Vanderbilt, and
        pays him to withdraw from business for ten years. Samuels goes to sea as
        a cabin boy. Richard Henry Dana embarks on two-year sailing voyage to
        California. Charles Marshall buys out the company that took over the
        Black Ball Line from its founders.

1835   Junius Smith forms British & American Steam Navigation Company.

1836   Collins starts the Dramatic Line of sailing packets to Europe.

1837   U.S. experiences severe financial panic affecting maritime operations.

1838   *Sirius* and *Great Western* participate in transatlantic steamship race. Brit-
        ish Admiralty proposes transatlantic steamship mail subsidy. Collins
        urges President Martin Van Buren to consider the need for a steam navy
        and subsidized mail carriers. Federal legislation requires inspection and
        supervision of passenger steam vessels.

1839   Cunard seeks mail subsidy in England, contracts with Napier and others
        for steamship operation, and wins first Admiralty subsidy in May. Lauch-
        lan McKay publishes *The Practical Shipbuilder,* first book on marine
        architecture. *Robert F. Stockton,* first iron-hulled, screw-propelled vessel,
        crosses Atlantic.

1840   Cunard's *Britannia* establishes Liverpool-Boston steamship route in July.

1841   McKay joins with William Currier to build two New York packets.
        Robert Bennett Forbes patents the double topsail, which McKay adopts
        for the *Reindeer.* Smith loses steamship *President* on its second voyage.

1842   McKay produces the *Courier,* his first ship as solo designer and builder.

1843   Samuels becomes master of sail. Cunard loses *Columbia* off Cape Sable.

1844   McKay produces packet *John R. Skiddy;* meets Train and produces *Joshua
        Bates* for Train's transatlantic packet trade. Train loses *Dorchester* in a gale.

1845   Congress authorizes government aid through mail contracts.

1846   Collins proposes a line of steam packets and forms United States Mail
        Steamship Company, known widely as Collins Line. Vanderbilt launches
        Cornelius Vanderbilt, part of Hudson River fleet. McKay's *Anglo Saxon,*
        produced for Train, is lost off Cape Sable. The Irish famine begins.

1847   Ocean Steam Navigation Company becomes first American company to
        operate under subsidy. Vanderbilt races *Cornelius Vanderbilt* against Law's
        Oregon. Train adds *Ocean Monarch* for immigrant trade.

1848   Gold is discovered in California. *Ocean Monarch* burns in the Irish Sea.

1849   Collins Line launches *Atlantic* and *Pacific*. Cunard inaugurates port facilities in New York for Liverpool service. George Francis Train becomes partner in Enoch Train's White Diamond Line and encourages McKay to build clippers for the California route.

1850   Maiden voyages of *Atlantic* and *Pacific;* latter takes the Blue Riband. McKay launches first clipper ship. Vanderbilt looks westward and acquires Nicaraguan charter for Accessory Transit Company. Train adds *Daniel Webster* and *Stag Hound*. Cunard and Collins establish a secret fare-fixing agreement. Jenny Lind arrives in New York on *Atlantic*.

1851   Vanderbilt Line establishes New York to San Francisco route via Nicaragua. Commodore Vanderbilt becomes opponent of William Walker. British Inman Line joins competition for transatlantic trade. *Atlantic* survives long, perilous voyage. *Baltic* wins Blue Riband. McKay builds *Flying Cloud* and *Staffordshire* for Enoch Train; Train sells *Flying Cloud* before its launching.

1852   *Pacific* sets westward crossing record. Train sells *Anglo-American* to British. McKay produces *Sovereign of the Seas* for himself and brother Lauchlan. Cunard's losses to Collins continue. Collins sends *Baltic* up Potomac River to Washington to lobby for subsidy increase.

1853   Currier and Townsend build semiclipper *Dreadnought* under Samuels's direction; first voyage is highly profitable and sets eastbound sailing record. McKay builds *Star of Empire* and *Chariot of Fame* for Train, the latter his last purchase from McKay. Crimean War starts. McKay's *Great Republic* burns. Vanderbilt takes private steam yacht *North Star* on European cruise, loses control of Accessory Transit and the intercoastal route to Morgan and Garrison, allied with Walker. Junius Smith dies in New York.

1854   Vanderbilt threatens ruin for those who took control of his line. Warner fails in invasion of Lower California and is acquitted of violating neutrality laws. Cunard withdraws ships from the Atlantic under Admiralty wartime rules. *Dreadnought* makes six one-way fast passages, breaks all sail packet records in December, New York to Liverpool in thirteen days and eleven hours and beats Cunard steamships. *Arctic* sinks after collision, and Collins loses wife, son, and daughter. Collins confronts Vanderbilt on his application for a competing transatlantic subsidy. Vanderbilt orders building of *North Star* and *Ariel*. Train loses *Staffordshire* off Nova Scotia.

1855   Warner captures Granada. Vanderbilt fails in bid for subsidy. Collins's subsidy is renewed. Vanderbilt starts European Line, offers New York–Le Havre service with *North Star,* and follows with *Ariel.* Crimean War ends. Cunard restores New York–Liverpool operation. Collins arranges suspension of agreement with Cunard until *Adriatic* is operational.

1856 Vanderbilt regains control of Accessory Transit; coerces payments from Panama lines for closing Nicaragua service; with three large vessels, enters into competition with Cunard and Collins; sells *North Star.* Warner obtains U.S. recognition of new Nicaraguan government and declares himself president. Collins's *Pacific* vanishes at sea.

1857 *Adriatic* is launched. Congress withdraws Collins's subsidy and contracts with Vanderbilt for transatlantic mail. Third financial panic occurs. Train sells White Diamond Line. Cope ends operation. Inman, Cunard, and Vanderbilt lead in transatlantic passenger transport figures. Central American states force Warner's defeat and his surrender to U.S. Navy, but he is again acquitted of violating neutrality.

1858 *Adriatic* makes Collins Line's last voyage. Vanderbilt's threat to reopen Accessory Transit gains him a stipend of $56,000. Bankrupt, Collins turns to development of Ohio mineral properties. Vanderbilt, sole American steamship operator on the North Atlantic, offers irregular service.

1859 Samuels establishes packet ship speed record, New York to Liverpool, and quells a mutiny on *Dreadnought.* McKay studies ironclads in Europe.

1860 Warner, forced to surrender to British navy, is turned over to Honduras and shot by firing squad at Trujillo.

1861 Firing on Union's Fort Sumter starts war between Union and Confederacy. Vanderbilt sells Atlantic Line, fits out *Vanderbilt* as Union warship, and joins in unsuccessful raiding expedition to New Orleans as chartered vessels prove unseaworthy.

1862 Samuels completes eight years of sailing *Dreadnought* in a drastic last cruise. Vanderbilt buys stock in New York & Harlem Railroad. Cunard introduces the *Scotia,* last of the company's paddlers.

1863 McKay begins production of iron ships and marine engines. Civil War, iron hulls, and screw propulsion spell end of sail transport. Samuels commands steamer *John Rice.* Vanderbilt avoids U.S. Senate resolution of censure and receives medal for donation of the *Vanderbilt.*

1864 Congress initiates the transcontinental railroad.

1865 Samuels commands *G. B. McClellan,* part of Union fleet, in last major battle of Civil War. Samuel Cunard dies in London. Charles Marshall dies in New York.

1866   Samuels captains the *Fulton* steam packet to Havre and wins first trans-
       atlantic yacht race as commander of *Henrietta* for James Gordon Bennett.

1867   Vanderbilt takes control of New York Central Railroad.

1868   Enoch Train dies in Saugus, Massachusetts.

1869   McKay builds his last sailing ship, *Glory of the Seas,* and sells his yard.

1877   Vanderbilt dies in New York.

1878   Collins dies in New York. Black Ball Line ends operations.

1880   McKay dies in Hamilton, Massachusetts.

1887   Samuels publishes memoirs.

1908   Samuels dies in Brooklyn.

1998   Carnival Corporation takes control of Cunard Line.

Bibliography

Albion, Robert Greenhalgh. *The Rise of New York Port, 1815–1860.* New York: Scribner's, 1939. Reprint, 1964.

——. *Square-Riggers on Schedule: The New York Sailing Packets to England and France.* Princeton: Princeton University Press, 1938. Reprint, New York: Archon Books, 1965.

Armstrong, Warren. *The Collins Story.* London: R. Hale, 1957.

Bain, David Haward. *Empire Express.* New York: Viking Penguin, 1999.

Bauer, K. Jack. *A Maritime History of the United States.* Columbia: University of South Carolina Press, 1988.

Berry, Lawrence F. "Early Dorchester." *Dorchester Beacon,* November 7, 14, 21, and 28, 1957. Four-part series about Enoch Train, merchant-shipowner.

Blom, Eric. "Rule, Britannia." Vol. 7, 330, in *Grove's Dictionary of Music and Musicians.* New York: St. Martin's Press, 1954.

Blume, Kenneth John. "The Hairy Ape Reconsidered: The American Merchant Seaman and the Transition from Sail to Steam in the Late Nineteenth Century." *American Neptune* 44 (winter 1984).

Bolster, W. Jeffrey. *Black Jacks: African American Seamen in the Age of Sail.* Cambridge: Harvard University Press, 1997.

Bonsor, N. R. P. *North Atlantic Seaway,* 4 vols. Newton Abbot, England: David & Charles, 1955, 1975, 1980.

Bradlee, F. B. C. "The Dreadnought of Newburyport." *Essex Institute Historical Collections,* vol. LVI, 1920.

Braynard, Frank O. *S.S. Savannah: The Elegant Steam Ship.* Athens: University of Georgia Press, 1963.

Brinnin, John Malcolm. *The Sway of the Grand Saloon, a Social History of the North Atlantic.* New York: Delacorte Press, 1971.

Butler, John A. *Sailing on Friday: The Perilous Voyage of America's Merchant Marine.* Washington, D.C.: Brassey's, 1997.

Chapelle, Howard I. *The Search for Speed under Sail 1700–1855.* New York: W. W. Norton, 1967.

Cheney, Robert K. *Maritime History of the Merrimac—Shipbuilding.* Newburyport, Mass.: Newburyport Press, 1964.

Choules, John Overton. *The Cruise of the Steam Yacht* North Star: *A Narrative of Mr. Vanderbilt's Party.* Boston: Gould and Lincoln; New York: Evans and Dickerson, 1854.

Coleman, Terry. *Going to America.* New York: Doubleday, 1973.

Cutler, Carl C. *Queens of the Western Ocean: The Story of America's Mail and Passenger Sailing Lines.* Annapolis: Naval Institute Press, 1961.

———. *Greyhounds of the Sea: The Story of the American Clipper Ships.* 1930. Reprint, Annapolis: Naval Institute Press, 1984.

Dana, Richard Henry, Jr. *The Seaman's Friend: A Treatise on Practical Seamanship.* Mineola, N.Y.: Dover Publications, 1997; unabridged republication of 14th ed. Boston: Thomas Groom, 1879.

Davis, Charles G. *American Sailing Ships: Their Plans and History.* New York: Dover Publications, 1984; unabridged republication of *Ships of the Past,* Salem: Marine Research Society, 1929.

De La Pedraja, René. *A Historical Dictionary of the U.S. Merchant Marine and Shipping Industry: Since the Introduction of Steam.* Westport, Conn.: Greenwood Press, 1994.

Delgado, James P. *To California by Sea.* Columbia: University of South Carolina Press, 1990.

de Tocqueville, Alexis. *Democracy in America.* Edited by J. P. Mayer, 1848 edition. Translated by George Lawrence. New York: HarperCollins, 1966.

Dickens, Charles. *American Notes.* 1842. Reprint, N.Y.: Fromm International Publishing, 1985.

Druett, Joan. *Hen Frigates: Wives of Merchant Captains under Sail.* New York: Simon & Schuster, 1998.

Fairburn, William Armstrong, ed. *Merchant Sail.* 6 vols. Center Lovell, Maine: Fairburn Marine Educational Foundation, 1945–55.

Folkman, David I, Jr. *The Nicaraguan Route.* Salt Lake City: University of Utah Press, 1972.

Gardiner, Robert, and Basil Greenhill, eds. *The Advent of Steam—The Merchant Steamship before 1900.* London: Conway Maritime Press, 1993.

Gibson, Andrew, and Arthur Donovan. *The Abandoned Ocean: A History of United States Maritime Policy.* Columbia: University of South Carolina Press, 2000.

Griffiths, Denis. *Steam at Sea: Two Centuries of Steam-Powered Ships.* London: Brassey's, 1997.

Guedalla, Philip. *The Hundred Year.* As extracted in "Washington Wheel of Fortune," *Harper's,* May 1998, 49–54.

Hardenberg, Horst O. *Middle Ages of the Internal Combustion Engine.* Warrendale, Pa.: Society of Automotive Engineers, 1999.

Hargest, George E. *History of Letter Post Communication between the United States and Europe, 1845–1875.* Washington, D.C.: Smithsonian Institution Press, 1971.

Hubbard, Walter, and Richard F. Winter. *North Atlantic Mail Sailings, 1840–75.* Wheeling, Ill.: United States Philatelic Classics Society, 1988.

Hunter, Louis C., with Beatrice Jones Hunter. *Steamboats on the Western Rivers: An Economic and Technological History.* New York: Octagon Books, 1969; original edition, Cambridge: Harvard University Press, 1949.

Hyde, Francis E. *Cunard and the North Atlantic, 1840–1973.* Atlantic Highlands, N.J.: Humanities Press, 1975.

Ingham, John M., ed. *Biographical Dictionary of American Business Leaders.* Westport, Conn.: Greenwood Press, 1983.

Kemble, J[ohn] H. *The Panama Route 1848–1868.* Berkeley: University of California Press, 1943.

——. "The Pacific Mail." *American Neptune* 10 (April 1950), 123.

Kinder, Gary. *Ship of Gold in the Deep Blue Sea.* New York: Atlantic Monthly Press, 1998.

Kunhardt, Philip B., Jr., Philip B. Kunhardt III, and Peter W. Kunhardt. *P. T. Barnum: America's Greatest Showman.* New York: Knopf, 1995.

Labaree, Benjamin W., ed. *The Atlantic World of Robert G. Albion.* Middletown, Conn.: Wesleyan University Press, 1975.

Laing, Alexander. *American Sail: A Pictorial History.* New York: Dutton, 1961.

Lane, Wheaton J. *Commodore Vanderbilt: An Epic of the Steam Age.* New York: Knopf, 1942.

Laxton, Edward. *The Famine Ships.* New York: Henry Holt, 1996.

Lindsay, William S. *History of Merchant Shipping and Ancient Commerce.* Vol. IV. London: London Society, 1876.

Maddocks, Melvin, ed. *The Atlantic Crossing.* Alexandria, Va.: Time-Life Books, 1981.

Magoun, F. Alexander. *The Frigate* Constitution *and Other Historic Ships.* Salem, Mass.: Marine Research Society, 1928. Reprint, New York: Dover Publications, 1987.

Marvel, William. *The* Alabama *and the* Kearsarge: *The Sailor's Civil War.* Chapel Hill: University of North Carolina Press, 1996.

McKay, Richard C. *Donald McKay and His Famous Sailing Ships.* New York: Dover Publications, 1995. Unabridged and slightly altered republication of

Some Famous Sailing Ships and Their Builder Donald McKay, New York: G. P. Putnam, 1928.

———. *South Street: A Maritime History of New York.* Riverside, Conn.: 7 C's Press, 1969.

McNeil, Ian, ed. *An Encyclopaedia of the History of Technology.* London and New York: Routledge, 1990. Reprint (paperback), 1996.

McPherson, James M. *Battle Cry of Freedom: The Civil War Era.* New York: Oxford University Press, 1988.

Melville, Herman. *Redburn: His First Voyage.* 1849. Reprint, New York: Double-day, 1957.

Morison, Samuel Eliot. *The Maritime History of Massachusetts: 1783–1860.* Cambridge, Mass.: Houghton Mifflin, 1961.

Morris, James M. *Our Maritime Heritage: Maritime Developments and Their Impact on American Life.* Newport News, Virginia: University Press of America, 1979.

Paine, Lincoln P. *Ships of the World: An Historical Encyclopedia.* Boston: Houghton Mifflin, 1997.

Riesenberg, Felix. *Under Sail.* New York: Macmillan, 1918.

Samuels, Samuel. *From the Forecastle to the Cabin.* Boston: Charles E. Lauriet, 1924. Reprint of original 1887 edition with an added introduction by Ralph D. Paine.

Scheele, Carl H. *A Short History of the Mail Service.* Washington, D.C.: Smithsonian Institution Press, 1970.

Shufeldt, R. W. "Account of the Passage and Safety of the Steamship Atlantic." *New York Herald,* February 16, 1851, 1.

Sloan, Edward W. "The Roots of a Maritime Fortune: E. K. Collins and the New York–Gulf Coast Trade, 1821–1848." *Gulf Coast Historical Review* 5 (spring 1990), 104–13.

———. "The *Baltic* Goes to Washington: Lobbying for a Congressional Steamship Subsidy, 1852." *The Northern Mariner,* V, no. 1 (January 1995), 19–32.

Spikes, Judith Doolin. *Larchmont, NY: People and Places.* Larchmont, New York: Fountain Square Books, 1991.

Staff, Frank. *The Transatlantic Mail.* New York: John De Graff; London: Alard Coles, 1956.

Taylor, David B. *Steam Conquers the Atlantic.* New York: Appleton-Century, 1939.

Thompson, David Whittet. "The Great Steamboat Monopolies, Part II: The Hudson." *American Neptune,* 16 (October 1956), 270.

Train, Arthur. *Puritan's Progress.* New York: Charles Scribner's, 1931.

Train, George Francis. *My Life in Many States and Foreign Lands.* New York: Appleton, 1902.

Tute, Warren. *Atlantic Conquest: The Men and Ships of the Glorious Age of Steam.* Boston: Little, Brown, 1962.

Whitney, Ralph. "The Unlucky Collins Line." *American Heritage,* February 1957, 48–53, 100–102.

Willmer and Smith's Times. "The Ocean Monarch Burnt at Sea." *The Boston Atlas,* September 9, 1848, 2.

Winiarski, Kathryn. "Historian: Man Who Named Larchmont Deserves a Tombstone." *Mamaroneck Daily Times,* October 5, 1992, 1.

Wood, Virginia Steele. *Live Oaking: Southern Timbers for Tall Ships.* Annapolis: Naval Institute Press, 1981. Reprint, 1995.

Wright, Esmond. *Franklin of Philadelphia.* Cambridge: Harvard University Press, 1986.

Subject Index of Patents for Inventions 1790–1873, Series. New York: Arno Press, 1976.

"Railroad, Canal, and Steamboat Statistics." Hunt's *Merchants' Magazine,* September 1851, 379–80.

"Railroad, Canal, and Steamboat Statistics." Hunt's *Merchants' Magazine,* March 1852, 379–81.

"Railroad, Canal, and Steamboat Statistics." Hunt's *Merchants' Magazine,* April 1853, 506.

"Commercial Statistics." Hunt's *Merchants' Magazine,* April 1853, 506–7.

"Railroad, Canal, and Steamboat Statistics." Hunt's *Merchants' Magazine,* May 1858, 630–31.

"Arrival of the Britannia Steamship." *The Boston Atlas,* July 20, 1840, 1, 2.

"Cunard Festival at East Boston." *The Boston Atlas,* July 22, 1840, 2.

"Passage to the Sea." *The Boston Atlas,* February 2, 1844, 2.

"Joyful News: Safety of the Steamship Atlantic." *New York Herald,* February 16, 1851, 1.

"Non-Arrival of the Arctic." *New York Herald,* October 7, 1854, 3.

"News by Telegraph . . . Destruction of the Steamer E. K. Collins by Fire." *New York Herald,* October 10, 1854, 1.

"Distressing News . . . Total Loss of the Arctic." *New York Herald,* October 11, 1854, 1.

"Shipwrecks in the Late Storm." *New York Herald,* January 13, 1856, 1.

"Arrival of the Persia." *New York Herald,* February 10, 1856, 1.

"The News," editorial. *New York Herald,* February 10, 1856, 4.

"The News," editorial. *New York Herald,* February 12, 1856, 4.

"Great Conflagration." *New York Times,* December 26, 1853, 1.

"Obituary, Edward K. Collins." *New York Times,* January 23, 1878, 5.

"Capt. Samuels Dead." *New York Times,* May 19, 1908, 7.

"Jenny Lind's Reception—Anticipatory." *New York Tribune,* August 19, 1850, 1.

"Arrival of Jenny Lind." *New York Tribune,* September 2, 1850, 1.

Congressional Globe. 34th Cong., 1st sess., 2162–66.

Congressional Globe. 35th Cong., 1st sess., June 9, 1858, 2219–22.

Statutes at Large of the United States of America. V, 748–50; IX, 187, 378; X, 21; XI, 102.

U.S. Senate Document 237. 29th Cong., 1st sess., 6.

U.S. House Executive Document 91. 32nd Cong., 1st sess., 36, 76.

U.S. Senate Executive Document No. 68. 34th Cong., 1st sess., 1856, 2843.

Notes on Sources

Epigraphs at the opening of each section are extracted, respectively, from William Shakespeare, *Julius Caesar,* IV, iii; Thomas Paine, *The American Crisis,* no. 1; Shakespeare, *King Henry the Sixth, Part III,* IV, iii.

As noted in the preface, the two major works definitive of the period are Albion, *Square-Riggers on Schedule* and *Rise of New York Port.* I use them for much of the background detail. *American Biographical Dictionary's* twenty volumes provide concise lives of each of the American principals. This is a good starting point because many of the essays and short bibliographies therein were produced by noteworthy maritime writers, such as Samuel Eliot Morison and Robert Albion. Lane, *Commodore Vanderbilt,* and the memoirs of Samuels, *From Forecastle to Cabin,* are the only reliable histories of the Americans; some suspect the truthfulness of the latter, albeit without proof to the contrary. Armstrong, *Collins Story,* is just that, a well-indexed fictionalized history. Under its imaginative gloss lie many obscure details that helped in compiling the life of Edward Collins. Hyde, *Cunard and the North Atlantic,* is the source of much of Samuel Cunard's early life, nearly all of the particulars on the origin of the Cunard Line, and the correspondence with Robert Napier.

A narrowly distributed book intended for stamp collectors, Hubbard and Winter, *North Atlantic Mail Sailings,* lists all transatlantic steamship sailings from American and European ports by shipping line and date of departure. It thereby gives a picture, practically in photographic detail, of the British-American competition.

Comparisons of life on board steam and sail packets stem from both an early chapter and a late chapter in Dickens, *American Notes: A Journey.* With his customary droll humor, Charles Dickens describes the miseries of a wintry crossing on the *Britannia* and the pleasures of returning in the late spring on the well-known sailing packet *George Washington.* His tale is recommended reading for those interested in what cabin-class life was like during the mid–eighteenth century. I drew cultural background from Brinnin, *Sway of the Grand Saloon,* and Tute, *Atlantic Conquest.* With respect to the latter, it was interesting to trace to its source a minor error in Tute's mention of Enoch Train and Donald McKay. Tute appears to have drawn on Richard McKay's history of his grandfather's ships and McKay, in turn, on the memoirs of Train. Train's lively imagination sometimes deviated from the facts as reported in contemporary newspapers. Nothing of importance to the essential history was lost in the transcriptions.

Fiction can be a reliable source of colorful details if one understands the context in which it was written. Such is the case with Melville, *Redburn,* written before *Typee* and *Moby Dick* and practically autobiographical in telling the story of Redburn's (Melville's) first sea voyage. My descriptions of the River Mersey and Liverpool are based on his account.

Newspapers were plentiful in every major city during the nineteenth century, with a dozen or more published daily or weekly in Boston alone. They tended to specialize in their news coverage to draw readership from particular community interests. *The Boston Atlas* provides the best source on the sailing packets and the Cunard Line's early years in Boston. The shipping-oriented *New York Herald* thoroughly covers the business activities of Edward Collins and routinely carried Collins Line advertisements for its New York sailings.

Lengthy authoritative materials on Collins based on personal papers are hard to find, a situation that fortunately is unlikely to continue. Whitney, "Unlucky Collins Line," is useful. Sloan, who has written several scholarly articles for narrowly distributed historical journals, including "*Baltic* Goes to Washington" and "Roots of Maritime Fortune," is at work on a full text about Collins. Sloan's articles have been a generous source of detail on both the early years of the Dramatic Line and the Cunard-Collins cartel. I look forward to his biography of Collins.

Whether or not Samuel Samuels achieved a new record on the *Dreadnought* in 1859 remains an issue. Bradlee, in his monograph, Dreadnought *of Newburyport,* disputes claims that no such fast passage ever took place and cites letters from agent David Ogden and Samuels himself that testify to the accomplishment. Here is another life that deserves the spotlight, if for no other reason than to affirm the basic truth of a remarkable tale.

Chapelle, *Search for Speed under Sail,* takes an objective look at Donald McKay and finds much of the adulation overdone. I have drawn on Chapelle's comments but cannot deny the evidence, supported by footnotes in Morison, *Maritime History of Massachusetts,* that no builder, American or foreign, could improve on the McKay clippers for ships of their size.

Cutler, *Greyhounds of the Sea* and *Queens of the Western Ocean,* proves helpful in putting sail and steam vessels in perspective. From the latter, as well as other technical sources, I conclude that the slow, century-long development of steam vessels was due primarily to material limitations, overcome eventually by the

Bessemer process as the armies of North and South drew America's attention from the sea.

The life story of Enoch Train, dependent on brief newspaper articles and his cousin's somewhat suspect memoirs, was the most challenging to piece together. Fitting together other independently written pieces, advertisements, and elements of Donald McKay's quasi-biography helped to fill some of the gaps.

The peaking of the Industrial Revolution during the middle of the nineteenth century was accompanied by the vigorous activity of a host of talented writers and illustrators. Newspapers, magazines, and book publishers benefited from their work. I don't feel that my comparison to the Sumerian invention of writing constitutes an exaggeration. Thanks to the proliferation of libraries by 1860, another blessing derived from that glorious age, we are able to step back into the lives of the observers.

Index

About the Author

Philosopher and historian of American maritime affairs, John A. Butler is the author of *Strike Able-Peter: The Stranding and Salvage of the USS* Missouri and *Sailing on Friday: The Perilous Voyage of America's Merchant Marine.* A graduate of the Massachusetts Maritime Academy and Holy Cross College, he later served as an officer in both the United States Lines and the U.S. Navy. For more than thirty years, he worked for IBM in marketing and technical education. The author retains memberships in the National Maritime Historical Society and the Steamship Historical Society of America. He lives in Potomac, Maryland.